Denmark Air Force Handbook

Just The

facts101

Textbook Key Facts

by Cram101
Texbook NOT Included

Table of Contents

Index: Answers

Just The Facts101

Exam Prep for

Denmark Air Force Handbook

Just The Facts101 Exam Prep is your link from
the textbook and lecture to your exams.

**Just The Facts101 Exam Preps are unauthorized and comprehensive reviews
of your textbooks.**

All material provided by CTI Publications (c) 2019

Textbook publishers and textbook authors do not participate in or contribute to these reviews.

Just The Facts101 Exam Prep

eAIN 444580

Foundations of Business

A business, also known as an enterprise, agency or a firm, is an entity involved in the provision of goods and/or services to consumers. Businesses are prevalent in capitalist economies, where most of them are privately owned and provide goods and services to customers in exchange for other goods, services, or money.

:: Business law ::

A _____ is an arrangement where parties, known as partners, agree to cooperate to advance their mutual interests. The partners in a _____ may be individuals, businesses, interest-based organizations, schools, governments or combinations. Organizations may partner to increase the likelihood of each achieving their mission and to amplify their reach. A _____ may result in issuing and holding equity or may be only governed by a contract.

Exam Probability: **Low**

1. *Answer choices:*

(see index for correct answer)

- a. Partnership
- b. Tax patent
- c. Refusal to deal
- d. Consularization

Guidance: level 1

:: Globalization-related theories ::

_____ is an economic system based on the private ownership of the means of production and their operation for profit. Characteristics central to _____ include private property, capital accumulation, wage labor, voluntary exchange, a price system, and competitive markets. In a capitalist market economy, decision-making and investment are determined by every owner of wealth, property or production ability in financial and capital markets, whereas prices and the distribution of goods and services are mainly determined by competition in goods and services markets.

2. *Answer choices:*

- a. Economic Development
- b. post-industrial
- c. Capitalism

Guidance: level 1

:: Financial accounting ::

_____ is a financial metric which represents operating liquidity available to a business, organisation or other entity, including governmental entities. Along with fixed assets such as plant and equipment, _____ is considered a part of operating capital. Gross _____ is equal to current assets. _____ is calculated as current assets minus current liabilities. If current assets are less than current liabilities, an entity has a _____ deficiency, also called a _____ deficit.

3. *Answer choices:*

- a. Commuted cash value
- b. Money measurement

- c. Certified Public Accountants Association
- d. Accounting identity

Guidance: level 1

:: Cash flow ::

_____ s are narrowly interconnected with the concepts of value, interest rate and liquidity. A _____ that shall happen on a future day tN can be transformed into a _____ of the same value in t0.

Exam Probability: **Medium**

4. *Answer choices:*

(see index for correct answer)

- a. Discounted payback period
- b. Cash carrier
- c. Operating cash flow
- d. Cash flow loan

Guidance: level 1

:: Market research ::

_____ is "the process or set of processes that links the producers, customers, and end users to the marketer through information used to identify and define marketing opportunities and problems; generate, refine, and evaluate marketing actions; monitor marketing performance; and improve understanding of marketing as a process. _____ specifies the information required to address these issues, designs the method for collecting information, manages and implements the data collection process, analyzes the results, and communicates the findings and their implications."

Exam Probability: **High**

5. *Answer choices:*

(see index for correct answer)

- a. Media-Analyse
- b. Marketing research
- c. Offshore 2020
- d. Competitive intelligence

Guidance: level 1

:: Insolvency ::

_____ is a legal process through which people or other entities who cannot repay debts to creditors may seek relief from some or all of their debts. In most jurisdictions, _____ is imposed by a court order, often initiated by the debtor.

6. *Answer choices:*

(see index for correct answer)

- a. Insolvency law of Russia
- b. Bankruptcy
- c. Financial distress
- d. United Kingdom insolvency law

Guidance: level 1

:: Semiconductor companies ::

_____ Corporation is a Japanese multinational conglomerate corporation headquartered in Konan, Minato, Tokyo. Its diversified business includes consumer and professional electronics, gaming, entertainment and financial services. The company owns the largest music entertainment business in the world, the largest video game console business and one of the largest video game publishing businesses, and is one of the leading manufacturers of electronic products for the consumer and professional markets, and a leading player in the film and television entertainment industry. _____ was ranked 97th on the 2018 Fortune Global 500 list.

Exam Probability: **Low**

7. *Answer choices:*

(see index for correct answer)

- a. Qulsar
- b. Everspin Technologies
- c. Semitool
- d. Sony

Guidance: level 1

:: Workplace ::

_____ is asystematic determination of a subject's merit, worth and significance, using criteria governed by a set of standards. It can assist an organization, program, design, project or any other intervention or initiative to assess any aim, realisable concept/proposal, or any alternative, to help in decision-making; or to ascertain the degree of achievement or value in regard to the aim and objectives and results of any such action that has been completed. The primary purpose of _____ , in addition to gaining insight into prior or existing initiatives, is to enable reflection and assist in the identification of future change.

Exam Probability: **High**

8. *Answer choices:*
(see index for correct answer)

- a. Evaluation
- b. labour turnover
- c. Feminisation of the workplace
- d. Open allocation

:: Generally Accepted Accounting Principles ::

In accounting, _____ is the income that a business have from its normal business activities, usually from the sale of goods and services to customers. _____ is also referred to as sales or turnover. Some companies receive _____ from interest, royalties, or other fees. _____ may refer to business income in general, or it may refer to the amount, in a monetary unit, earned during a period of time, as in "Last year, Company X had _____ of $42 million". Profits or net income generally imply total _____ minus total expenses in a given period. In accounting, in the balance statement it is a subsection of the Equity section and _____ increases equity, it is often referred to as the "top line" due to its position on the income statement at the very top. This is to be contrasted with the "bottom line" which denotes net income .

Exam Probability: **High**

9. *Answer choices:*

(see index for correct answer)

- a. Depreciation
- b. Statement of recommended practice
- c. Construction in progress
- d. Earnings before interest, taxes, depreciation, and amortization

:: Management ::

The term _____ refers to measures designed to increase the degree of autonomy and self-determination in people and in communities in order to enable them to represent their interests in a responsible and self-determined way, acting on their own authority. It is the process of becoming stronger and more confident, especially in controlling one's life and claiming one's rights. _____ as action refers both to the process of self- _____ and to professional support of people, which enables them to overcome their sense of powerlessness and lack of influence, and to recognize and use their resources. To do work with power.

Exam Probability: **Low**

10. *Answer choices:*

(see index for correct answer)

- a. Empowerment
- b. Management cockpit
- c. Submission management
- d. Business rule

Guidance: level 1

:: Generally Accepted Accounting Principles ::

Expenditure is an outflow of money to another person or group to pay for an item or service, or for a category of costs. For a tenant, rent is an _____ . For students or parents, tuition is an _____ . Buying food, clothing, furniture or an automobile is often referred to as an _____ . An _____ is a cost that is "paid" or "remitted", usually in exchange for something of value. Something that seems to cost a great deal is "expensive". Something that seems to cost little is "inexpensive". " _____ s of the table" are _____ s of dining, refreshments, a feast, etc.

Exam Probability: **Low**

11. *Answer choices:*

(see index for correct answer)

- a. Paid in capital
- b. Financial position of the United States
- c. Depreciation
- d. Provision

Guidance: level 1

:: ::

_____ is an abstract concept of management of complex systems according to a set of rules and trends. In systems theory, these types of rules exist in various fields of biology and society, but the term has slightly different meanings according to context. For example.

12. *Answer choices:*

(see index for correct answer)

- a. levels of analysis
- b. Regulation
- c. empathy
- d. functional perspective

Guidance: level 1

:: Macroeconomics ::

A foreign _____ is an investment in the form of a controlling ownership in a business in one country by an entity based in another country. It is thus distinguished from a foreign portfolio investment by a notion of direct control.

Exam Probability: **Medium**

13. *Answer choices:*

(see index for correct answer)

- a. Modern Monetary Theory
- b. Indexed unit of account
- c. Direct investment

- d. Consensus forecast

Guidance: level 1

:: Consumer theory ::

_____ is the quantity of a good that consumers are willing and able to purchase at various prices during a given period of time.

Exam Probability: **Low**

14. *Answer choices:*

(see index for correct answer)

- a. Demand
- b. Revealed preference
- c. Joint demand
- d. Income elasticity of demand

Guidance: level 1

:: Management occupations ::

_____ ship is the process of designing, launching and running a new business, which is often initially a small business. The people who create these businesses are called _____ s.

Exam Probability: **Low**

15. *Answer choices:*

(see index for correct answer)

- a. Entrepreneur
- b. Arts administration
- c. Hayward
- d. Vorstandsassistent

Guidance: level 1

:: Production and manufacturing ::

_____ is a set of techniques and tools for process improvement. Though as a shortened form it may be found written as 6S, it should not be confused with the methodology known as 6S .

Exam Probability: **High**

16. *Answer choices:*

(see index for correct answer)

- a. Turret lathe
- b. PA512
- c. Variable rate feeder
- d. Pegging report

Guidance: level 1

:: Office administration ::

An _____ is generally a room or other area where an organization's employees perform administrative work in order to support and realize objects and goals of the organization. The word " _____ " may also denote a position within an organization with specific duties attached to it ; the latter is in fact an earlier usage, _____ as place originally referring to the location of one's duty. When used as an adjective, the term " _____ " may refer to business-related tasks. In law, a company or organization has _____ s in any place where it has an official presence, even if that presence consists of a storage silo rather than an establishment with desk-and-chair. An _____ is also an architectural and design phenomenon: ranging from a small _____ such as a bench in the corner of a small business of extremely small size , through entire floors of buildings, up to and including massive buildings dedicated entirely to one company. In modern terms an _____ is usually the location where white-collar workers carry out their functions. As per James Stephenson, " _____ is that part of business enterprise which is devoted to the direction and co-ordination of its various activities."

Exam Probability: **Low**

17. *Answer choices:*

(see index for correct answer)

- a. Activity management
- b. Fish! Philosophy
- c. Office
- d. Inter departmental communication

Guidance: level 1

:: International trade ::

An _____ is a good brought into a jurisdiction, especially across a national border, from an external source. The party bringing in the good is called an _____ er. An _____ in the receiving country is an export from the sending country. _____ ation and exportation are the defining financial transactions of international trade.

Exam Probability: **High**

18. *Answer choices:*

(see index for correct answer)

- a. Reimportation
- b. Indian Ocean trade
- c. Letter of credit
- d. Import

Guidance: level 1

:: Management ::

> _____ is a process by which entities review the quality of all factors involved in production. ISO 9000 defines _____ as "A part of quality management focused on fulfilling quality requirements".

Exam Probability: **High**

19. *Answer choices:*

(see index for correct answer)

- a. Quality control
- b. Knowledge ecosystem
- c. Core competency
- d. Productive efficiency

Guidance: level 1

:: International trade ::

_____ or globalisation is the process of interaction and integration among people, companies, and governments worldwide. As a complex and multifaceted phenomenon, _____ is considered by some as a form of capitalist expansion which entails the integration of local and national economies into a global, unregulated market economy. _____ has grown due to advances in transportation and communication technology. With the increased global interactions comes the growth of international trade, ideas, and culture. _____ is primarily an economic process of interaction and integration that's associated with social and cultural aspects. However, conflicts and diplomacy are also large parts of the history of _____ , and modern _____ .

Exam Probability: **Low**

20. *Answer choices:*

(see index for correct answer)

- a. Trade route from the Varangians to the Greeks
- b. Home country control
- c. UNeDocs
- d. Globalization

Guidance: level 1

:: Systems theory ::

A _____ is a group of interacting or interrelated entities that form a unified whole. A _____ is delineated by its spatial and temporal boundaries, surrounded and influenced by its environment, described by its structure and purpose and expressed in its functioning.

Exam Probability: **Low**

21. *Answer choices:*

(see index for correct answer)

- a. System
- b. subsystem
- c. equifinality
- d. co-design

Guidance: level 1

:: ::

Competition arises whenever at least two parties strive for a goal which cannot be shared: where one's gain is the other's loss .

Exam Probability: **Low**

22. *Answer choices:*

(see index for correct answer)

- a. functional perspective
- b. Character
- c. personal values
- d. Competitor

Guidance: level 1

:: Financial statements ::

In financial accounting, a _____ or statement of financial position or statement of financial condition is a summary of the financial balances of an individual or organization, whether it be a sole proprietorship, a business partnership, a corporation, private limited company or other organization such as Government or not-for-profit entity. Assets, liabilities and ownership equity are listed as of a specific date, such as the end of its financial year. A _____ is often described as a "snapshot of a company's financial condition". Of the four basic financial statements, the _____ is the only statement which applies to a single point in time of a business' calendar year.

Exam Probability: **Low**

23. *Answer choices:*

(see index for correct answer)

- a. Financial report
- b. Balance sheet
- c. Emphasis of matter
- d. Statement of retained earnings

:: Supply chain management ::

_____ is the process of finding and agreeing to terms, and acquiring goods, services, or works from an external source, often via a tendering or competitive bidding process. _____ is used to ensure the buyer receives goods, services, or works at the best possible price when aspects such as quality, quantity, time, and location are compared. Corporations and public bodies often define processes intended to promote fair and open competition for their business while minimizing risks such as exposure to fraud and collusion.

Exam Probability: **Low**

24. *Answer choices:*

(see index for correct answer)

- a. Design for logistics
- b. Enterprise resource planning
- c. Capconn
- d. Procurement

:: Marketing ::

The _____ is a foundation model for businesses. The _____ has been defined as the "set of marketing tools that the firm uses to pursue its marketing objectives in the target market". Thus the _____ refers to four broad levels of marketing decision, namely: product, price, place, and promotion. Marketing practice has been occurring for millennia, but marketing theory emerged in the early twentieth century. The contemporary _____, or the 4 Ps, which has become the dominant framework for marketing management decisions, was first published in 1960. In services marketing, an extended _____ is used, typically comprising 7 Ps, made up of the original 4 Ps extended by process, people, and physical evidence. Occasionally service marketers will refer to 8 Ps, comprising these 7 Ps plus performance.

Exam Probability: **Low**

25. *Answer choices:*

(see index for correct answer)

- a. Marketing mix
- b. Cumulative prospect theory
- c. Call to action
- d. Positioning

Guidance: level 1

:: Property ::

The right to property or right to own property is often classified as a human right for natural persons regarding their possessions. A general recognition of a right to private property is found more rarely and is typically heavily constrained insofar as property is owned by legal persons and where it is used for production rather than consumption.

Exam Probability: **High**

26. *Answer choices:*

(see index for correct answer)

- a. Lockean proviso
- b. The Great Transformation
- c. Property rights
- d. Non-property system

Guidance: level 1

:: Business models ::

_____ es are privately owned corporations, partnerships, or sole proprietorships that have fewer employees and/or less annual revenue than a regular-sized business or corporation. Businesses are defined as "small" in terms of being able to apply for government support and qualify for preferential tax policy varies depending on the country and industry.

_____ es range from fifteen employees under the Australian Fair Work Act 2009, fifty employees according to the definition used by the European Union, and fewer than five hundred employees to qualify for many U.S. _____ Administration programs. While _____ es can also be classified according to other methods, such as annual revenues, shipments, sales, assets, or by annual gross or net revenue or net profits, the number of employees is one of the most widely used measures.

Exam Probability: **Medium**

27. *Answer choices:*

(see index for correct answer)

- a. Dependent growth business model
- b. Open Music Model
- c. Small business
- d. Subscription business model

Guidance: level 1

:: Packaging ::

In work place, _____ or job _____ means good ranking with the hypothesized conception of requirements of a role. There are two types of job _____ s: contextual and task. Task _____ is related to cognitive ability while contextual _____ is dependent upon personality. Task _____ are behavioral roles that are recognized in job descriptions and by remuneration systems, they are directly related to organizational _____ , whereas, contextual _____ are value based and additional behavioral roles that are not recognized in job descriptions and covered by compensation; they are extra roles that are indirectly related to organizational _____ . Citizenship _____ like contextual _____ means a set of individual activity/contribution that supports the organizational culture.

Exam Probability: **Low**

28. *Answer choices:*

(see index for correct answer)

- a. Oxygen scavenger
- b. Sustainable packaging
- c. Keep case
- d. Performance

Guidance: level 1

:: Debt ::

_____ is when something, usually money, is owed by one party, the borrower or _____ or, to a second party, the lender or creditor. _____ is a deferred payment, or series of payments, that is owed in the future, which is what differentiates it from an immediate purchase. The _____ may be owed by sovereign state or country, local government, company, or an individual. Commercial _____ is generally subject to contractual terms regarding the amount and timing of repayments of principal and interest. Loans, bonds, notes, and mortgages are all types of _____ . The term can also be used metaphorically to cover moral obligations and other interactions not based on economic value. For example, in Western cultures, a person who has been helped by a second person is sometimes said to owe a " _____ of gratitude" to the second person.

Exam Probability: **Low**

29. *Answer choices:*

(see index for correct answer)

- a. Debt
- b. Odious debt
- c. Recourse debt
- d. Vulture fund

Guidance: level 1

:: Currency ::

A _____ , in the most specific sense is money in any form when in use or circulation as a medium of exchange, especially circulating banknotes and coins. A more general definition is that a _____ is a system of money in common use, especially for people in a nation. Under this definition, US dollars , pounds sterling , Australian dollars , European euros , Russian rubles and Indian Rupees are examples of currencies. These various currencies are recognized as stores of value and are traded between nations in foreign exchange markets, which determine the relative values of the different currencies. Currencies in this sense are defined by governments, and each type has limited boundaries of acceptance.

Exam Probability: **Medium**

30. *Answer choices:*

(see index for correct answer)

- a. Currency
- b. Cross currency swap
- c. Fiat money
- d. Decimalisation

Guidance: level 1

:: Business law ::

A _____ is a group of people who jointly supervise the activities of an organization, which can be either a for-profit business, nonprofit organization, or a government agency. Such a board's powers, duties, and responsibilities are determined by government regulations and the organization's own constitution and bylaws. These authorities may specify the number of members of the board, how they are to be chosen, and how often they are to meet.

31. *Answer choices:*

(see index for correct answer)

- a. Commercial law
- b. General assignment
- c. Voting trust
- d. Company mortgage

Guidance: level 1

:: Television commercials ::

_____ is a phenomenon whereby something new and somehow valuable is formed. The created item may be intangible or a physical object .

32. *Answer choices:*

- a. Lamp
- b. The Program Exchange
- c. Frozen Peas
- d. Creativity

Guidance: level 1

:: Real estate valuation ::

_____ or OMV is the price at which an asset would trade in a competitive auction setting. _____ is often used interchangeably with open _____ , fair value or fair _____ , although these terms have distinct definitions in different standards, and may or may not differ in some circumstances.

Exam Probability: **High**

33. *Answer choices:*

- a. Market value
- b. Rate base
- c. Appraisal Standards Board
- d. Real estate benchmarking

:: International trade ::

_____ involves the transfer of goods or services from one person or entity to another, often in exchange for money. A system or network that allows _____ is called a market.

Exam Probability: **High**

34. *Answer choices:*

(see index for correct answer)

- a. Trade Act of 1974
- b. FAST Card
- c. Trade
- d. Combined Nomenclature

:: Information science ::

A _____ is a written, drawn, presented, or memorialized representation of thought. a _____ is a form, or written piece that trains a line of thought or as in history, a significant event. The word originates from the Latin _____ um, which denotes a "teaching" or "lesson": the verb doceo denotes "to teach". In the past, the word was usually used to denote a written proof useful as evidence of a truth or fact. In the computer age, " _____ " usually denotes a primarily textual computer file, including its structure and format, e.g. fonts, colors, and images. Contemporarily, " _____ " is not defined by its transmission medium, e.g., paper, given the existence of electronic _____ s. " _____ ation" is distinct because it has more denotations than " _____ ". _____ s are also distinguished from "realia", which are three-dimensional objects that would otherwise satisfy the definition of " _____ " because they memorialize or represent thought; _____ s are considered more as 2 dimensional representations. While _____ s are able to have large varieties of customization, all _____ s are able to be shared freely, and have the right to do so, creativity can be represented by _____ s, also. History, events, examples, opinion, etc. all can be expressed in _____ s.

Exam Probability: **High**

35. *Answer choices:*

(see index for correct answer)

- a. Schema.org
- b. Information audit
- c. Integrated Operations in the High North
- d. Document

Guidance: level 1

:: Business ethics ::

_____ is a type of harassment technique that relates to a sexual nature and the unwelcome or inappropriate promise of rewards in exchange for sexual favors. _____ includes a range of actions from mild transgressions to sexual abuse or assault. Harassment can occur in many different social settings such as the workplace, the home, school, churches, etc. Harassers or victims may be of any gender.

Exam Probability: **High**

36. *Answer choices:*

(see index for correct answer)

- a. Corporate sustainable profitability
- b. Enron Code of Ethics
- c. Sexual harassment
- d. Bribery Act 2010

Guidance: level 1

:: Industrial Revolution ::

The _____ , now also known as the First _____ , was the transition to new manufacturing processes in Europe and the US, in the period from about 1760 to sometime between 1820 and 1840. This transition included going from hand production methods to machines, new chemical manufacturing and iron production processes, the increasing use of steam power and water power, the development of machine tools and the rise of the mechanized factory system. The _____ also led to an unprecedented rise in the rate of population growth.

Exam Probability: **Low**

37. *Answer choices:*

(see index for correct answer)

- a. Pocasset Manufacturing Company
- b. Bernat Mill
- c. Moira Furnace
- d. Roberts Loom

Guidance: level 1

:: Quality management ::

_____ ensures that an organization, product or service is consistent. It has four main components: quality planning, quality assurance, quality control and quality improvement. _____ is focused not only on product and service quality, but also on the means to achieve it. _____ , therefore, uses quality assurance and control of processes as well as products to achieve more consistent quality. What a customer wants and is willing to pay for it determines quality. It is written or unwritten commitment to a known or unknown consumer in the market . Thus, quality can be defined as fitness for intended use or, in other words, how well the product performs its intended function

Exam Probability: **High**

38. *Answer choices:*

(see index for correct answer)

- a. PQASSO
- b. Dana Ulery
- c. Registro Italiano Navale
- d. Quality management

Guidance: level 1

:: Management accounting ::

_____ s are costs that change as the quantity of the good or service that a business produces changes. _____ s are the sum of marginal costs over all units produced. They can also be considered normal costs. Fixed costs and _____ s make up the two components of total cost. Direct costs are costs that can easily be associated with a particular cost object. However, not all _____ s are direct costs. For example, variable manufacturing overhead costs are _____ s that are indirect costs, not direct costs. _____ s are sometimes called unit-level costs as they vary with the number of units produced.

Exam Probability: **Low**

39. *Answer choices:*

(see index for correct answer)

- a. Chartered Institute of Management Accountants
- b. Fixed assets management
- c. Management control system
- d. Variable cost

Guidance: level 1

:: Commercial item transport and distribution ::

A _____ is a commitment or expectation to perform some action in general or if certain circumstances arise. A _____ may arise from a system of ethics or morality, especially in an honor culture. Many duties are created by law, sometimes including a codified punishment or liability for non-performance. Performing one's _____ may require some sacrifice of self-interest.

Exam Probability: **Medium**

40. *Answer choices:*

(see index for correct answer)

- a. Weigh station
- b. Multimodal transport
- c. SAP EWM
- d. Duty

Guidance: level 1

:: Service industries ::

_____ are the economic services provided by the finance industry, which encompasses a broad range of businesses that manage money, including credit unions, banks, credit-card companies, insurance companies, accountancy companies, consumer-finance companies, stock brokerages, investment funds, individual managers and some government-sponsored enterprises. _____ companies are present in all economically developed geographic locations and tend to cluster in local, national, regional and international financial centers such as London, New York City, and Tokyo.

41. *Answer choices:*

(see index for correct answer)

- a. Financial services
- b. Allotment
- c. Language industry
- d. Maid service

Guidance: level 1

:: Business law ::

_____ is where a person's financial liability is limited to a fixed sum, most commonly the value of a person's investment in a company or partnership. If a company with _____ is sued, then the claimants are suing the company, not its owners or investors. A shareholder in a limited company is not personally liable for any of the debts of the company, other than for the amount already invested in the company and for any unpaid amount on the shares in the company, if any. The same is true for the members of a _____ partnership and the limited partners in a limited partnership. By contrast, sole proprietors and partners in general partnerships are each liable for all the debts of the business .

42. *Answer choices:*

(see index for correct answer)

- a. Retained interest
- b. Time-and-a-half
- c. Registered agent
- d. Personal Property Security Act

Guidance: level 1

:: Employment ::

The _____ is an individual's metaphorical "journey" through learning, work and other aspects of life. There are a number of ways to define _____ and the term is used in a variety of ways.

Exam Probability: **High**

43. *Answer choices:*

(see index for correct answer)

- a. Career
- b. Cyberloafing
- c. Extra role performance
- d. ThinkTalk

Guidance: level 1

:: Energy and fuel journals ::

In physics, energy is the quantitative property that must be transferred to an object in order to perform work on, or to heat, the object. Energy is a conserved quantity; the law of conservation of energy states that energy can be converted in form, but not created or destroyed. The SI unit of energy is the joule, which is the energy transferred to an object by the work of moving it a distance of 1 metre against a force of 1 newton.

Exam Probability: **Medium**

44. *Answer choices:*

(see index for correct answer)

- a. Energies
- b. Journal of Power Sources
- c. Applied Thermal Engineering
- d. Renewable and Sustainable Energy Reviews

Guidance: level 1

:: Marketing analytics ::

_____ is a long-term, forward-looking approach to planning with the fundamental goal of achieving a sustainable competitive advantage. Strategic planning involves an analysis of the company's strategic initial situation prior to the formulation, evaluation and selection of market-oriented competitive position that contributes to the company's goals and marketing objectives.

45. *Answer choices:*

(see index for correct answer)

- a. Return on marketing investment
- b. Perceptual map
- c. Marketing strategy
- d. Marketing resource management

Guidance: level 1

:: Environmental economics ::

_____ is the process of people maintaining change in a balanced environment, in which the exploitation of resources, the direction of investments, the orientation of technological development and institutional change are all in harmony and enhance both current and future potential to meet human needs and aspirations. For many in the field, _____ is defined through the following interconnected domains or pillars: environment, economic and social, which according to Fritjof Capra is based on the principles of Systems Thinking. Sub-domains of sustainable development have been considered also: cultural, technological and political. While sustainable development may be the organizing principle for _____ for some, for others, the two terms are paradoxical . Sustainable development is the development that meets the needs of the present without compromising the ability of future generations to meet their own needs. Brundtland Report for the World Commission on Environment and Development introduced the term of sustainable development.

46. *Answer choices:*

- a. Mitigation banking
- b. Ecolabel
- c. Genuine progress indicator
- d. Travel cost analysis

Guidance: level 1

:: Stock market ::

_____ is a form of corporate equity ownership, a type of security. The terms voting share and ordinary share are also used frequently in other parts of the world; " _____ " being primarily used in the United States. They are known as Equity shares or Ordinary shares in the UK and other Commonwealth realms. This type of share gives the stockholder the right to share in the profits of the company, and to vote on matters of corporate policy and the composition of the members of the board of directors.

Exam Probability: **Medium**

47. *Answer choices:*

- a. International Retail Service
- b. Somalia Stock Exchange
- c. Secondary market offering

- d. Red chip

Guidance: level 1

:: Management ::

A _____ describes the rationale of how an organization creates, delivers, and captures value, in economic, social, cultural or other contexts. The process of _____ construction and modification is also called _____ innovation and forms a part of business strategy.

Exam Probability: **High**

48. *Answer choices:*

(see index for correct answer)

- a. Business model
- b. Tata Management Training Centre
- c. Instruction creep
- d. Systems analysis

Guidance: level 1

:: Marketing ::

A _____ is something that is necessary for an organism to live a healthy life. _____ s are distinguished from wants in that, in the case of a _____ , a deficiency causes a clear adverse outcome: a dysfunction or death. In other words, a _____ is something required for a safe, stable and healthy life while a want is a desire, wish or aspiration. When _____ s or wants are backed by purchasing power, they have the potential to become economic demands.

Exam Probability: **High**

49. *Answer choices:*

(see index for correct answer)

- a. Impulse buying
- b. Editorial calendar
- c. Need
- d. Carrying cost

Guidance: level 1

:: Business ::

A _____ is a mathematical object used to count, measure, and label. The original examples are the natural _____ s 1, 2, 3, 4, and so forth. A written symbol like "5" that represents a _____ is called a numeral. A numeral system is an organized way to write and manipulate this type of symbol, for example the Hindu–Arabic numeral system allows combinations of numerical digits like "5" and "0" to represent larger _____ s like 50. A numeral in linguistics can refer to a symbol like 5, the words or phrase that names a _____ , like "five hundred", or other words that mean a specific _____ , like "dozen". In addition to their use in counting and measuring, numerals are often used for labels , for ordering , and for codes . In common usage, _____ may refer to a symbol, a word or phrase, or the mathematical object.

Exam Probability: **High**

50. *Answer choices:*

(see index for correct answer)

- a. Number
- b. Legal governance, risk management, and compliance
- c. First party leads
- d. Les Vergers du Mekong

Guidance: level 1

:: Stochastic processes ::

_____ in its modern meaning is a "new idea, creative thoughts, new imaginations in form of device or method". _____ is often also viewed as the application of better solutions that meet new requirements, unarticulated needs, or existing market needs. Such _____ takes place through the provision of more-effective products, processes, services, technologies, or business models that are made available to markets, governments and society. An _____ is something original and more effective and, as a consequence, new, that "breaks into" the market or society. _____ is related to, but not the same as, invention, as _____ is more apt to involve the practical implementation of an invention to make a meaningful impact in the market or society, and not all _____ s require an invention. _____ often manifests itself via the engineering process, when the problem being solved is of a technical or scientific nature. The opposite of _____ is exnovation.

Exam Probability: **High**

51. *Answer choices:*

(see index for correct answer)

- a. Continuous-time stochastic process
- b. Diffusion process
- c. Loss network
- d. Innovation

Guidance: level 1

:: Association of Southeast Asian Nations ::

The Association of Southeast Asian Nations is a regional intergovernmental organization comprising ten countries in Southeast Asia, which promotes intergovernmental cooperation and facilitates economic, political, security, military, educational, and sociocultural integration among its members and other countries in Asia. It also regularly engages other countries in the Asia-Pacific region and beyond. A major partner of Shanghai Cooperation Organisation, _____ maintains a global network of alliances and dialogue partners and is considered by many as a global powerhouse, the central union for cooperation in Asia-Pacific, and a prominent and influential organization. It is involved in numerous international affairs, and hosts diplomatic missions throughout the world.

Exam Probability: **Medium**

52. *Answer choices:*

(see index for correct answer)

- a. ASEAN Intergovernmental Commission on Human Rights
- b. ASEAN Rise
- c. Flag of the Association of Southeast Asian Nations
- d. ASEAN Human Rights Declaration

Guidance: level 1

:: Market research ::

_____ , an acronym for Information through Disguised Experimentation is an annual market research fair conducted by the students of IIM-Lucknow. Students create games and use various other simulated environments to capture consumers' subconscious thoughts. This innovative method of market research removes the sensitization effect that might bias peoples answers to questions. This ensures that the most truthful answers are captured to research questions. The games are designed in such a way that the observers can elicit all the required information just by observing and noting down the behaviour and the responses of the participants.

Exam Probability: **Medium**

53. *Answer choices:*

(see index for correct answer)

- a. INDEX
- b. Competitive intelligence
- c. DigitalMR
- d. The ESPN Sports Poll

Guidance: level 1

:: Data management ::

_____ is a form of intellectual property that grants the creator of an original creative work an exclusive legal right to determine whether and under what conditions this original work may be copied and used by others, usually for a limited term of years. The exclusive rights are not absolute but limited by limitations and exceptions to _____ law, including fair use. A major limitation on _____ on ideas is that _____ protects only the original expression of ideas, and not the underlying ideas themselves.

Exam Probability: **High**

54. *Answer choices:*

(see index for correct answer)

- a. Consumer relationship system
- b. Small data
- c. Distributed transaction
- d. Lean integration

Guidance: level 1

:: Stock market ::

A _____ , equity market or share market is the aggregation of buyers and sellers of stocks , which represent ownership claims on businesses; these may include securities listed on a public stock exchange, as well as stock that is only traded privately. Examples of the latter include shares of private companies which are sold to investors through equity crowdfunding platforms. Stock exchanges list shares of common equity as well as other security types, e.g. corporate bonds and convertible bonds.

55. *Answer choices:*

(see index for correct answer)

- a. Stock market
- b. Xetra
- c. Program trading
- d. Indian Depository Receipt

Guidance: level 1

:: Asset ::

In financial accounting, an _____ is any resource owned by the business. Anything tangible or intangible that can be owned or controlled to produce value and that is held by a company to produce positive economic value is an _____ . Simply stated, _____ s represent value of ownership that can be converted into cash . The balance sheet of a firm records the monetary value of the _____ s owned by that firm. It covers money and other valuables belonging to an individual or to a business.

Exam Probability: **Medium**

56. *Answer choices:*

(see index for correct answer)

- a. Current asset

- b. Asset

Guidance: level 1

:: Business ::

_____ is a trade policy that does not restrict imports or exports; it can also be understood as the free market idea applied to international trade. In government, _____ is predominantly advocated by political parties that hold liberal economic positions while economically left-wing and nationalist political parties generally support protectionism, the opposite of _____ .

Exam Probability: **Low**

57. *Answer choices:*

(see index for correct answer)

- a. Staff and line
- b. Operating agreement
- c. Free trade
- d. Customer experience

Guidance: level 1

:: Macroeconomics ::

_____ is the increase in the inflation-adjusted market value of the goods and services produced by an economy over time. It is conventionally measured as the percent rate of increase in real gross domestic product, or real GDP.

Exam Probability: **Medium**

58. *Answer choices:*

(see index for correct answer)

- a. Economic growth
- b. Crowding out
- c. Life-cycle hypothesis
- d. Endogenous money

Guidance: level 1

:: ::

_____ is a means of protection from financial loss. It is a form of risk management, primarily used to hedge against the risk of a contingent or uncertain loss

Exam Probability: **Low**

59. *Answer choices:*

(see index for correct answer)

- a. Insurance
- b. levels of analysis
- c. hierarchical perspective
- d. imperative

Guidance: level 1

Management

Management is the administration of an organization, whether it is a business, a not-for-profit organization, or government body. Management includes the activities of setting the strategy of an organization and coordinating the efforts of its employees (or of volunteers) to accomplish its objectives through the application of available resources, such as financial, natural, technological, and human resources.

:: Employment compensation ::

_____ refers to various incentive plans introduced by businesses that provide direct or indirect payments to employees that depend on company`s profitability in addition to employees` regular salary and bonuses. In publicly traded companies these plans typically amount to allocation of shares to employees. One of the earliest pioneers of _____ was Englishman Theodore Cooke Taylor, who is known to have introduced the practice in his woollen mills during the late 1800s .

Exam Probability: **High**

1. *Answer choices:*

(see index for correct answer)

- a. The Theory of Wages
- b. State Compensation Insurance Fund
- c. Interactive accommodation process
- d. Profit sharing

Guidance: level 1

:: ::

A _____ is a research instrument consisting of a series of questions for the purpose of gathering information from respondents. The _____ was invented by the Statistical Society of London in 1838.

Exam Probability: **Medium**

2. *Answer choices:*

(see index for correct answer)

- a. Questionnaire
- b. personal values
- c. cultural
- d. surface-level diversity

Guidance: level 1

:: Commercial item transport and distribution ::

In commerce, supply-chain management , the management of the flow of goods and services, involves the movement and storage of raw materials, of work-in-process inventory, and of finished goods from point of origin to point of consumption. Interconnected or interlinked networks, channels and node businesses combine in the provision of products and services required by end customers in a supply chain. Supply-chain management has been defined as the "design, planning, execution, control, and monitoring of supply-chain activities with the objective of creating net value, building a competitive infrastructure, leveraging worldwide logistics, synchronizing supply with demand and measuring performance globally."SCM practice draws heavily from the areas of industrial engineering, systems engineering, operations management, logistics, procurement, information technology, and marketing and strives for an integrated approach. Marketing channels play an important role in supply-chain management. Current research in supply-chain management is concerned with topics related to sustainability and risk management, among others. Some suggest that the "people dimension" of SCM, ethical issues, internal integration, transparency/visibility, and human capital/talent management are topics that have, so far, been underrepresented on the research agenda.

3. *Answer choices:*

(see index for correct answer)

- a. Skid unit
- b. Best Way Technologies
- c. Skid mount
- d. Dimensional weight

Guidance: level 1

:: International trade ::

_____ involves the transfer of goods or services from one person or entity to another, often in exchange for money. A system or network that allows _____ is called a market.

Exam Probability: **Low**

4. *Answer choices:*

(see index for correct answer)

- a. International Centre for Trade and Sustainable Development
- b. Bureau de change
- c. Banana Framework Agreement
- d. Trade

:: ::

_____ is the amount of time someone works beyond normal working hours. The term is also used for the pay received for this time. Normal hours may be determined in several ways.

Exam Probability: **Medium**

5. *Answer choices:*

(see index for correct answer)

- a. Overtime
- b. hierarchical
- c. levels of analysis
- d. corporate values

:: Summary statistics ::

_____ is the number of occurrences of a repeating event per unit of time. It is also referred to as temporal _____ , which emphasizes the contrast to spatial _____ and angular _____ . The period is the duration of time of one cycle in a repeating event, so the period is the reciprocal of the _____ . For example: if a newborn baby's heart beats at a _____ of 120 times a minute, its period—the time interval between beats—is half a second . _____ is an important parameter used in science and engineering to specify the rate of oscillatory and vibratory phenomena, such as mechanical vibrations, audio signals , radio waves, and light.

Exam Probability: **High**

6. *Answer choices:*

- a. Generalized entropy index
- b. Quartile
- c. Frequency
- d. Scan statistic

Guidance: level 1

:: Quality management ::

A _____ or quality control circle is a group of workers who do the same or similar work, who meet regularly to identify, analyze and solve work-related problems. Normally small in size, the group is usually led by a supervisor or manager and presents its solutions to management; where possible, workers implement the solutions themselves in order to improve the performance of the organization and motivate employees. _____ s were at their most popular during the 1980s, but continue to exist in the form of Kaizen groups and similar worker participation schemes.

Exam Probability: **Medium**

7. *Answer choices:*

(see index for correct answer)

- a. Management by wandering around
- b. Quality circle
- c. Product quality risk in supply chain
- d. External quality assessment

Guidance: level 1

:: ::

In organizational behavior and industrial/organizational psychology, proactivity or _____ behavior by individuals refers to anticipatory, change-oriented and self-initiated behavior in situations. _____ behavior involves acting in advance of a future situation, rather than just reacting. It means taking control and making things happen rather than just adjusting to a situation or waiting for something to happen. _____ employees generally do not need to be asked to act, nor do they require detailed instructions.

Exam Probability: **Low**

8. *Answer choices:*

(see index for correct answer)

- a. information systems assessment
- b. Proactive
- c. similarity-attraction theory
- d. imperative

Guidance: level 1

:: Workplace ::

A _____ , also referred to as a performance review, performance evaluation, development discussion, or employee appraisal is a method by which the job performance of an employee is documented and evaluated. _____ s are a part of career development and consist of regular reviews of employee performance within organizations.

9. *Answer choices:*

(see index for correct answer)

- a. Workplace spirituality
- b. performance review
- c. Hostile environment sexual harassment
- d. Performance appraisal

Guidance: level 1

:: Management ::

_____ is the process of thinking about the activities required to achieve a desired goal. It is the first and foremost activity to achieve desired results. It involves the creation and maintenance of a plan, such as psychological aspects that require conceptual skills. There are even a couple of tests to measure someone's capability of _____ well. As such, _____ is a fundamental property of intelligent behavior. An important further meaning, often just called " _____ " is the legal context of permitted building developments.

10. *Answer choices:*

(see index for correct answer)

- a. Vorstand
- b. Planning
- c. Crisis plan
- d. Management buyout

Guidance: level 1

:: Marketing ::

_____ , in marketing, manufacturing, call centres and management, is the use of flexible computer-aided manufacturing systems to produce custom output. Such systems combine the low unit costs of mass production processes with the flexibility of individual customization.

Exam Probability: **High**

11. *Answer choices:*

(see index for correct answer)

- a. The customer is always right
- b. Market development
- c. Franchise disclosure document
- d. Mass customization

Guidance: level 1

:: Outsourcing ::

_____ is the relocation of a business process from one country to another—typically an operational process, such as manufacturing, or supporting processes, such as accounting. Typically this refers to a company business, although state governments may also employ _____ . More recently, technical and administrative services have been offshored.

Exam Probability: **Low**

12. *Answer choices:*

(see index for correct answer)

- a. Telarus
- b. Virtual Staff Finder
- c. Chris Ducker
- d. Application Management Services Framework

Guidance: level 1

:: ::

_____ is the collection of mechanisms, processes and relations by which corporations are controlled and operated. Governance structures and principles identify the distribution of rights and responsibilities among different participants in the corporation and include the rules and procedures for making decisions in corporate affairs. _____ is necessary because of the possibility of conflicts of interests between stakeholders, primarily between shareholders and upper management or among shareholders.

Exam Probability: **Low**

13. *Answer choices:*

(see index for correct answer)

- a. information systems assessment
- b. Corporate governance
- c. process perspective
- d. deep-level diversity

Guidance: level 1

:: Human resource management ::

_____ encompasses values and behaviors that contribute to the unique social and psychological environment of a business. The _____ influences the way people interact, the context within which knowledge is created, the resistance they will have towards certain changes, and ultimately the way they share knowledge. _____ represents the collective values, beliefs and principles of organizational members and is a product of factors such as history, product, market, technology, strategy, type of employees, management style, and national culture; culture includes the organization's vision, values, norms, systems, symbols, language, assumptions, environment, location, beliefs and habits.

Exam Probability: **High**

14. *Answer choices:*

(see index for correct answer)

- a. Employment testing
- b. Talent management
- c. Organizational culture
- d. Pay in lieu of notice

Guidance: level 1

:: Project management ::

Some scenarios associate "this kind of planning" with learning "life skills".
_____ s are necessary, or at least useful, in situations where individuals need to know what time they must be at a specific location to receive a specific service, and where people need to accomplish a set of goals within a set time period.

Exam Probability: **High**

15. *Answer choices:*

(see index for correct answer)

- a. Test and evaluation master plan
- b. Deployment Plan
- c. Drag cost
- d. Project charter

Guidance: level 1

:: Management ::

_____ is the identification, evaluation, and prioritization of risks followed by coordinated and economical application of resources to minimize, monitor, and control the probability or impact of unfortunate events or to maximize the realization of opportunities.

Exam Probability: **Low**

16. *Answer choices:*

(see index for correct answer)

- a. Managerialism
- b. Risk management
- c. Reval
- d. Defensive expenditures

Guidance: level 1

:: Elementary mathematics ::

_____ is a numerical measurement of how far apart objects are. In physics or everyday usage, _____ may refer to a physical length or an estimation based on other criteria . In most cases, " _____ from A to B" is interchangeable with " _____ from B to A". In mathematics, a _____ function or metric is a generalization of the concept of physical _____ . A metric is a function that behaves according to a specific set of rules, and is a way of describing what it means for elements of some space to be "close to" or "far away from" each other.

Exam Probability: **Low**

17. *Answer choices:*

(see index for correct answer)

- a. Unary numeral system
- b. Identity function

- c. Distance
- d. Abscissa

Guidance: level 1

:: Employee relations ::

_____ ownership, or employee share ownership, is an ownership interest in a company held by the company's workforce. The ownership interest may be facilitated by the company as part of employees' remuneration or incentive compensation for work performed, or the company itself may be employee owned.

Exam Probability: **Low**

18. *Answer choices:*

(see index for correct answer)

- a. employee stock ownership
- b. Employee morale
- c. Employee engagement
- d. Employee stock

Guidance: level 1

:: Marketing ::

A _____ is an overall experience of a customer that distinguishes an organization or product from its rivals in the eyes of the customer. _____ s are used in business, marketing, and advertising. Name _____ s are sometimes distinguished from generic or store _____ s.

Exam Probability: **Low**

19. *Answer choices:*

(see index for correct answer)

- a. Marketing automation
- b. Markup
- c. Brand
- d. Promise marketing

Guidance: level 1

:: ::

_____ , in its broadest context, includes both the attainment of that which is just and the philosophical discussion of that which is just. The concept of _____ is based on numerous fields, and many differing viewpoints and perspectives including the concepts of moral correctness based on ethics, rationality, law, religion, equity and fairness. Often, the general discussion of _____ is divided into the realm of social _____ as found in philosophy, theology and religion, and, procedural _____ as found in the study and application of the law.

20. *Answer choices:*

(see index for correct answer)

- a. personal values
- b. hierarchical
- c. corporate values
- d. Justice

Guidance: level 1

:: Project management ::

A _____ is a professional in the field of project management. _____ s have the responsibility of the planning, procurement and execution of a project, in any undertaking that has a defined scope, defined start and a defined finish; regardless of industry. _____ s are first point of contact for any issues or discrepancies arising from within the heads of various departments in an organization before the problem escalates to higher authorities. Project management is the responsibility of a _____ . This individual seldom participates directly in the activities that produce the end result, but rather strives to maintain the progress, mutual interaction and tasks of various parties in such a way that reduces the risk of overall failure, maximizes benefits, and minimizes costs.

Exam Probability: **Medium**

21. *Answer choices:*

(see index for correct answer)

- a. Advanced Integrated Practice
- b. Trenegy Incorporated
- c. Product description
- d. Project manager

Guidance: level 1

:: Business terms ::

A _____ is a short statement of why an organization exists, what its overall goal is, identifying the goal of its operations: what kind of product or service it provides, its primary customers or market, and its geographical region of operation. It may include a short statement of such fundamental matters as the organization's values or philosophies, a business's main competitive advantages, or a desired future state—the "vision".

Exam Probability: **Low**

22. *Answer choices:*

(see index for correct answer)

- a. strategic plan
- b. Mission statement
- c. organizational capital
- d. churn rate

:: Teams ::

A _____ usually refers to a group of individuals who work together from different geographic locations and rely on communication technology such as email, FAX, and video or voice conferencing services in order to collaborate. The term can also refer to groups or teams that work together asynchronously or across organizational levels. Powell, Piccoli and Ives define _____ s as "groups of geographically, organizationally and/or time dispersed workers brought together by information and telecommunication technologies to accomplish one or more organizational tasks." According to Ale Ebrahim et. al. , _____ s can also be defined as "small temporary groups of geographically, organizationally and/or time dispersed knowledge workers who coordinate their work predominantly with electronic information and communication technologies in order to accomplish one or more organization tasks."

Exam Probability: **Low**

23. *Answer choices:*

(see index for correct answer)

- a. Team-building
- b. Virtual team

:: Human resource management ::

_____ involves improving the effectiveness of organizations and the individuals and teams within them. Training may be viewed as related to immediate changes in organizational effectiveness via organized instruction, while development is related to the progress of longer-term organizational and employee goals. While _____ technically have differing definitions, the two are oftentimes used interchangeably and/or together. _____ has historically been a topic within applied psychology but has within the last two decades become closely associated with human resources management, talent management, human resources development, instructional design, human factors, and knowledge management.

Exam Probability: **High**

24. *Answer choices:*

(see index for correct answer)

- a. Four-day week
- b. Herrmann Brain Dominance Instrument
- c. Training and development
- d. Competency-based recruitment

Guidance: level 1

:: Types of marketing ::

In microeconomics and management, _____ is an arrangement in which the supply chain of a company is owned by that company. Usually each member of the supply chain produces a different product or service, and the products combine to satisfy a common need. It is contrasted with horizontal integration, wherein a company produces several items which are related to one another. _____ has also described management styles that bring large portions of the supply chain not only under a common ownership, but also into one corporation .

Exam Probability: **High**

25. *Answer choices:*

(see index for correct answer)

- a. Vertical integration
- b. Guerrilla marketing
- c. Ambush marketing
- d. Shopper marketing

Guidance: level 1

:: Game theory ::

_____ is the idea that rationality is limited when individuals make decisions: by the tractability of the decision problem, the cognitive limitations of the mind, and the time available to make the decision. Decision-makers, in this view, act as satisficers, seeking a satisfactory solution rather than an optimal one.

26. *Answer choices:*

(see index for correct answer)

- a. Complete information
- b. Bounded rationality
- c. Two-level game theory
- d. Dictator game

Guidance: level 1

:: Production and manufacturing ::

_____ is a set of techniques and tools for process improvement. Though as a shortened form it may be found written as 6S, it should not be confused with the methodology known as 6S .

Exam Probability: **Medium**

27. *Answer choices:*

(see index for correct answer)

- a. Fixed position assembly
- b. Six Sigma
- c. Process control
- d. Low rate initial production

:: Labor rights ::

A _____ is a wrong or hardship suffered, real or supposed, which forms legitimate grounds of complaint. In the past, the word meant the infliction or cause of hardship.

Exam Probability: **Medium**

28. *Answer choices:*

(see index for correct answer)

- a. Kate Mullany House
- b. China Labor Watch
- c. Grievance
- d. Swift raids

:: Management ::

_____ is a process by which entities review the quality of all factors involved in production. ISO 9000 defines _____ as "A part of quality management focused on fulfilling quality requirements".

Exam Probability: **Low**

29. *Answer choices:*

(see index for correct answer)

- a. Distributed management
- b. Quality control
- c. Mobile sales enablement
- d. Event management

Guidance: level 1

:: Supply chain management ::

_____ is the process of finding and agreeing to terms, and acquiring goods, services, or works from an external source, often via a tendering or competitive bidding process. _____ is used to ensure the buyer receives goods, services, or works at the best possible price when aspects such as quality, quantity, time, and location are compared. Corporations and public bodies often define processes intended to promote fair and open competition for their business while minimizing risks such as exposure to fraud and collusion.

Exam Probability: **Low**

30. *Answer choices:*

(see index for correct answer)

- a. Enterprise resource planning

- b. Procurement
- c. Enterprise carbon accounting
- d. Confirmed line item performance

:: Information science ::

_____ is the resolution of uncertainty; it is that which answers the question of "what an entity is" and thus defines both its essence and nature of its characteristics. _____ relates to both data and knowledge, as data is meaningful _____ representing values attributed to parameters, and knowledge signifies understanding of a concept. _____ is uncoupled from an observer, which is an entity that can access _____ and thus discern what it specifies; _____ exists beyond an event horizon for example. In the case of knowledge, the _____ itself requires a cognitive observer to be obtained.

Exam Probability: **Low**

31. *Answer choices:*

(see index for correct answer)

- a. Primary source
- b. Information
- c. Computational informatics
- d. Retrievability

:: Planning ::

_____ is a high level plan to achieve one or more goals under conditions of uncertainty. In the sense of the "art of the general," which included several subsets of skills including tactics, siegecraft, logistics etc., the term came into use in the 6th century C.E. in East Roman terminology, and was translated into Western vernacular languages only in the 18th century. From then until the 20th century, the word "_____" came to denote "a comprehensive way to try to pursue political ends, including the threat or actual use of force, in a dialectic of wills" in a military conflict, in which both adversaries interact.

Exam Probability: **High**

32. *Answer choices:*

(see index for correct answer)

- a. Commercial area
- b. Strategic communication
- c. Resource-Task Network
- d. Interactive planning

Guidance: level 1

:: Mereology ::

_____ , in the abstract, is what belongs to or with something, whether as an attribute or as a component of said thing. In the context of this article, it is one or more components , whether physical or incorporeal, of a person's estate; or so belonging to, as in being owned by, a person or jointly a group of people or a legal entity like a corporation or even a society. Depending on the nature of the _____ , an owner of _____ has the right to consume, alter, share, redefine, rent, mortgage, pawn, sell, exchange, transfer, give away or destroy it, or to exclude others from doing these things, as well as to perhaps abandon it; whereas regardless of the nature of the _____ , the owner thereof has the right to properly use it , or at the very least exclusively keep it.

Exam Probability: **Low**

33. *Answer choices:*

(see index for correct answer)

- a. Mereology
- b. Property
- c. Gunk
- d. Meronomy

Guidance: level 1

:: Production and manufacturing ::

_____ is a theory of management that analyzes and synthesizes workflows. Its main objective is improving economic efficiency, especially labor productivity. It was one of the earliest attempts to apply science to the engineering of processes and to management. _____ is sometimes known as Taylorism after its founder, Frederick Winslow Taylor.

Exam Probability: **High**

34. *Answer choices:*

(see index for correct answer)

- a. Total quality management
- b. Scientific management
- c. Mockup
- d. Nuffield Tools and Gauges

Guidance: level 1

:: ::

_____ , known in Europe as research and technological development , refers to innovative activities undertaken by corporations or governments in developing new services or products, or improving existing services or products. _____ constitutes the first stage of development of a potential new service or the production process.

Exam Probability: **Medium**

35. *Answer choices:*

(see index for correct answer)

- a. co-culture
- b. levels of analysis
- c. Research and development
- d. imperative

Guidance: level 1

:: Scientific method ::

In the social sciences and life sciences, a _____ is a research method involving an up-close, in-depth, and detailed examination of a subject of study , as well as its related contextual conditions.

Exam Probability: **Low**

36. *Answer choices:*

(see index for correct answer)

- a. pilot project
- b. Causal research
- c. Preference test
- d. explanatory research

Guidance: level 1

The _____ is a political and economic union of 28 member states that are located primarily in Europe. It has an area of 4,475,757 km2 and an estimated population of about 513 million. The EU has developed an internal single market through a standardised system of laws that apply in all member states in those matters, and only those matters, where members have agreed to act as one. EU policies aim to ensure the free movement of people, goods, services and capital within the internal market, enact legislation in justice and home affairs and maintain common policies on trade, agriculture, fisheries and regional development. For travel within the Schengen Area, passport controls have been abolished. A monetary union was established in 1999 and came into full force in 2002 and is composed of 19 EU member states which use the euro currency.

Exam Probability: **Medium**

37. *Answer choices:*

(see index for correct answer)

- a. interpersonal communication
- b. information systems assessment
- c. empathy
- d. European Union

Guidance: level 1

_____ broadly refers to those factors of effectively functioning social groups that include such things as interpersonal relationships, a shared sense of identity, a shared understanding, shared norms, shared values, trust, cooperation, and reciprocity. However, the many views of this complex subject make a single definition difficult.

Exam Probability: **Low**

38. *Answer choices:*

(see index for correct answer)

- a. First Tuesday
- b. Studyplaces
- c. Social capital
- d. Social invisibility

Guidance: level 1

:: ::

_____ is the process of two or more people or organizations working together to complete a task or achieve a goal. _____ is similar to cooperation. Most _____ requires leadership, although the form of leadership can be social within a decentralized and egalitarian group. Teams that work collaboratively often access greater resources, recognition and rewards when facing competition for finite resources.

Exam Probability: **Low**

39. *Answer choices:*

(see index for correct answer)

- a. empathy
- b. Collaboration
- c. Sarbanes-Oxley act of 2002
- d. co-culture

Guidance: level 1

:: ::

A _____ is a problem offering two possibilities, neither of which is unambiguously acceptable or preferable. The possibilities are termed the horns of the _____ , a clichéd usage, but distinguishing the _____ from other kinds of predicament as a matter of usage.

Exam Probability: **Medium**

40. *Answer choices:*

(see index for correct answer)

- a. levels of analysis
- b. open system
- c. interpersonal communication
- d. hierarchical perspective

:: Statistical terminology ::

_____ is the magnitude or dimensions of a thing. _____ can be measured as length, width, height, diameter, perimeter, area, volume, or mass.

Exam Probability: **High**

41. *Answer choices:*

(see index for correct answer)

- a. Deviation
- b. Collectively exhaustive events
- c. Univariate distribution
- d. Innovations vector

:: Production and manufacturing ::

_____ consists of organization-wide efforts to "install and make permanent climate where employees continuously improve their ability to provide on demand products and services that customers will find of particular value." "Total" emphasizes that departments in addition to production are obligated to improve their operations; "management" emphasizes that executives are obligated to actively manage quality through funding, training, staffing, and goal setting. While there is no widely agreed-upon approach, TQM efforts typically draw heavily on the previously developed tools and techniques of quality control. TQM enjoyed widespread attention during the late 1980s and early 1990s before being overshadowed by ISO 9000, Lean manufacturing, and Six Sigma.

Exam Probability: **Medium**

42. *Answer choices:*

(see index for correct answer)

- a. Industrial engineering
- b. Earned value
- c. Seweasy
- d. Total quality management

Guidance: level 1

:: Business models ::

A _____, _____ company or daughter company is a company that is owned or controlled by another company, which is called the parent company, parent, or holding company. The _____ can be a company, corporation, or limited liability company. In some cases it is a government or state-owned enterprise. In some cases, particularly in the music and book publishing industries, subsidiaries are referred to as imprints.

Exam Probability: **High**

43. *Answer choices:*

(see index for correct answer)

- a. Brainsworking
- b. Subsidiary
- c. What if chart
- d. Defensive patent aggregation

Guidance: level 1

:: Human resource management ::

A _____ is a group of people with different functional expertise working toward a common goal. It may include people from finance, marketing, operations, and human resources departments. Typically, it includes employees from all levels of an organization. Members may also come from outside an organization .

Exam Probability: **Low**

44. *Answer choices:*

(see index for correct answer)

- a. Progressive discipline
- b. Hemsley Fraser
- c. Cross-functional team
- d. Job sharing

Guidance: level 1

:: Organizational structure ::

An _____ defines how activities such as task allocation, coordination, and supervision are directed toward the achievement of organizational aims.

Exam Probability: **High**

45. *Answer choices:*

(see index for correct answer)

- a. Organizational structure
- b. Organization of the New York City Police Department
- c. Automated Bureaucracy
- d. The Starfish and the Spider

Guidance: level 1

:: Business planning ::

_____ is an organization's process of defining its strategy, or direction, and making decisions on allocating its resources to pursue this strategy. It may also extend to control mechanisms for guiding the implementation of the strategy. _____ became prominent in corporations during the 1960s and remains an important aspect of strategic management. It is executed by strategic planners or strategists, who involve many parties and research sources in their analysis of the organization and its relationship to the environment in which it competes.

Exam Probability: **Low**

46. *Answer choices:*

(see index for correct answer)

- a. Strategic planning
- b. Community Futures
- c. Gap analysis
- d. Customer Demand Planning

Guidance: level 1

:: ::

An _____ is a process where candidates are examined to determine their suitability for specific types of employment, especially management or military command. The candidates' personality and aptitudes are determined by techniques including interviews, group exercises, presentations, examinations and psychometric testing.

Exam Probability: **High**

47. *Answer choices:*

(see index for correct answer)

- a. surface-level diversity
- b. imperative
- c. Assessment center
- d. functional perspective

Guidance: level 1

:: Personality tests ::

The Myers–Briggs Type Indicator is an introspective self-report questionnaire with the purpose of indicating differing psychological preferences in how people perceive the world around them and make decisions. . Though the test superficially resembles some psychological theories it is commonly classified as pseudoscience, especially as pertains to its supposed predictive abilities.

Exam Probability: **Medium**

48. *Answer choices:*

(see index for correct answer)

- a. personality quiz
- b. Myers-Briggs type
- c. Keirsey Temperament Sorter
- d. Myers-Briggs Type Indicator

Guidance: level 1

:: Office administration ::

An _____ is generally a room or other area where an organization`s employees perform administrative work in order to support and realize objects and goals of the organization. The word " _____ " may also denote a position within an organization with specific duties attached to it ; the latter is in fact an earlier usage, _____ as place originally referring to the location of one`s duty. When used as an adjective, the term " _____ " may refer to business-related tasks. In law, a company or organization has _____ s in any place where it has an official presence, even if that presence consists of a storage silo rather than an establishment with desk-and-chair. An _____ is also an architectural and design phenomenon: ranging from a small _____ such as a bench in the corner of a small business of extremely small size , through entire floors of buildings, up to and including massive buildings dedicated entirely to one company. In modern terms an _____ is usually the location where white-collar workers carry out their functions. As per James Stephenson, " _____ is that part of business enterprise which is devoted to the direction and co-ordination of its various activities."

Exam Probability: **High**

49. *Answer choices:*

(see index for correct answer)

- a. Activity management
- b. Fish! Philosophy
- c. Inter departmental communication
- d. Office administration

Guidance: level 1

:: Social psychology ::

In social psychology, _____ is the phenomenon of a person exerting less effort to achieve a goal when he or she works in a group than when working alone. This is seen as one of the main reasons groups are sometimes less productive than the combined performance of their members working as individuals, but should be distinguished from the accidental coordination problems that groups sometimes experience.

Exam Probability: **Low**

50. *Answer choices:*

(see index for correct answer)

- a. Prosocial
- b. Impression formation
- c. fear appeal
- d. Social loafing

:: Statistical terminology ::

_____ es can be learned implicitly within cultural contexts. People may develop _____ es toward or against an individual, an ethnic group, a sexual or gender identity, a nation, a religion, a social class, a political party, theoretical paradigms and ideologies within academic domains, or a species. _____ ed means one-sided, lacking a neutral viewpoint, or not having an open mind. _____ can come in many forms and is related to prejudice and intuition.

Exam Probability: **High**

51. *Answer choices:*

(see index for correct answer)

- a. Univariate distribution
- b. Stability
- c. Fisher consistency
- d. Bias

:: Critical thinking ::

In psychology, _____ is regarded as the cognitive process resulting in the selection of a belief or a course of action among several alternative possibilities. Every _____ process produces a final choice, which may or may not prompt action.

Exam Probability: **Low**

52. *Answer choices:*

(see index for correct answer)

- a. Critical reading
- b. Project Reason
- c. TregoED
- d. Decision-making

Guidance: level 1

:: Classification systems ::

_____ is the practice of comparing business processes and performance metrics to industry bests and best practices from other companies. Dimensions typically measured are quality, time and cost.

Exam Probability: **Medium**

53. *Answer choices:*

(see index for correct answer)

- a. Alpine Club classification of the Eastern Alps
- b. Uniclass
- c. Benchmarking
- d. Military taxonomy

Guidance: level 1

:: Marketing ::

_____ or stock control can be broadly defined as "the activity of checking a shop's stock." However, a more focused definition takes into account the more science-based, methodical practice of not only verifying a business' inventory but also focusing on the many related facets of inventory management "within an organisation to meet the demand placed upon that business economically." Other facets of _____ include supply chain management, production control, financial flexibility, and customer satisfaction. At the root of _____ , however, is the _____ problem, which involves determining when to order, how much to order, and the logistics of those decisions.

Exam Probability: **Medium**

54. *Answer choices:*

(see index for correct answer)

- a. Back to school
- b. Bluetooth advertising
- c. Interruption marketing

- d. Inventory control

Guidance: level 1

:: Monopoly (economics) ::

_____ is a category of property that includes intangible creations of the human intellect. _____ encompasses two types of rights: industrial property rights and copyright. It was not until the 19th century that the term "_____" began to be used, and not until the late 20th century that it became commonplace in the majority of the world.

Exam Probability: **Low**

55. *Answer choices:*

(see index for correct answer)

- a. Barriers to exit
- b. Tesco Town
- c. Privatization
- d. Chamberlinian monopolistic competition

Guidance: level 1

:: ::

A _____ is an organization, usually a group of people or a company, authorized to act as a single entity and recognized as such in law. Early incorporated entities were established by charter . Most jurisdictions now allow the creation of new _____ s through registration.

Exam Probability: **Low**

56. *Answer choices:*

(see index for correct answer)

- a. Character
- b. Corporation
- c. information systems assessment
- d. functional perspective

Guidance: level 1

:: Monopoly (economics) ::

A _____ is a form of intellectual property that gives its owner the legal right to exclude others from making, using, selling, and importing an invention for a limited period of years, in exchange for publishing an enabling public disclosure of the invention. In most countries _____ rights fall under civil law and the _____ holder needs to sue someone infringing the _____ in order to enforce his or her rights. In some industries _____ s are an essential form of competitive advantage; in others they are irrelevant.

57. *Answer choices:*

(see index for correct answer)

- a. Complementary monopoly
- b. Patent
- c. Dominance
- d. Trust

Guidance: level 1

:: ::

_____ is the process of making predictions of the future based on past and present data and most commonly by analysis of trends. A commonplace example might be estimation of some variable of interest at some specified future date. Prediction is a similar, but more general term. Both might refer to formal statistical methods employing time series, cross-sectional or longitudinal data, or alternatively to less formal judgmental methods. Usage can differ between areas of application: for example, in hydrology the terms "forecast" and "_____" are sometimes reserved for estimates of values at certain specific future times, while the term "prediction" is used for more general estimates, such as the number of times floods will occur over a long period.

Exam Probability: **High**

58. *Answer choices:*

(see index for correct answer)

- a. Forecasting
- b. information systems assessment
- c. hierarchical perspective
- d. empathy

Guidance: level 1

:: Leadership ::

_____ is a theory of leadership where a leader works with teams to identify needed change, creating a vision to guide the change through inspiration, and executing the change in tandem with committed members of a group; it is an integral part of the Full Range Leadership Model. _____ serves to enhance the motivation, morale, and job performance of followers through a variety of mechanisms; these include connecting the follower`s sense of identity and self to a project and to the collective identity of the organization; being a role model for followers in order to inspire them and to raise their interest in the project; challenging followers to take greater ownership for their work, and understanding the strengths and weaknesses of followers, allowing the leader to align followers with tasks that enhance their performance.

Exam Probability: **Low**

59. *Answer choices:*

(see index for correct answer)

- a. Transformational leadership
- b. Leadership analysis

- c. Integral leadership
- d. Superleadership

Guidance: level 1

Business law

Corporate law (also known as business law) is the body of law governing the rights, relations, and conduct of persons, companies, organizations and businesses. It refers to the legal practice relating to, or the theory of corporations. Corporate law often describes the law relating to matters which derive directly from the life-cycle of a corporation. It thus encompasses the formation, funding, governance, and death of a corporation.

:: ::

_____, also referred to as orthostasis, is a human position in which the body is held in an upright position and supported only by the feet.

Exam Probability: **Low**

1. *Answer choices:*

(see index for correct answer)

- a. interpersonal communication
- b. Standing
- c. functional perspective
- d. deep-level diversity

Guidance: level 1

:: Forgery ::

_____ is a white-collar crime that generally refers to the false making or material alteration of a legal instrument with the specific intent to defraud anyone . Tampering with a certain legal instrument may be forbidden by law in some jurisdictions but such an offense is not related to _____ unless the tampered legal instrument was actually used in the course of the crime to defraud another person or entity. Copies, studio replicas, and reproductions are not considered forgeries, though they may later become forgeries through knowing and willful misrepresentations.

Exam Probability: **Medium**

2. *Answer choices:*

(see index for correct answer)

- a. False evidence
- b. Catacomb saints
- c. Forgery
- d. Forgery Act 1861

:: Business law ::

A _____ is a group of people who jointly supervise the activities of an organization, which can be either a for-profit business, nonprofit organization, or a government agency. Such a board's powers, duties, and responsibilities are determined by government regulations and the organization's own constitution and bylaws. These authorities may specify the number of members of the board, how they are to be chosen, and how often they are to meet.

Exam Probability: **Medium**

3. *Answer choices:*

(see index for correct answer)

- a. Partnership
- b. Doing business as
- c. License
- d. Board of directors

:: ::

A _____ is a formal presentation of a matter such as a complaint, indictment or bill of exchange. In early-medieval England, juries of _____ would hear inquests in order to establish whether someone should be presented for a crime.

Exam Probability: **Medium**

4. *Answer choices:*

(see index for correct answer)

- a. cultural
- b. deep-level diversity
- c. levels of analysis
- d. Presentment

Guidance: level 1

:: Commercial item transport and distribution ::

A _____ in common law countries is a person or company that transports goods or people for any person or company and that is responsible for any possible loss of the goods during transport. A _____ offers its services to the general public under license or authority provided by a regulatory body. The regulatory body has usually been granted "ministerial authority" by the legislation that created it. The regulatory body may create, interpret, and enforce its regulations upon the _____ with independence and finality, as long as it acts within the bounds of the enabling legislation.

5. *Answer choices:*

- a. Toll Specialised and Domestic Freight
- b. Common carrier
- c. Ocean transportation intermediary
- d. Hold

Guidance: level 1

:: Business ::

An _____ is a key document used by limited liability companies to outline the business' financial and functional decisions including rules, regulations and provisions. The purpose of the document is to govern the internal operations of the business in a way that suits the specific needs of the business owners. Once the document is signed by the members of the limited liability company, it acts as an official contract binding them to its terms. _____ is mandatory as per laws only in 5 states - California, Delaware, Maine, Missouri, and New York LLCs operating without an _____ are governed by the state's default rules contained in the relevant statute and developed through state court decisions. An _____ is similar in function to corporate by-laws, or analogous to a partnership agreement in multi-member LLCs. In single-member LLCs, an _____ is a declaration of the structure that the member has chosen for the company and sometimes used to prove in court that the LLC structure is separate from that of the individual owner and thus necessary so that the owner has documentation to prove that he or she is indeed separate from the entity itself.

6. *Answer choices:*

(see index for correct answer)

- a. Legal governance, risk management, and compliance
- b. Corporate housing
- c. Professional services
- d. Co-creation

Guidance: level 1

:: International trade ::

_____ involves the transfer of goods or services from one person or entity to another, often in exchange for money. A system or network that allows _____ is called a market.

Exam Probability: **Low**

7. *Answer choices:*

(see index for correct answer)

- a. Foreign Sales Corporation
- b. Trade
- c. Westline
- d. The Observatory of Economic Complexity

:: ::

In law, a _____ is the formal finding of fact made by a jury on matters
or questions submitted to the jury by a judge. In a bench trial, the judge's
decision near the end of the trial is simply referred to as a finding. In
England and Wales, a coroner's findings are called _____ s .

Exam Probability: **Low**

8. *Answer choices:*

(see index for correct answer)

- a. hierarchical
- b. Sarbanes-Oxley act of 2002
- c. Verdict
- d. similarity-attraction theory

:: Real property law ::

_____ is the judicial process whereby a will is "proved" in a court of law and accepted as a valid public document that is the true last testament of the deceased, or whereby the estate is settled according to the laws of intestacy in the state of residence [or real property] of the deceased at time of death in the absence of a legal will.

Exam Probability: **Medium**

9. *Answer choices:*

(see index for correct answer)

- a. Mesne profits
- b. Palestinian land laws
- c. Attornment
- d. Probate

Guidance: level 1

:: Real property law ::

_____ is an area of criminal law or tort law broadly divided into three groups: _____ to the person, _____ to chattels and _____ to land.

Exam Probability: **High**

10. *Answer choices:*

(see index for correct answer)

- a. Probate
- b. Trespass
- c. Land court
- d. Real Estate Settlement Procedures Act

Guidance: level 1

:: ::

_____ is the act or practice of forbidding something by law; more particularly the term refers to the banning of the manufacture, storage , transportation, sale, possession, and consumption of alcoholic beverages. The word is also used to refer to a period of time during which such bans are enforced.

Exam Probability: **High**

11. *Answer choices:*

(see index for correct answer)

- a. co-culture
- b. functional perspective
- c. hierarchical
- d. Character

:: Meetings ::

A _____ is a body of one or more persons that is subordinate to a deliberative assembly. Usually, the assembly sends matters into a _____ as a way to explore them more fully than would be possible if the assembly itself were considering them. _____ s may have different functions and their type of work differ depending on the type of the organization and its needs.

Exam Probability: **High**

12. *Answer choices:*

(see index for correct answer)

- a. Future workshop
- b. AEI World Forum
- c. Middle East Electricity
- d. Candlelight vigil

:: ::

_____ is the administration of an organization, whether it is a business, a not-for-profit organization, or government body. _____ includes the activities of setting the strategy of an organization and coordinating the efforts of its employees to accomplish its objectives through the application of available resources, such as financial, natural, technological, and human resources. The term " _____ " may also refer to those people who manage an organization.

Exam Probability: **High**

13. *Answer choices:*

(see index for correct answer)

- a. cultural
- b. surface-level diversity
- c. Management
- d. hierarchical

Guidance: level 1

:: Marketing ::

_____ or stock is the goods and materials that a business holds for the ultimate goal of resale .

Exam Probability: **High**

14. *Answer choices:*

(see index for correct answer)

- a. Inventory
- b. Need
- c. Preference-rank translation
- d. Partnerized inventory management

Guidance: level 1

:: Utilitarianism ::

_____ is a family of consequentialist ethical theories that promotes actions that maximize happiness and well-being for the majority of a population. Although different varieties of _____ admit different characterizations, the basic idea behind all of them is to in some sense maximize utility, which is often defined in terms of well-being or related concepts. For instance, Jeremy Bentham, the founder of _____ , described utility as

Exam Probability: **High**

15. *Answer choices:*

(see index for correct answer)

- a. Hedonism
- b. Utilitarianism
- c. The Methods of Ethics

- d. Utilitarian bioethics

Guidance: level 1

:: ::

Advertising is a marketing communication that employs an openly sponsored, non-personal message to promote or sell a product, service or idea. Sponsors of advertising are typically businesses wishing to promote their products or services. Advertising is differentiated from public relations in that an advertiser pays for and has control over the message. It differs from personal selling in that the message is non-personal, i.e., not directed to a particular individual.Advertising is communicated through various mass media, including traditional media such as newspapers, magazines, television, radio, outdoor advertising or direct mail; and new media such as search results, blogs, social media, websites or text messages. The actual presentation of the message in a medium is referred to as an _____ , or "ad" or advert for short.

Exam Probability: **Low**

16. *Answer choices:*

(see index for correct answer)

- a. personal values
- b. Advertisement
- c. functional perspective
- d. interpersonal communication

Guidance: level 1

:: Stock market ::

The _____ of a corporation is all of the shares into which ownership of the corporation is divided. In American English, the shares are commonly known as "_____ s". A single share of the _____ represents fractional ownership of the corporation in proportion to the total number of shares. This typically entitles the _____ holder to that fraction of the company's earnings, proceeds from liquidation of assets , or voting power, often dividing these up in proportion to the amount of money each _____ holder has invested. Not all _____ is necessarily equal, as certain classes of _____ may be issued for example without voting rights, with enhanced voting rights, or with a certain priority to receive profits or liquidation proceeds before or after other classes of shareholders.

Exam Probability: **High**

17. *Answer choices:*

(see index for correct answer)

- a. Bombay Stock Exchange
- b. Penny stock
- c. Stock market data systems
- d. Foolish Four

Guidance: level 1

:: Business ethics ::

_____ is a type of harassment technique that relates to a sexual nature and the unwelcome or inappropriate promise of rewards in exchange for sexual favors. _____ includes a range of actions from mild transgressions to sexual abuse or assault. Harassment can occur in many different social settings such as the workplace, the home, school, churches, etc. Harassers or victims may be of any gender.

Exam Probability: **Medium**

18. *Answer choices:*

(see index for correct answer)

- a. Linda Peeno
- b. Anti-sweatshop movement
- c. Sexual harassment
- d. Ethical consumerism

Guidance: level 1

:: Contract law ::

_____ is the act of recall or annulment. It is the cancelling of an act, the recalling of a grant or privilege, or the making void of some deed previously existing.

Exam Probability: **Low**

19. *Answer choices:*

- a. Anticipatory repudiation
- b. Rescission
- c. Duress
- d. Per minas

Guidance: level 1

:: ::

_____ is a marketing communication that employs an openly sponsored, non-personal message to promote or sell a product, service or idea. Sponsors of _____ are typically businesses wishing to promote their products or services. _____ is differentiated from public relations in that an advertiser pays for and has control over the message. It differs from personal selling in that the message is non-personal, i.e., not directed to a particular individual. _____ is communicated through various mass media, including traditional media such as newspapers, magazines, television, radio, outdoor _____ or direct mail; and new media such as search results, blogs, social media, websites or text messages. The actual presentation of the message in a medium is referred to as an advertisement, or "ad" or advert for short.

Exam Probability: **High**

20. *Answer choices:*

- a. levels of analysis
- b. hierarchical perspective
- c. Advertising
- d. cultural

Guidance: level 1

:: Debt ::

_____ is the trust which allows one party to provide money or resources to another party wherein the second party does not reimburse the first party immediately , but promises either to repay or return those resources at a later date. In other words, _____ is a method of making reciprocity formal, legally enforceable, and extensible to a large group of unrelated people.

Exam Probability: **Low**

21. *Answer choices:*

(see index for correct answer)

- a. Recourse debt
- b. Debt crisis
- c. Borrowing base
- d. Credit

Guidance: level 1

In law, an _____ is the process in which cases are reviewed, where parties request a formal change to an official decision. _____ s function both as a process for error correction as well as a process of clarifying and interpreting law. Although appellate courts have existed for thousands of years, common law countries did not incorporate an affirmative right to _____ into their jurisprudence until the 19th century.

Exam Probability: **Medium**

22. *Answer choices:*

(see index for correct answer)

- a. similarity-attraction theory
- b. Sarbanes-Oxley act of 2002
- c. cultural
- d. co-culture

Guidance: level 1

:: Patent law ::

A _____ is generally any statement intended to specify or delimit the scope of rights and obligations that may be exercised and enforced by parties in a legally recognized relationship. In contrast to other terms for legally operative language, the term _____ usually implies situations that involve some level of uncertainty, waiver, or risk.

23. *Answer choices:*

(see index for correct answer)

- a. Disclaimer
- b. Coverture
- c. Patent application
- d. Patent watch

Guidance: level 1

:: ::

A _____ is a request to do something, most commonly addressed to a government official or public entity. _____ s to a deity are a form of prayer called supplication.

24. *Answer choices:*

(see index for correct answer)

- a. levels of analysis
- b. functional perspective
- c. Sarbanes-Oxley act of 2002
- d. Petition

:: Contract law ::

A _____ cannot be enforced by law. _____ s are different from voidable contracts, which are contracts that may be nullified. However, when a contract is being written and signed, there is no automatic mechanism available in every situation that can be utilized to detect the validity or enforceability of that contract. Practically, a contract can be declared to be void by a court of law. So the main question is that under what conditions can a contract be deemed as void

Exam Probability: **Low**

25. *Answer choices:*

(see index for correct answer)

- a. Implied warranty
- b. Good faith
- c. Choice of law clause
- d. Void contract

:: Business models ::

A _____ is "an autonomous association of persons united voluntarily to meet their common economic, social, and cultural needs and aspirations through a jointly-owned and democratically-controlled enterprise". _____ s may include.

Exam Probability: **Medium**

26. *Answer choices:*

(see index for correct answer)

- a. Market game
- b. Business model pattern
- c. Professional open source
- d. Cooperative

Guidance: level 1

:: Majority–minority relations ::

_____ , also known as reservation in India and Nepal, positive discrimination / action in the United Kingdom, and employment equity in Canada and South Africa, is the policy of promoting the education and employment of members of groups that are known to have previously suffered from discrimination. Historically and internationally, support for _____ has sought to achieve goals such as bridging inequalities in employment and pay, increasing access to education, promoting diversity, and redressing apparent past wrongs, harms, or hindrances.

27. *Answer choices:*

(see index for correct answer)

- a. positive discrimination
- b. Affirmative action
- c. cultural Relativism

Guidance: level 1

:: Business models ::

A _____ , _____ company or daughter company is a company that is owned or controlled by another company, which is called the parent company, parent, or holding company. The _____ can be a company, corporation, or limited liability company. In some cases it is a government or state-owned enterprise. In some cases, particularly in the music and book publishing industries, subsidiaries are referred to as imprints.

28. *Answer choices:*

(see index for correct answer)

- a. Business-agile enterprise
- b. Consumer cooperative
- c. Dependent growth business model

- d. InnovationXchange

Guidance: level 1

:: ::

In financial markets, a share is a unit used as mutual funds, limited partnerships, and real estate investment trusts. The owner of _____ in the corporation/company is a shareholder of the corporation. A share is an indivisible unit of capital, expressing the ownership relationship between the company and the shareholder. The denominated value of a share is its face value, and the total of the face value of issued _____ represent the capital of a company, which may not reflect the market value of those _____ .

Exam Probability: **Low**

29. *Answer choices:*

(see index for correct answer)

- a. similarity-attraction theory
- b. levels of analysis
- c. deep-level diversity
- d. Shares

Guidance: level 1

:: Legal doctrines and principles ::

In the common law of torts, _____ loquitur is a doctrine that infers negligence from the very nature of an accident or injury in the absence of direct evidence on how any defendant behaved. Although modern formulations differ by jurisdiction, common law originally stated that the accident must satisfy the necessary elements of negligence: duty, breach of duty, causation, and injury. In _____ loquitur, the elements of duty of care, breach, and causation are inferred from an injury that does not ordinarily occur without negligence.

Exam Probability: **Low**

30. *Answer choices:*

(see index for correct answer)

- a. Res ipsa
- b. Attractive nuisance doctrine
- c. Mutual mistake
- d. Acquiescence

Guidance: level 1

:: American legal terms ::

The phrase "by _____" is a legal term that indicates that a right or liability has been created for a party, irrespective of the intent of that party, because it is dictated by existing legal principles. For example, if a person dies without a will, his or her heirs are determined by _____. Similarly, if a person marries or has a child after his or her will has been executed, the law writes this pretermitted spouse or pretermitted heir into the will if no provision for this situation was specifically included. Adverse possession, in which title to land passes because non-owners have occupied it for a certain period of time, is another important right that vests by _____ .

Exam Probability: **Low**

31. *Answer choices:*

(see index for correct answer)

- a. Operation of law
- b. Reasonable time

Guidance: level 1

:: Debt ::

_____ , in finance and economics, is payment from a borrower or deposit-taking financial institution to a lender or depositor of an amount above repayment of the principal sum , at a particular rate. It is distinct from a fee which the borrower may pay the lender or some third party. It is also distinct from dividend which is paid by a company to its shareholders from its profit or reserve, but not at a particular rate decided beforehand, rather on a pro rata basis as a share in the reward gained by risk taking entrepreneurs when the revenue earned exceeds the total costs.

Exam Probability: **Medium**

32. *Answer choices:*

(see index for correct answer)

- a. Troubled Debt Restructuring
- b. Interest
- c. Museum of Foreign Debt
- d. Bad debt

Guidance: level 1

:: ::

A contract is a legally-binding agreement which recognises and governs the rights and duties of the parties to the agreement. A contract is legally enforceable because it meets the requirements and approval of the law. An agreement typically involves the exchange of goods, services, money, or promises of any of those. In the event of breach of contract, the law awards the injured party access to legal remedies such as damages and cancellation.

33. *Answer choices:*

- a. Contract law
- b. cultural
- c. corporate values
- d. imperative

Guidance: level 1

:: Legal terms ::

An _____ is a legal and equitable remedy in the form of a special court order that compels a party to do or refrain from specific acts. "When a court employs the extraordinary remedy of _____ , it directs the conduct of a party, and does so with the backing of its full coercive powers." A party that fails to comply with an _____ faces criminal or civil penalties, including possible monetary sanctions and even imprisonment. They can also be charged with contempt of court. Counter _____ s are _____ s that stop or reverse the enforcement of another _____ .

34. *Answer choices:*

- a. Felony
- b. Injunction
- c. Man-made law
- d. Indirect liability

Guidance: level 1

:: ::

Punishment is the imposition of an undesirable or unpleasant outcome upon a group or individual, meted out by an authority—in contexts ranging from child discipline to criminal law—as a response and deterrent to a particular action or behaviour that is deemed undesirable or unacceptable. The reasoning may be to condition a child to avoid self-endangerment, to impose social conformity , to defend norms, to protect against future harms , and to maintain the law—and respect for rule of law—under which the social group is governed. Punishment may be self-inflicted as with self-flagellation and mortification of the flesh in the religious setting, but is most often a form of social coercion.

Exam Probability: **Low**

35. *Answer choices:*

(see index for correct answer)

- a. Punitive
- b. deep-level diversity
- c. surface-level diversity
- d. Sarbanes-Oxley act of 2002

:: Business law ::

A _____ , also known as the sole trader, individual entrepreneurship or proprietorship, is a type of enterprise that is owned and run by one person and in which there is no legal distinction between the owner and the business entity. A sole trader does not necessarily work `alone`—it is possible for the sole trader to employ other people.

Exam Probability: **Medium**

36. *Answer choices:*

(see index for correct answer)

- a. Joint venture
- b. Partnership
- c. Time-and-a-half
- d. Certificate of incorporation

:: ::

In contract law, rescission is an equitable remedy which allows a contractual party to cancel the contract. Parties may _____ if they are the victims of a vitiating factor, such as misrepresentation, mistake, duress, or undue influence. Rescission is the unwinding of a transaction. This is done to bring the parties, as far as possible, back to the position in which they were before they entered into a contract .

Exam Probability: **Medium**

37. *Answer choices:*

(see index for correct answer)

- a. cultural
- b. empathy
- c. imperative
- d. levels of analysis

Guidance: level 1

:: Statutory law ::

_____ or statute law is written law set down by a body of legislature or by a singular legislator . This is as opposed to oral or customary law; or regulatory law promulgated by the executive or common law of the judiciary. Statutes may originate with national, state legislatures or local municipalities.

Exam Probability: **Medium**

38. *Answer choices:*

(see index for correct answer)

- a. ratification
- b. Statutory Law
- c. incorporation by reference
- d. Statute of repose

Guidance: level 1

:: Contract law ::

_____ is an equitable remedy in the law of contract, whereby a court issues an order requiring a party to perform a specific act, such as to complete performance of the contract. It is typically available in the sale of land, but otherwise is not generally available if damages are an appropriate alternative. _____ is almost never available for contracts of personal service, although performance may also be ensured through the threat of proceedings for contempt of court.

Exam Probability: **Medium**

39. *Answer choices:*

(see index for correct answer)

- a. enforceable
- b. Non est factum
- c. Fundamental breach

- d. ConsensusDOCS

Guidance: level 1

:: ::

The _____ is the highest court within the hierarchy of courts in many legal jurisdictions. Other descriptions for such courts include court of last resort, apex court, and high court of appeal. Broadly speaking, the decisions of a _____ are not subject to further review by any other court. _____ s typically function primarily as appellate courts, hearing appeals from decisions of lower trial courts, or from intermediate-level appellate courts.

Exam Probability: **Medium**

40. *Answer choices:*

(see index for correct answer)

- a. hierarchical perspective
- b. Supreme Court
- c. process perspective
- d. cultural

Guidance: level 1

:: ::

The _____ is one of the several United States Uniform Acts proposed by the National Conference of Commissioners on Uniform State Laws . Forty-seven states, the District of Columbia, and the U.S. Virgin Islands have adopted the UETA. Its purpose is to harmonize state laws concerning retention of paper records and the validity of electronic signatures.

Exam Probability: **Low**

41. *Answer choices:*

(see index for correct answer)

- a. co-culture
- b. interpersonal communication
- c. Uniform Electronic Transactions Act
- d. open system

Guidance: level 1

:: Fraud ::

_____ is the deliberate use of someone else's identity, usually as a method to gain a financial advantage or obtain credit and other benefits in the other person's name, and perhaps to the other person's disadvantage or loss. The person whose identity has been assumed may suffer adverse consequences, especially if they are held responsible for the perpetrator's actions.

_____ occurs when someone uses another's personally identifying information, like their name, identifying number, or credit card number, without their permission, to commit fraud or other crimes. The term _____ was coined in 1964. Since that time, the definition of _____ has been statutorily prescribed throughout both the U.K. and the United States as the theft of personally identifying information, generally including a person's name, date of birth, social security number, driver's license number, bank account or credit card numbers, PIN numbers, electronic signatures, fingerprints, passwords, or any other information that can be used to access a person's financial resources.

Exam Probability: **Medium**

42. *Answer choices:*

(see index for correct answer)

- a. Fraud Alert
- b. Identity theft
- c. Control fraud
- d. Paternity fraud

Guidance: level 1

:: ::

_____ is the body of law that governs the activities of administrative agencies of government. Government agency action can include rule making, adjudication, or the enforcement of a specific regulatory agenda. _____ is considered a branch of public law. As a body of law, _____ deals with the decision-making of the administrative units of government that are part of a national regulatory scheme in such areas as police law, international trade, manufacturing, the environment, taxation, broadcasting, immigration and transport. _____ expanded greatly during the twentieth century, as legislative bodies worldwide created more government agencies to regulate the social, economic and political spheres of human interaction.

Exam Probability: **Low**

43. *Answer choices:*

(see index for correct answer)

- a. cultural
- b. functional perspective
- c. Administrative law
- d. interpersonal communication

Guidance: level 1

:: Sexual harassment in the United States ::

In law, a _____ , reasonable man, or the man on the Clapham omnibus is a hypothetical person of legal fiction crafted by the courts and communicated through case law and jury instructions.

44. *Answer choices:*

(see index for correct answer)

- a. Sandy Gallin
- b. Reasonable person
- c. Sexual harassment in education in the United States
- d. Blakey v. Continental Airlines

Guidance: level 1

:: Marketing ::

A _____ is an overall experience of a customer that distinguishes an organization or product from its rivals in the eyes of the customer. _____ s are used in business, marketing, and advertising. Name _____ s are sometimes distinguished from generic or store _____ s.

Exam Probability: **High**

45. *Answer choices:*

(see index for correct answer)

- a. Customer lifetime value
- b. Brand
- c. Call centre

- d. Brand content management

Guidance: level 1

:: Legal doctrines and principles ::

_____ , land acquisition , compulsory purchase , resumption , resumption/compulsory acquisition , or expropriation is the power of a state, provincial, or national government to take private property for public use. However, this power can be legislatively delegated by the state to municipalities, government subdivisions, or even to private persons or corporations, when they are authorized by the legislature to exercise the functions of public character.

Exam Probability: **Low**

46. *Answer choices:*

(see index for correct answer)

- a. Act of state
- b. negligence
- c. Eminent domain
- d. Mutual assent

Guidance: level 1

:: Manufactured goods ::

A _____ or final good is any commodity that is produced or consumed by the consumer to satisfy current wants or needs. _____ s are ultimately consumed, rather than used in the production of another good. For example, a microwave oven or a bicycle that is sold to a consumer is a final good or _____ , but the components that are sold to be used in those goods are intermediate goods. For example, textiles or transistors can be used to make some further goods.

Exam Probability: **High**

47. *Answer choices:*

(see index for correct answer)

- a. Household goods
- b. Consumer Good
- c. Tarpaulin
- d. Final good

Guidance: level 1

:: Finance ::

A _____ , in the law of the United States, is a contract that governs the relationship between the parties to a kind of financial transaction known as a secured transaction. In a secured transaction, the Grantor assigns, grants and pledges to the grantee a security interest in personal property which is referred to as the collateral. Examples of typical collateral are shares of stock, livestock, and vehicles. A _____ is not used to transfer any interest in real property , only personal property. The document used by lenders to obtain a lien on real property is a mortgage or deed of trust.

Exam Probability: **High**

48. *Answer choices:*

(see index for correct answer)

- a. Security agreement
- b. Marginal conditional stochastic dominance
- c. Shoe leather cost
- d. Structured settlement factoring transaction

Guidance: level 1

:: Real estate ::

_____ , real estate, realty, or immovable property In English common law refers to landed properties belonging to some person. It include all structures, crops, buildings, machinery, wells, dams, ponds, mines, canals, and roads, among other things. The term is historic, arising from the now-discontinued form of action, which distinguish between _____ disputes and personal property disputes. Personal property was, and continues to refer to all properties that are not real properties.

Exam Probability: **Low**

49. *Answer choices:*

(see index for correct answer)

- a. Real property
- b. Transfer deed
- c. Land terrier
- d. Estate agent

Guidance: level 1

:: Commercial item transport and distribution ::

_____ s may be negotiable or non-negotiable. Negotiable _____ s allow transfer of ownership of that commodity without having to deliver the physical commodity. See Delivery order.

Exam Probability: **Low**

50. *Answer choices:*

(see index for correct answer)

- a. Voice-directed warehousing
- b. Yacht transport
- c. Containerlift
- d. Megalister

Guidance: level 1

:: Commercial item transport and distribution ::

A _____ is a commitment or expectation to perform some action in general or if certain circumstances arise. A _____ may arise from a system of ethics or morality, especially in an honor culture. Many duties are created by law, sometimes including a codified punishment or liability for non-performance. Performing one's _____ may require some sacrifice of self-interest.

Exam Probability: **Medium**

51. *Answer choices:*

(see index for correct answer)

- a. Duty
- b. Paper pallet
- c. Skid unit
- d. Shore Porters Society

:: Contract law ::

A _____ is an event or state of affairs that is required before something else will occur. In contract law, a _____ is an event which must occur, unless its non-occurrence is excused, before performance under a contract becomes due, i.e., before any contractual duty exists.

Exam Probability: **Low**

52. *Answer choices:*

(see index for correct answer)

- a. Condition precedent
- b. Baseball business rules
- c. Frustration of purpose
- d. Cost-plus-incentive fee

:: Finance ::

_____ is the investigation or exercise of care that a reasonable business or person is expected to take before entering into an agreement or contract with another party, or an act with a certain standard of care.

53. *Answer choices:*

(see index for correct answer)

- a. Structured sale
- b. Due diligence
- c. XBRL assurance
- d. Penalized present value

Guidance: level 1

:: Contract law ::

_____ is a legal process for collecting a monetary judgment on behalf of a plaintiff from a defendant. _____ allows the plaintiff to take the money or property of the debtor from the person or institution that holds that property . A similar legal mechanism called execution allows the seizure of money or property held directly by the debtor.

54. *Answer choices:*

(see index for correct answer)

- a. Garnishment
- b. Voidable contract
- c. Essentialia negotii
- d. The Death of Contract

Guidance: level 1

:: ::

_____ is the study and management of exchange relationships. _____ is the business process of creating relationships with and satisfying customers. With its focus on the customer, _____ is one of the premier components of business management.

Exam Probability: **High**

55. *Answer choices:*
(see index for correct answer)

- a. empathy
- b. Marketing
- c. co-culture
- d. process perspective

Guidance: level 1

:: Decision theory ::

A _____ is a deliberate system of principles to guide decisions and achieve rational outcomes. A _____ is a statement of intent, and is implemented as a procedure or protocol. Policies are generally adopted by a governance body within an organization. Policies can assist in both subjective and objective decision making. Policies to assist in subjective decision making usually assist senior management with decisions that must be based on the relative merits of a number of factors, and as a result are often hard to test objectively, e.g. work-life balance _____ . In contrast policies to assist in objective decision making are usually operational in nature and can be objectively tested, e.g. password _____ .

Exam Probability: **Medium**

56. *Answer choices:*

(see index for correct answer)

- a. Emotional bias
- b. Subjective expected utility
- c. Trade-off talking rational economic person
- d. Policy

Guidance: level 1

:: Insolvency ::

_____ is the state of being unable to pay the money owed, by a person or company, on time; those in a state of _____ are said to be insolvent. There are two forms: cash-flow _____ and balance-sheet _____ .

Exam Probability: **Medium**

57. *Answer choices:*

(see index for correct answer)

- a. Personal Insolvency Arrangement
- b. Insolvency
- c. Financial distress
- d. Liquidation

Guidance: level 1

:: ::

At common law, _____ are a remedy in the form of a monetary award to be paid to a claimant as compensation for loss or injury. To warrant the award, the claimant must show that a breach of duty has caused foreseeable loss. To be recognised at law, the loss must involve damage to property, or mental or physical injury; pure economic loss is rarely recognised for the award of _____ .

Exam Probability: **Low**

58. *Answer choices:*

(see index for correct answer)

- a. corporate values
- b. process perspective
- c. Damages
- d. hierarchical perspective

Guidance: level 1

:: ::

A concept of English law, a _____ is an untrue or misleading statement of fact made during negotiations by one party to another, the statement then inducing that other party into the contract. The misled party may normally rescind the contract, and sometimes may be awarded damages as well

Exam Probability: **High**

59. *Answer choices:*

(see index for correct answer)

- a. Character
- b. surface-level diversity
- c. Misrepresentation
- d. corporate values

Guidance: level 1

Finance

Finance is a field that is concerned with the allocation (investment) of assets and liabilities over space and time, often under conditions of risk or uncertainty. Finance can also be defined as the science of money management. Participants in the market aim to price assets based on their risk level, fundamental value, and their expected rate of return. Finance can be split into three sub-categories: public finance, corporate finance and personal finance.

:: ::

A tax is a compulsory financial charge or some other type of levy imposed upon a taxpayer by a governmental organization in order to fund various public expenditures. A failure to pay, along with evasion of or resistance to _____ , is punishable by law. Taxes consist of direct or indirect taxes and may be paid in money or as its labour equivalent.

Exam Probability: **Medium**

1. *Answer choices:*

(see index for correct answer)

- a. co-culture
- b. similarity-attraction theory
- c. Taxation
- d. interpersonal communication

Guidance: level 1

:: Leasing ::

A finance lease is a type of lease in which a finance company is typically the legal owner of the asset for the duration of the lease, while the lessee not only has operating control over the asset, but also has a some share of the economic risks and returns from the change in the valuation of the underlying asset.

Exam Probability: **Low**

2. *Answer choices:*

(see index for correct answer)

- a. Capital lease
- b. Synthetic lease

Guidance: level 1

:: Investment ::

In finance, the benefit from an _____ is called a return. The return may consist of a gain realised from the sale of property or an _____, unrealised capital appreciation , or _____ income such as dividends, interest, rental income etc., or a combination of capital gain and income. The return may also include currency gains or losses due to changes in foreign currency exchange rates.

Exam Probability: **High**

3. *Answer choices:*

(see index for correct answer)

- a. Separately managed account
- b. Market sentiment
- c. Hybrid Investment
- d. MarketSmith

Guidance: level 1

The _____ of a function of a real variable measures the sensitivity to change of the function value with respect to a change in its argument .
_____ s are a fundamental tool of calculus. For example, the _____ of the position of a moving object with respect to time is the object`s velocity: this measures how quickly the position of the object changes when time advances.

Exam Probability: **High**

4. *Answer choices:*

(see index for correct answer)

- a. empathy
- b. levels of analysis
- c. imperative
- d. Derivative

Guidance: level 1

:: Expense ::

A company's _____ , or As a result, the computation of the _____
is considerably more complex. Tax law may provide for different treatment of
items of income and expenses as a result of tax policy. The differences may be
of permanent or temporary nature. Permanent items are in the form of non
taxable income and non taxable expenses. Things such as expenses considered not
deductible by taxing authorities , the range of tax rates applicable to
various levels of income, different tax rates in different jurisdictions,
multiple layers of tax on income, and other issues.

Exam Probability: **Low**

5. *Answer choices:*

(see index for correct answer)

- a. Corporate travel
- b. expenditure
- c. Tax expense
- d. Expense account

Guidance: level 1

:: Inventory ::

Costs are associated with particular goods using one of the several formulas, including specific identification, first-in first-out , or average cost. Costs include all costs of purchase, costs of conversion and other costs that are incurred in bringing the inventories to their present location and condition. Costs of goods made by the businesses include material, labor, and allocated overhead. The costs of those goods which are not yet sold are deferred as costs of inventory until the inventory is sold or written down in value.

Exam Probability: **Low**

6. *Answer choices:*

- a. Reorder point
- b. Order picking
- c. Inventory bounce
- d. Cost of goods sold

Guidance: level 1

:: Finance ::

The _____ of a corporation is the accumulated net income of the corporation that is retained by the corporation at a particular point of time, such as at the end of the reporting period. At the end of that period, the net income at that point is transferred from the Profit and Loss Account to the _____ account. If the balance of the _____ account is negative it may be called accumulated losses, retained losses or accumulated deficit, or similar terminology.

7. *Answer choices:*

(see index for correct answer)

- a. Retained earnings
- b. Downside beta
- c. Replicating strategy
- d. Putty-putty

Guidance: level 1

:: Monopoly (economics) ::

A _____ is a form of intellectual property that gives its owner the legal right to exclude others from making, using, selling, and importing an invention for a limited period of years, in exchange for publishing an enabling public disclosure of the invention. In most countries _____ rights fall under civil law and the _____ holder needs to sue someone infringing the _____ in order to enforce his or her rights. In some industries _____ s are an essential form of competitive advantage; in others they are irrelevant.

Exam Probability: **High**

8. *Answer choices:*

(see index for correct answer)

- a. Patent
- b. Monopsony
- c. Wartime Law on Industrial Property
- d. Revenue-cap regulation

Guidance: level 1

:: ::

In the field of analysis of algorithms in computer science, the _____ is a method of amortized analysis based on accounting. The _____ often gives a more intuitive account of the amortized cost of an operation than either aggregate analysis or the potential method. Note, however, that this does not guarantee such analysis will be immediately obvious; often, choosing the correct parameters for the _____ requires as much knowledge of the problem and the complexity bounds one is attempting to prove as the other two methods.

Exam Probability: **Low**

9. *Answer choices:*

(see index for correct answer)

- a. process perspective
- b. hierarchical perspective
- c. information systems assessment
- d. personal values

:: Accounting terminology ::

_____ is money owed by a business to its suppliers shown as a liability on a company's balance sheet. It is distinct from notes payable liabilities, which are debts created by formal legal instrument documents.

Exam Probability: **Low**

10. *Answer choices:*

(see index for correct answer)

- a. revenue recognition principle
- b. managerial accounting
- c. Accounts payable
- d. Fund accounting

:: Generally Accepted Accounting Principles ::

In accounting, _____ , gross margin, sales profit, or credit sales is the difference between revenue and the cost of making a product or providing a service, before deducting overheads, payroll, taxation, and interest payments. This is different from operating profit . Gross margin is the term normally used in the U.S., while _____ is the more common usage in the UK and Australia.

Exam Probability: **Medium**

11. *Answer choices:*

(see index for correct answer)

- a. Treasury stock
- b. Contributed capital
- c. Engagement letter
- d. Historical cost

Guidance: level 1

:: Financial accounting ::

_____ in accounting is the process of treating investments in associate companies. Equity accounting is usually applied where an investor entity holds 20–50% of the voting stock of the associate company. The investor records such investments as an asset on its balance sheet. The investor's proportional share of the associate company's net income increases the investment , and proportional payments of dividends decrease it. In the investor's income statement, the proportional share of the investor's net income or net loss is reported as a single-line item.

12. *Answer choices:*

(see index for correct answer)

- a. Valuation
- b. Equity method
- c. Deferred financing cost
- d. Capital account

Guidance: level 1

:: Stock market ::

_____ or stock market launch is a type of public offering in which shares of a company are sold to institutional investors and usually also retail investors; an IPO is underwritten by one or more investment banks, who also arrange for the shares to be listed on one or more stock exchanges. Through this process, colloquially known as floating, or going public, a privately held company is transformed into a public company. _____ s can be used: to raise new equity capital for the company concerned; to monetize the investments of private shareholders such as company founders or private equity investors; and to enable easy trading of existing holdings or future capital raising by becoming publicly traded enterprises.

Exam Probability: **Medium**

13. *Answer choices:*

(see index for correct answer)

- a. Avanza
- b. Initial public offering
- c. Squeeze out
- d. Market-based valuation

Guidance: level 1

:: ::

_____ is the collection of techniques, skills, methods, and processes used in the production of goods or services or in the accomplishment of objectives, such as scientific investigation. _____ can be the knowledge of techniques, processes, and the like, or it can be embedded in machines to allow for operation without detailed knowledge of their workings. Systems applying _____ by taking an input, changing it according to the system's use, and then producing an outcome are referred to as _____ systems or technological systems.

Exam Probability: **High**

14. *Answer choices:*

(see index for correct answer)

- a. personal values
- b. similarity-attraction theory
- c. Technology
- d. Character

:: ::

_____ is the field of accounting concerned with the summary, analysis and reporting of financial transactions related to a business. This involves the preparation of financial statements available for public use. Stockholders, suppliers, banks, employees, government agencies, business owners, and other stakeholders are examples of people interested in receiving such information for decision making purposes.

Exam Probability: **Medium**

15. *Answer choices:*

(see index for correct answer)

- a. functional perspective
- b. interpersonal communication
- c. co-culture
- d. hierarchical

:: ::

_____ is the collection of mechanisms, processes and relations by which corporations are controlled and operated. Governance structures and principles identify the distribution of rights and responsibilities among different participants in the corporation and include the rules and procedures for making decisions in corporate affairs. _____ is necessary because of the possibility of conflicts of interests between stakeholders, primarily between shareholders and upper management or among shareholders.

Exam Probability: **High**

16. *Answer choices:*

(see index for correct answer)

- a. similarity-attraction theory
- b. hierarchical
- c. Corporate governance
- d. process perspective

Guidance: level 1

:: Pharmaceutical industry ::

A _____ is a document in which data collected for a clinical trial is first recorded. This data is usually later entered in the case report form. The International Conference on Harmonisation of Technical Requirements for Registration of Pharmaceuticals for Human Use guidelines define _____ s as "original documents, data, and records." _____ s contain source data, which is defined as "all information in original records and certified copies of original records of clinical findings, observations, or other activities in a clinical trial necessary for the reconstruction and evaluation of the trial."

Exam Probability: **High**

17. *Answer choices:*

(see index for correct answer)

- a. Title 21 CFR Part 11
- b. First DataBank
- c. Insulated shipping container
- d. Clinical research coordinator

Guidance: level 1

:: Generally Accepted Accounting Principles ::

Expenditure is an outflow of money to another person or group to pay for an item or service, or for a category of costs. For a tenant, rent is an _____ . For students or parents, tuition is an _____ . Buying food, clothing, furniture or an automobile is often referred to as an _____ . An _____ is a cost that is "paid" or "remitted", usually in exchange for something of value. Something that seems to cost a great deal is "expensive". Something that seems to cost little is "inexpensive". " _____ s of the table" are _____ s of dining, refreshments, a feast, etc.

Exam Probability: **Medium**

18. *Answer choices:*

(see index for correct answer)

- a. Expense
- b. Fin 48
- c. Deprival value
- d. Statement of recommended practice

Guidance: level 1

:: ::

Pharmaceutical _____ is the creation of a particular pharmaceutical product to fit the unique need of a patient. To do this, _____ pharmacists combine or process appropriate ingredients using various tools.

Exam Probability: **Medium**

19. *Answer choices:*

(see index for correct answer)

- a. deep-level diversity
- b. information systems assessment
- c. levels of analysis
- d. Compounding

Guidance: level 1

:: Accounting terminology ::

Accounts are typically defined by an identifier and a caption or header and are coded by account type. In computerized accounting systems with computable quantity accounting, the accounts can have a quantity measure definition.

Exam Probability: **High**

20. *Answer choices:*

(see index for correct answer)

- a. Enterprise liquidity
- b. Account
- c. Accounts payable
- d. Record to report

Guidance: level 1

:: Business ::

The seller, or the provider of the goods or services, completes a sale in response to an acquisition, appropriation, requisition or a direct interaction with the buyer at the point of sale. There is a passing of title of the item, and the settlement of a price, in which agreement is reached on a price for which transfer of ownership of the item will occur. The seller, not the purchaser typically executes the sale and it may be completed prior to the obligation of payment. In the case of indirect interaction, a person who sells goods or service on behalf of the owner is known as a _____ man or _____ woman or _____ person, but this often refers to someone selling goods in a store/shop, in which case other terms are also common, including _____ clerk, shop assistant, and retail clerk.

Exam Probability: **Medium**

21. *Answer choices:*

(see index for correct answer)

- a. Sales
- b. Les Vergers du Mekong
- c. Office broker
- d. Customer experience

Guidance: level 1

:: Occupations ::

An _____ is a practitioner of accounting or accountancy, which is the measurement, disclosure or provision of assurance about financial information that helps managers, investors, tax authorities and others make decisions about allocating resource.

Exam Probability: **Medium**

22. *Answer choices:*

(see index for correct answer)

- a. Technogypsie
- b. Monumental masonry
- c. Carpentry
- d. Private investigator

Guidance: level 1

:: Business law ::

A _____ is an arrangement where parties, known as partners, agree to cooperate to advance their mutual interests. The partners in a _____ may be individuals, businesses, interest-based organizations, schools, governments or combinations. Organizations may partner to increase the likelihood of each achieving their mission and to amplify their reach. A _____ may result in issuing and holding equity or may be only governed by a contract.

Exam Probability: **High**

23. *Answer choices:*

(see index for correct answer)

- a. Enhanced use lease
- b. Partnership
- c. Limited liability limited partnership
- d. Installment sale

Guidance: level 1

:: Stock market ::

_____ is a form of stock which may have any combination of features not possessed by common stock including properties of both an equity and a debt instrument, and is generally considered a hybrid instrument. _____ s are senior to common stock, but subordinate to bonds in terms of claim and may have priority over common stock in the payment of dividends and upon liquidation. Terms of the _____ are described in the issuing company's articles of association or articles of incorporation.

Exam Probability: **High**

24. *Answer choices:*

(see index for correct answer)

- a. Secondary shares
- b. Order book
- c. Preferred stock

- d. Volume-weighted average price

Guidance: level 1

:: Accounting ::

It is the period for which books are balanced and the financial statements are prepared. Generally, the _____ consists of 12 months. However the beginning of the _____ differs according to the jurisdiction. For example, one entity may follow the regular calendar year, i.e. January to December as the accounting year, while another entity may follow April to March as the _____ .

Exam Probability: **High**

25. *Answer choices:*

(see index for correct answer)

- a. European training programs
- b. Financing cost
- c. Comfort letter
- d. Accounting period

Guidance: level 1

:: Valuation (finance) ::

_____ refers to an assessment of the viability, stability, and profitability of a business, sub-business or project.

Exam Probability: **High**

26. *Answer choices:*

(see index for correct answer)

- a. Russian Society of Appraisers
- b. Graham number
- c. Valuation using multiples
- d. Value-in-use

Guidance: level 1

:: Bonds (finance) ::

In finance, a _____ or convertible note or convertible debt is a type of bond that the holder can convert into a specified number of shares of common stock in the issuing company or cash of equal value. It is a hybrid security with debt- and equity-like features. It originated in the mid-19th century, and was used by early speculators such as Jacob Little and Daniel Drew to counter market cornering.

Exam Probability: **Medium**

27. *Answer choices:*

(see index for correct answer)

- a. Global bond
- b. Securities Industry and Financial Markets Association
- c. Fixed rate bond
- d. Dirty price

Guidance: level 1

:: ::

_____ is an eight-block-long street running roughly northwest to southeast from Broadway to South Street, at the East River, in the Financial District of Lower Manhattan in New York City. Over time, the term has become a metonym for the financial markets of the United States as a whole, the American financial services industry , or New York–based financial interests.

Exam Probability: **High**

28. *Answer choices:*

(see index for correct answer)

- a. process perspective
- b. Character
- c. cultural
- d. interpersonal communication

:: Accounting terminology ::

_____ is a legally enforceable claim for payment held by a business for goods supplied and/or services rendered that customers/clients have ordered but not paid for. These are generally in the form of invoices raised by a business and delivered to the customer for payment within an agreed time frame.
_____ is shown in a balance sheet as an asset. It is one of a series of accounting transactions dealing with the billing of a customer for goods and services that the customer has ordered. These may be distinguished from notes receivable, which are debts created through formal legal instruments called promissory notes.

Exam Probability: **Medium**

29. *Answer choices:*

(see index for correct answer)

- a. Accounts receivable
- b. Adjusting entries
- c. Chart of accounts
- d. Mark-to-market

:: Costs ::

In economics, _____ is the total economic cost of production and is made up of variable cost, which varies according to the quantity of a good produced and includes inputs such as labour and raw materials, plus fixed cost, which is independent of the quantity of a good produced and includes inputs that cannot be varied in the short term: fixed costs such as buildings and machinery, including sunk costs if any. Since cost is measured per unit of time, it is a flow variable.

Exam Probability: **Medium**

30. *Answer choices:*

(see index for correct answer)

- a. Cost competitiveness of fuel sources
- b. Incremental cost-effectiveness ratio
- c. Average cost
- d. Total cost

Guidance: level 1

:: Accounting terminology ::

Total _____ is a method of Accounting cost which entails the full cost of manufacturing or providing a service. TAC includes not just the costs of materials and labour, but also of all manufacturing overheads . The cost of each cost center can be direct or indirect. The direct cost can be easily identified with individual cost centers. Whereas indirect cost cannot be easily identified with the cost center. The distribution of overhead among the departments is called apportionment.

31. *Answer choices:*

(see index for correct answer)

- a. Cash flow management
- b. Statement of financial position
- c. Share premium
- d. Absorption costing

Guidance: level 1

:: Derivatives (finance) ::

A _____ or _____ row is a line of closely spaced shrubs and sometimes trees, planted and trained to form a barrier or to mark the boundary of an area, such as between neighbouring properties. _____ s used to separate a road from adjoining fields or one field from another, and of sufficient age to incorporate larger trees, are known as _____ rows. Often they serve as windbreaks to improve conditions for the adjacent crops, as in bocage country. When clipped and maintained, _____ s are also a simple form of topiary.

Exam Probability: **Medium**

32. *Answer choices:*

(see index for correct answer)

- a. Credit default swap index
- b. Strike price
- c. Commodity index fund
- d. Hedge

:: Loans ::

In finance, a _____ is the lending of money by one or more individuals, organizations, or other entities to other individuals, organizations etc. The recipient incurs a debt, and is usually liable to pay interest on that debt until it is repaid, and also to repay the principal amount borrowed.

Exam Probability: **Low**

33. *Answer choices:*

(see index for correct answer)

- a. Loan
- b. Hard money loan
- c. Second lien
- d. Loan sale

:: Debt ::

_____ is when something, usually money, is owed by one party, the borrower or _____ or, to a second party, the lender or creditor. _____ is a deferred payment, or series of payments, that is owed in the future, which is what differentiates it from an immediate purchase. The _____ may be owed by sovereign state or country, local government, company, or an individual. Commercial _____ is generally subject to contractual terms regarding the amount and timing of repayments of principal and interest. Loans, bonds, notes, and mortgages are all types of _____ . The term can also be used metaphorically to cover moral obligations and other interactions not based on economic value. For example, in Western cultures, a person who has been helped by a second person is sometimes said to owe a " _____ of gratitude" to the second person.

Exam Probability: **Medium**

34. *Answer choices:*

(see index for correct answer)

- a. Crown debt
- b. Debt
- c. Least developed country
- d. Arrears

Guidance: level 1

:: ::

_____ is the consumption and saving opportunity gained by an entity within a specified timeframe, which is generally expressed in monetary terms. For households and individuals, " _____ is the sum of all the wages, salaries, profits, interest payments, rents, and other forms of earnings received in a given period of time."

Exam Probability: **High**

35. *Answer choices:*

(see index for correct answer)

- a. open system
- b. Character
- c. Income
- d. personal values

Guidance: level 1

:: Global systemically important banks ::

The _____ Corporation is an American multinational investment bank and financial services company based in Charlotte, North Carolina with central hubs in New York City, London, Hong Kong, Minneapolis, and Toronto. _____ was formed through NationsBank's acquisition of BankAmerica in 1998. It is the second largest banking institution in the United States, after JP Morgan Chase. As a part of the Big Four, it services approximately 10.73% of all American bank deposits, in direct competition with Citigroup, Wells Fargo, and JPMorgan Chase. Its primary financial services revolve around commercial banking, wealth management, and investment banking.

36. *Answer choices:*

(see index for correct answer)

- a. The Bank of New York Mellon
- b. The Bank of Tokyo-Mitsubishi UFJ
- c. BNP Paribas
- d. The Royal Bank of Scotland

Guidance: level 1

:: Payments ::

A _____ is the trade of value from one party to another for goods, or services, or to fulfill a legal obligation.

37. *Answer choices:*

(see index for correct answer)

- a. Subsidy
- b. VersaPay
- c. Payment
- d. Thirty pieces of silver

:: Asset ::

_____ s, also known as tangible assets or property, plant and equipment , is a term used in accounting for assets and property that cannot easily be converted into cash. This can be compared with current assets such as cash or bank accounts, described as liquid assets. In most cases, only tangible assets are referred to as fixed. IAS 16 defines _____ s as assets whose future economic benefit is probable to flow into the entity, whose cost can be measured reliably. _____ s belong to one of 2 types:"Freehold Assets" – assets which are purchased with legal right of ownership and used,and "Leasehold Assets" – assets used by owner without legal right for a particular period of time.

Exam Probability: **Low**

38. *Answer choices:*

(see index for correct answer)

- a. Current asset
- b. Fixed asset

:: Business economics ::

A _____ is a term used primarily in cost accounting to describe something to which costs are assigned. Common examples of _____ s are: product lines, geographic territories, customers, departments or anything else for which management would like to quantify cost.

Exam Probability: **High**

39. *Answer choices:*

(see index for correct answer)

- a. Units of transportation measurement
- b. Cost object
- c. Creditor Reference
- d. Willingness to pay

Guidance: level 1

:: Banking ::

_____ refers to a broad area of finance involving the collection, handling, and usage of cash. It involves assessing market liquidity, cash flow, and investments.

Exam Probability: **High**

40. *Answer choices:*

(see index for correct answer)

- a. Bank examiner
- b. Real-time posting
- c. Soft probe
- d. Cash management

Guidance: level 1

:: Stock market ::

The _____ of a corporation is all of the shares into which ownership of the corporation is divided. In American English, the shares are commonly known as " _____ s". A single share of the _____ represents fractional ownership of the corporation in proportion to the total number of shares. This typically entitles the _____ holder to that fraction of the company's earnings, proceeds from liquidation of assets , or voting power, often dividing these up in proportion to the amount of money each _____ holder has invested. Not all _____ is necessarily equal, as certain classes of _____ may be issued for example without voting rights, with enhanced voting rights, or with a certain priority to receive profits or liquidation proceeds before or after other classes of shareholders.

Exam Probability: **Medium**

41. *Answer choices:*

(see index for correct answer)

- a. Block premium
- b. Stock

- c. Contract for difference
- d. Hybrid market

Guidance: level 1

:: Marketing ::

_____ or stock is the goods and materials that a business holds for the ultimate goal of resale .

Exam Probability: **High**

42. *Answer choices:*

(see index for correct answer)

- a. Porter hypothesis
- b. Marketing Week
- c. Active adult retail
- d. Inventory

Guidance: level 1

:: Real estate ::

Amortisation is paying off an amount owed over time by making planned, incremental payments of principal and interest. To amortise a loan means "to kill it off". In accounting, amortisation refers to charging or writing off an intangible asset's cost as an operational expense over its estimated useful life to reduce a company's taxable income.

Exam Probability: **Medium**

43. *Answer choices:*

(see index for correct answer)

- a. Estate liquidation
- b. Amortization
- c. Cadastre
- d. Crown land

Guidance: level 1

:: ::

A _____ , or holiday, is a leave of absence from a regular occupation, or a specific trip or journey, usually for the purpose of recreation or tourism. People often take a _____ during specific holiday observances, or for specific festivals or celebrations. _____ s are often spent with friends or family.

Exam Probability: **Low**

44. *Answer choices:*

- a. surface-level diversity
- b. imperative
- c. functional perspective
- d. process perspective

Guidance: level 1

:: Commerce ::

Continuation of an entity as a _____ is presumed as the basis for financial reporting unless and until the entity`s liquidation becomes imminent. Preparation of financial statements under this presumption is commonly referred to as the _____ basis of accounting. If and when an entity`s liquidation becomes imminent, financial statements are prepared under the liquidation basis of accounting .

Exam Probability: **High**

45. *Answer choices:*

- a. Card association
- b. Purchasing manager
- c. Bill of sale
- d. Hauls

:: Stock market ::

A _____ , securities exchange or bourse, is a facility where stock brokers and traders can buy and sell securities, such as shares of stock and bonds and other financial instruments. _____ s may also provide for facilities the issue and redemption of such securities and instruments and capital events including the payment of income and dividends. Securities traded on a _____ include stock issued by listed companies, unit trusts, derivatives, pooled investment products and bonds. _____ s often function as "continuous auction" markets with buyers and sellers consummating transactions via open outcry at a central location such as the floor of the exchange or by using an electronic trading platform.

Exam Probability: **Medium**

46. *Answer choices:*

(see index for correct answer)

- a. All or none
- b. Avanza
- c. Piqqem
- d. Stock exchange

:: Financial ratios ::

The _____ shows the percentage of how profitable a company's assets are in generating revenue.

Exam Probability: **High**

47. *Answer choices:*

(see index for correct answer)

- a. Texas ratio
- b. Market-to-book
- c. Return on assets
- d. Net interest spread

Guidance: level 1

:: E-commerce ::

A _____ is a plastic payment card that can be used instead of cash when making purchases. It is similar to a credit card, but unlike a credit card, the money is immediately transferred directly from the cardholder's bank account when performing a transaction.

Exam Probability: **High**

48. *Answer choices:*

(see index for correct answer)

- a. Government-to-government
- b. ITransact
- c. Cyber Monday
- d. Debit card

Guidance: level 1

:: Actuarial science ::

_____ is the possibility of losing something of value. Values can be gained or lost when taking _____ resulting from a given action or inaction, foreseen or unforeseen . _____ can also be defined as the intentional interaction with uncertainty. Uncertainty is a potential, unpredictable, and uncontrollable outcome; _____ is a consequence of action taken in spite of uncertainty.

Exam Probability: **Medium**

49. *Answer choices:*

(see index for correct answer)

- a. Compound annual growth rate
- b. Risk parity
- c. Demography
- d. Risk

Guidance: level 1

:: Financial markets ::

A _____ is a financial market in which long-term debt or equity-backed securities are bought and sold. _____ s channel the wealth of savers to those who can put it to long-term productive use, such as companies or governments making long-term investments. Financial regulators like the Bank of England and the U.S. Securities and Exchange Commission oversee _____ s to protect investors against fraud, among other duties.

Exam Probability: **Medium**

50. *Answer choices:*

(see index for correct answer)

- a. Clearing balance requirement
- b. Capital market
- c. Alternative trading system
- d. Forex signal

Guidance: level 1

:: ::

In the broadest sense, _____ is any practice which contributes to the sale of products to a retail consumer. At a retail in-store level, _____ refers to the variety of products available for sale and the display of those products in such a way that it stimulates interest and entices customers to make a purchase.

51. *Answer choices:*

(see index for correct answer)

- a. levels of analysis
- b. Character
- c. hierarchical
- d. imperative

Guidance: level 1

:: Financial ratios ::

_____ is the difference between revenue and cost of goods sold divided by revenue. _____ is expressed as a percentage. Generally, it is calculated as the selling price of an item, less the cost of goods sold . _____ is often used interchangeably with Gross Profit, but the terms are different. When speaking about a monetary amount, it is technically correct to use the term Gross Profit; when referring to a percentage or ratio, it is correct to use _____ . In other words, _____ is a percentage value, while Gross Profit is a monetary value.

52. *Answer choices:*

(see index for correct answer)

- a. Debt service coverage ratio
- b. Statutory liquidity ratio
- c. Gross margin
- d. Return on assets

Guidance: level 1

:: Financial accounting ::

_____ is a financial metric which represents operating liquidity available to a business, organisation or other entity, including governmental entities. Along with fixed assets such as plant and equipment, _____ is considered a part of operating capital. Gross _____ is equal to current assets. _____ is calculated as current assets minus current liabilities. If current assets are less than current liabilities, an entity has a _____ deficiency, also called a _____ deficit.

Exam Probability: **High**

53. *Answer choices:*

(see index for correct answer)

- a. Valuation
- b. Accelerated depreciation
- c. Working capital
- d. Deferred financing cost

Guidance: level 1

In marketing, a _____ is a ticket or document that can be redeemed for a financial discount or rebate when purchasing a product.

Exam Probability: **Medium**

54. *Answer choices:*

(see index for correct answer)

- a. Coupon
- b. process perspective
- c. hierarchical perspective
- d. co-culture

Guidance: level 1

:: Mereology ::

_____ , in the abstract, is what belongs to or with something, whether as an attribute or as a component of said thing. In the context of this article, it is one or more components , whether physical or incorporeal, of a person's estate; or so belonging to, as in being owned by, a person or jointly a group of people or a legal entity like a corporation or even a society. Depending on the nature of the _____ , an owner of _____ has the right to consume, alter, share, redefine, rent, mortgage, pawn, sell, exchange, transfer, give away or destroy it, or to exclude others from doing these things, as well as to perhaps abandon it; whereas regardless of the nature of the _____ , the owner thereof has the right to properly use it , or at the very least exclusively keep it.

Exam Probability: **High**

55. *Answer choices:*

(see index for correct answer)

- a. Mereological essentialism
- b. Meronomy
- c. Mereotopology
- d. Property

Guidance: level 1

:: ::

_____ refers to a business or organization attempting to acquire goods or services to accomplish its goals. Although there are several organizations that attempt to set standards in the _____ process, processes can vary greatly between organizations. Typically the word "_____" is not used interchangeably with the word "procurement", since procurement typically includes expediting, supplier quality, and transportation and logistics in addition to _____ .

Exam Probability: **High**

56. *Answer choices:*

(see index for correct answer)

- a. personal values
- b. functional perspective
- c. Purchasing
- d. corporate values

Guidance: level 1

:: Decision theory ::

Within economics the concept of _____ is used to model worth or value, but its usage has evolved significantly over time. The term was introduced initially as a measure of pleasure or satisfaction within the theory of utilitarianism by moral philosophers such as Jeremy Bentham and John Stuart Mill. But the term has been adapted and reapplied within neoclassical economics, which dominates modern economic theory, as a _____ function that represents a consumer's preference ordering over a choice set. As such, it is devoid of its original interpretation as a measurement of the pleasure or satisfaction obtained by the consumer from that choice.

Exam Probability: **High**

57. *Answer choices:*

(see index for correct answer)

- a. Policy
- b. Subjective expected utility
- c. Sure-thing principle
- d. Dynamic decision-making

Guidance: level 1

:: Derivatives (finance) ::

_____ is any bodily activity that enhances or maintains physical fitness and overall health and wellness. It is performed for various reasons, to aid growth and improve strength, preventing aging, developing muscles and the cardiovascular system, honing athletic skills, weight loss or maintenance, improving health and also for enjoyment. Many individuals choose to _____ outdoors where they can congregate in groups, socialize, and enhance well-being.

Exam Probability: **Medium**

58. *Answer choices:*

(see index for correct answer)

- a. E-mini
- b. Dual currency deposit
- c. Option screener
- d. Credit derivative

Guidance: level 1

:: Accounting ::

_____ is a process of providing relief to shared service organization's cost centers that provide a product or service. In turn, the associated expense is assigned to internal clients' cost centers that consume the products and services. For example, the CIO may provide all IT services within the company and assign the costs back to the business units that consume each offering.

59. *Answer choices:*

(see index for correct answer)

- a. Special journals
- b. Earnings surprise
- c. Engineering Accounting
- d. Cost allocation

Guidance: level 1

Human resource management

Human resource (HR) management is the strategic approach to the effective management of organization workers so that they help the business gain a competitive advantage. It is designed to maximize employee performance in service of an employer's strategic objectives. HR is primarily concerned with the management of people within organizations, focusing on policies and on systems. HR departments are responsible for overseeing employee-benefits design, employee recruitment, training and development, performance appraisal, and rewarding (e.g., managing pay and benefit systems). HR also concerns itself with organizational change and industrial relations, that is, the balancing of organizational practices with requirements arising from collective bargaining and from governmental laws.

:: Occupational safety and health organizations ::

The _____ is the United States federal agency responsible for conducting research and making recommendations for the prevention of work-related injury and illness. NIOSH is part of the Centers for Disease Control and Prevention within the U.S. Department of Health and Human Services.

Exam Probability: **Low**

1. *Answer choices:*

(see index for correct answer)

- a. American Conference of Governmental Industrial Hygienists
- b. British Occupational Hygiene Society
- c. National Institute for Occupational Safety and Health
- d. Basic Occupational Health Services

Guidance: level 1

:: Recruitment ::

_____ is a tool companies and organizations use as a way to communicate the good and the bad characteristics of the job during the hiring process of new employees, or as a tool to reestablish job specificity for existing employees. _____ s should provide the individuals with a well-rounded description that details what obligations the individual can expect to perform while working for that specific company. Descriptions may include, but are not limited to, work environment, expectations, and Company policies .

2. *Answer choices:*

- a. Realistic job preview
- b. Staff Selection Commission
- c. Video resume
- d. The Select Family of Staffing Companies

Guidance: level 1

:: ::

_____ is overt or covert, often harmful, social interaction with the intention of inflicting damage or other unpleasantness upon another individual. It may occur either reactively or without provocation. In humans, frustration due to blocked goals can cause _____ . Human _____ can be classified into direct and indirect _____ ; whilst the former is characterized by physical or verbal behavior intended to cause harm to someone, the latter is characterized by behavior intended to harm the social relations of an individual or group.

3. *Answer choices:*

- a. Aggression
- b. interpersonal communication
- c. hierarchical
- d. empathy

Guidance: level 1

:: Management education ::

_____ is the implementation of government policy and also an academic discipline that studies this implementation and prepares civil servants for working in the public service. As a "field of inquiry with a diverse scope" whose fundamental goal is to "advance management and policies so that government can function". Some of the various definitions which have been offered for the term are: "the management of public programs"; the "translation of politics into the reality that citizens see every day"; and "the study of government decision making, the analysis of the policies themselves, the various inputs that have produced them, and the inputs necessary to produce alternative policies."

Exam Probability: **High**

4. *Answer choices:*

(see index for correct answer)

- a. Master of Commerce
- b. Public administration
- c. Certificate in Management Studies
- d. Executive DBA Council

:: Business process ::

Outsourcing is an agreement in which one company hires another company to be responsible for a planned or existing activity that is or could be done internally,and sometimes involves transferring employees and assets from one firm to another.

Exam Probability: **High**

5. *Answer choices:*

(see index for correct answer)

- a. Intention mining
- b. Business Motivation Model
- c. Open door policy
- d. Business process outsourcing

:: Systems thinking ::

Systems theory is the interdisciplinary study of systems. A system is a cohesive conglomeration of interrelated and interdependent parts that is either natural or man-made. Every system is delineated by its spatial and temporal boundaries, surrounded and influenced by its environment, described by its structure and purpose or nature and expressed in its functioning. In terms of its effects, a system can be more than the sum of its parts if it expresses synergy or emergent behavior. Changing one part of the system usually affects other parts and the whole system, with predictable patterns of behavior. For systems that are self-learning and self-adapting, the positive growth and adaptation depend upon how well the system is adjusted with its environment. Some systems function mainly to support other systems by aiding in the maintenance of the other system to prevent failure. The goal of systems theory is systematically discovering a system's dynamics, constraints, conditions and elucidating principles that can be discerned and applied to systems at every level of nesting, and in every field for achieving optimized equifinality.

Exam Probability: **Medium**

6. *Answer choices:*

(see index for correct answer)

- a. Ray Hammond
- b. Learning organization
- c. Delphi method
- d. Interdependence

Guidance: level 1

:: Survey methodology ::

_____ is often used to assess thoughts, opinions, and feelings. Surveys can be specific and limited, or they can have more global, widespread goals. Psychologists and sociologists often use surveys to analyze behavior, while it is also used to meet the more pragmatic needs of the media, such as, in evaluating political candidates, public health officials, professional organizations, and advertising and marketing directors. A survey consists of a predetermined set of questions that is given to a sample. With a representative sample, that is, one that is representative of the larger population of interest, one can describe the attitudes of the population from which the sample was drawn. Further, one can compare the attitudes of different populations as well as look for changes in attitudes over time. A good sample selection is key as it allows one to generalize the findings from the sample to the population, which is the whole purpose of _____ .

Exam Probability: **High**

7. *Answer choices:*

(see index for correct answer)

- a. Self-report study
- b. Total survey error
- c. Survey sampling
- d. World Association for Public Opinion Research

Guidance: level 1

:: ::

_____ consists of using generic or ad hoc methods in an orderly manner to find solutions to problems. Some of the problem-solving techniques developed and used in philosophy, artificial intelligence, computer science, engineering, mathematics, or medicine are related to mental problem-solving techniques studied in psychology.

Exam Probability: **Low**

8. *Answer choices:*

(see index for correct answer)

- a. Problem solving
- b. surface-level diversity
- c. Sarbanes-Oxley act of 2002
- d. levels of analysis

Guidance: level 1

:: Termination of employment ::

The _____ of 1988 is a US labor law which protects employees, their families, and communities by requiring most employers with 100 or more employees to provide 60 calendar-day advance notification of plant closings and mass layoffs of employees, as defined in the Act. In 2001, there were about 2,000 mass layoffs and plant closures which were subject to WARN advance notice requirements and which affected about 660,000 employees.

Exam Probability: **High**

9. *Answer choices:*

(see index for correct answer)

- a. Enforced retirement
- b. The Disposable American
- c. Luis Gabriel Aguilera
- d. Termination of Employment Convention, 1982

Guidance: level 1

:: United States federal labor legislation ::

The _____ of 1967 is a US labor law that forbids employment discrimination against anyone at least 40 years of age in the United States . In 1967, the bill was signed into law by President Lyndon B. Johnson. The ADEA prevents age discrimination and provides equal employment opportunity under conditions that were not explicitly covered in Title VII of the Civil Rights Act of 1964. It also applies to the standards for pensions and benefits provided by employers, and requires that information concerning the needs of older workers be provided to the general public.

Exam Probability: **Medium**

10. *Answer choices:*

(see index for correct answer)

- a. Age Discrimination in Employment Act
- b. Title 29 of the United States Code

- c. Drug-Free Workplace Act of 1988
- d. Contract Work Hours and Safety Standards Act

Guidance: level 1

:: Evaluation methods ::

In social psychology, _____ is the process of looking at oneself in order to assess aspects that are important to one's identity. It is one of the motives that drive self-evaluation, along with self-verification and self-enhancement. Sedikides suggests that the _____ motive will prompt people to seek information to confirm their uncertain self-concept rather than their certain self-concept and at the same time people use _____ to enhance their certainty of their own self-knowledge. However, the _____ motive could be seen as quite different from the other two self-evaluation motives. Unlike the other two motives through _____ people are interested in the accuracy of their current self view, rather than improving their self-view. This makes _____ the only self-evaluative motive that may cause a person's self-esteem to be damaged.

Exam Probability: **Low**

11. *Answer choices:*

(see index for correct answer)

- a. Self-assessment
- b. Economic impact analysis
- c. Qualitative research
- d. Electronic patient-reported outcome

:: Management ::

The term _____ refers to measures designed to increase the degree of autonomy and self-determination in people and in communities in order to enable them to represent their interests in a responsible and self-determined way, acting on their own authority. It is the process of becoming stronger and more confident, especially in controlling one's life and claiming one's rights. _____ as action refers both to the process of self-_____ and to professional support of people, which enables them to overcome their sense of powerlessness and lack of influence, and to recognize and use their resources. To do work with power.

Exam Probability: **Medium**

12. *Answer choices:*

(see index for correct answer)

- a. Iterative and incremental development
- b. Empowerment
- c. Fall guy
- d. Local management board

:: Human resource management ::

_____ is a continual process used to align the needs and priorities of the organization with those of its workforce to ensure it can meet its legislative, regulatory, service and production requirements and organizational objectives. _____ enables evidence based workforce development strategies.

Exam Probability: **Medium**

13. *Answer choices:*

(see index for correct answer)

- a. Progress, plans, problems
- b. Workforce planning
- c. Formal organization
- d. Disciplinary probation

Guidance: level 1

:: Labor ::

_____ s are workers whose main capital is knowledge. Examples include programmers, physicians, pharmacists, architects, engineers, scientists, design thinkers, public accountants, lawyers, and academics, and any other white-collar workers, whose line of work requires the one to "think for a living".

Exam Probability: **Low**

14. *Answer choices:*

- a. Andrew Davison
- b. Frisch elasticity of labor supply
- c. Knowledge worker
- d. Universal validity of collective labour agreements

Guidance: level 1

:: ::

Domestic violence is violence or other abuse by one person against another in a domestic setting, such as in marriage or cohabitation. It may be termed intimate partner violence when committed by a spouse or partner in an intimate relationship against the other spouse or partner, and can take place in heterosexual or same-sex relationships, or between former spouses or partners. Domestic violence can also involve violence against children, parents, or the elderly. It takes a number of forms, including physical, verbal, emotional, economic, religious, reproductive, and sexual abuse, which can range from subtle, coercive forms to marital rape and to violent physical abuse such as choking, beating, female genital mutilation, and acid throwing that results in disfigurement or death. Domestic murders include stoning, bride burning, honor killings, and dowry deaths.

Exam Probability: **Low**

15. *Answer choices:*

- a. Family violence
- b. empathy
- c. hierarchical perspective
- d. cultural

Guidance: level 1

:: Majority–minority relations ::

_____ , also known as reservation in India and Nepal, positive discrimination / action in the United Kingdom, and employment equity in Canada and South Africa, is the policy of promoting the education and employment of members of groups that are known to have previously suffered from discrimination. Historically and internationally, support for _____ has sought to achieve goals such as bridging inequalities in employment and pay, increasing access to education, promoting diversity, and redressing apparent past wrongs, harms, or hindrances.

Exam Probability: **Medium**

16. *Answer choices:*

(see index for correct answer)

- a. cultural dissonance
- b. positive discrimination
- c. cultural Relativism

Guidance: level 1

:: Recruitment ::

The _____ is an American nonprofit professional association established in 1956 in Bethlehem, Pennsylvania, for college career services, recruiting practitioners, and others who wish to hire the college educated.

Exam Probability: **Medium**

17. *Answer choices:*

(see index for correct answer)

- a. Military recruitment
- b. TalentScotland
- c. Skills-Based Hiring
- d. National Association of Colleges and Employers

Guidance: level 1

:: Hazard analysis ::

A _____ is an agent which has the potential to cause harm to a vulnerable target. The terms " _____ " and "risk" are often used interchangeably. However, in terms of risk assessment, they are two very distinct terms. A _____ is any agent that can cause harm or damage to humans, property, or the environment. Risk is defined as the probability that exposure to a _____ will lead to a negative consequence, or more simply, a _____ poses no risk if there is no exposure to that _____ .

Exam Probability: **Medium**

18. *Answer choices:*

(see index for correct answer)

- a. Hazard
- b. Hazardous Materials Identification System
- c. Risk assessment
- d. Hazard identification

Guidance: level 1

:: Employment compensation ::

A _____ , also known as a flexible spending arrangement, is one of a number of tax-advantaged financial accounts, resulting in payroll tax savings. Before the Patient Protection and Affordable Care Act, one significant disadvantage to using an FSA was that funds not used by the end of the plan year were forfeited to the employer, known as the "use it or lose it" rule. Under the terms of the Affordable Care Act, a plan may permit an employee to carry over up to $500 into the following year without losing the funds.

19. *Answer choices:*

(see index for correct answer)

- a. Protection of Wages Convention, 1949
- b. Maximum wage
- c. Flexible spending account
- d. Reservation wage

Guidance: level 1

:: Human resource management ::

The _____ is a free online database that contains hundreds of occupational definitions to help students, job seekers, businesses and workforce development professionals to understand today's world of work in the United States. It was developed under the sponsorship of the US Department of Labor/Employment and Training Administration through a grant to the North Carolina Employment Security Commission during the 1990s. John L. Holland's vocational model, often referred to as the Holland Codes, is used in the "Interests" section of the O*NET.

Exam Probability: **Medium**

20. *Answer choices:*

(see index for correct answer)

- a. Administrative services organization
- b. Managerial assessment of proficiency
- c. Occupational Information Network
- d. Management by observation

Guidance: level 1

:: ::

_____ is the formal act of giving up or quitting one's office or position. A _____ can occur when a person holding a position gained by election or appointment steps down, but leaving a position upon the expiration of a term, or choosing not to seek an additional term, is not considered _____ .

Exam Probability: **Medium**

21. *Answer choices:*

(see index for correct answer)

- a. Resignation
- b. hierarchical perspective
- c. Sarbanes-Oxley act of 2002
- d. deep-level diversity

Guidance: level 1

_____ is a method for employees to organize into a labor union in which a majority of employees in a bargaining unit sign authorization forms, or "cards", stating they wish to be represented by the union. Since the National Labor Relations Act became law in 1935, _____ has been an alternative to the National Labor Relations Board's election process. _____ and election are both overseen by the National Labor Relations Board. The difference is that with card sign-up, employees sign authorization cards stating they want a union, the cards are submitted to the NLRB and if more than 50% of the employees submitted cards, the NLRB requires the employer to recognize the union. The NLRA election process is an additional step with the NLRB conducting a secret ballot election after authorization cards are submitted. In both cases the employer never sees the authorization cards or any information that would disclose how individual employees voted.

Exam Probability: **Low**

22. *Answer choices:*

(see index for correct answer)

- a. similarity-attraction theory
- b. functional perspective
- c. cultural
- d. Card check

Guidance: level 1

_____ is the extraction of valuable minerals or other geological materials from the earth, usually from an ore body, lode, vein, seam, reef or placer deposit. These deposits form a mineralized package that is of economic interest to the miner.

Exam Probability: **Low**

23. *Answer choices:*

(see index for correct answer)

- a. information systems assessment
- b. similarity-attraction theory
- c. open system
- d. Mining

Guidance: level 1

:: Labour law ::

A _____ is a "shop-floor" organization representing workers that functions as a local/firm-level complement to trade unions but is independent of these at least in some countries. _____ s exist with different names in a variety of related forms in a number of European countries, including Britain ; Germany and Austria ; Luxembourg ; the Netherlands and Flanders in Belgium ; Italy ; France ; Wallonia in Belgium and Spain .

Exam Probability: **Medium**

24. *Answer choices:*

(see index for correct answer)

- a. Positive action
- b. The Burke Group
- c. Works council
- d. Bharat Forge Co Ltd v Uttam Manohar Nakate

Guidance: level 1

:: Trade unions ::

A _____ is an association of workers forming a legal unit or legal personhood, usually called a "bargaining unit", which acts as bargaining agent and legal representative for a unit of employees in all matters of law or right arising from or in the administration of a collective agreement. Labour unions typically fund the formal organisation, head office, and legal team functions of the labour union through regular fees or union dues. The delegate staff of the labour union representation in the workforce are made up of workplace volunteers who are appointed by members in democratic elections.

Exam Probability: **High**

25. *Answer choices:*

(see index for correct answer)

- a. Union democracy
- b. TU

- c. Trade union
- d. Paper local

Guidance: level 1

:: Human resource management ::

_____ expands the capacity of individuals to perform in leadership roles within organizations. Leadership roles are those that facilitate execution of a company's strategy through building alignment, winning mindshare and growing the capabilities of others. Leadership roles may be formal, with the corresponding authority to make decisions and take responsibility, or they may be informal roles with little official authority .

Exam Probability: **Low**

26. *Answer choices:*

(see index for correct answer)

- a. Job performance
- b. Disciplinary probation
- c. Leadership development
- d. Inclusion

Guidance: level 1

:: Business law ::

An _____ is a natural person, business, or corporation that provides goods or services to another entity under terms specified in a contract or within a verbal agreement. Unlike an employee, an _____ does not work regularly for an employer but works as and when required, during which time they may be subject to law of agency. _____s are usually paid on a freelance basis. Contractors often work through a limited company or franchise, which they themselves own, or may work through an umbrella company.

Exam Probability: **High**

27. *Answer choices:*

(see index for correct answer)

- a. Negotiable instrument
- b. De facto corporation and corporation by estoppel
- c. Complex structured finance transactions
- d. Independent contractor

Guidance: level 1

:: Employment compensation ::

The formula commonly used by compensation professionals to assess the competitiveness of an employee's pay level involves calculating a ""_____ "". _____ is the short form for Comparative ratio.

Exam Probability: **Medium**

28. *Answer choices:*

(see index for correct answer)

- a. Maximum wage
- b. IDS Pay Report
- c. Anderson v. Mt. Clemens Pottery Co.
- d. WorkCover Authority of New South Wales

Guidance: level 1

:: Recruitment ::

A _____ , also referred commonly as a career fair or career expo, is an event in which employers, recruiters, and schools give information to potential employees. Job seekers attend these while trying to make a good impression to potential coworkers by speaking face-to-face with one another, filling out résumés, and asking questions in attempt to get a good feel on the work needed. Likewise, online _____ s are held, giving job seekers another way to get in contact with probable employers using the internet.

Exam Probability: **Medium**

29. *Answer choices:*

(see index for correct answer)

- a. National Association of Colleges and Employers
- b. Job fair
- c. Europass

- d. Job fraud

:: Unemployment by country ::

Unemployment benefits are payments made by back authorized bodies to unemployed people. In the United States, benefits are funded by a compulsory governmental insurance system, not taxes on individual citizens. Depending on the jurisdiction and the status of the person, those sums may be small, covering only basic needs, or may compensate the lost time proportionally to the previous earned salary.

Exam Probability: **Low**

30. *Answer choices:*

(see index for correct answer)

- a. Unemployment insurance
- b. Unemployment in Spain
- c. Unemployment in Poland

:: Income ::

In business and accounting, net income is an entity's income minus cost of goods sold, expenses and taxes for an accounting period. It is computed as the residual of all revenues and gains over all expenses and losses for the period, and has also been defined as the net increase in shareholders' equity that results from a company's operations. In the context of the presentation of financial statements, the IFRS Foundation defines net income as synonymous with profit and loss. The difference between revenue and the cost of making a product or providing a service, before deducting overheads, payroll, taxation, and interest payments. This is different from operating income .

Exam Probability: **Low**

31. *Answer choices:*

(see index for correct answer)

- a. Bottom line
- b. Pay grade
- c. Property investment calculator
- d. Real estate investing

Guidance: level 1

:: Network theory ::

A _____ is a social structure made up of a set of social actors , sets of dyadic ties, and other social interactions between actors. The _____ perspective provides a set of methods for analyzing the structure of whole social entities as well as a variety of theories explaining the patterns observed in these structures. The study of these structures uses _____ analysis to identify local and global patterns, locate influential entities, and examine network dynamics.

32. *Answer choices:*

(see index for correct answer)

- a. Assortative mixing
- b. Network science
- c. Modularity
- d. Exponential random graph models

Guidance: level 1

:: Unemployment benefits ::

_____ are payments made by back authorized bodies to unemployed people. In the United States, benefits are funded by a compulsory governmental insurance system, not taxes on individual citizens. Depending on the jurisdiction and the status of the person, those sums may be small, covering only basic needs, or may compensate the lost time proportionally to the previous earned salary.

33. *Answer choices:*

(see index for correct answer)

- a. Kela
- b. Unemployment benefits in Sweden
- c. Unemployment benefits
- d. Unemployment benefits in Spain

Guidance: level 1

:: Employee relations ::

_____ are tools used by organizational leadership to gain feedback on and measure employee engagement, employee morale, and performance. Usually answered anonymously, surveys are also used to gain a holistic picture of employees' feelings on such areas as working conditions, supervisory impact, and motivation that regular channels of communication may not. Surveys are considered effective in this regard provided they are well-designed, effectively administered, have validity, and evoke changes and improvements.

Exam Probability: **Low**

34. *Answer choices:*

(see index for correct answer)

- a. Industry Federation of the State of Rio de Janeiro

- b. Employee handbook
- c. Employee motivation
- d. Employee surveys

Guidance: level 1

:: ::

_____ is the moral stance, political philosophy, ideology, or social outlook that emphasizes the moral worth of the individual. Individualists promote the exercise of one's goals and desires and so value independence and self-reliance and advocate that interests of the individual should achieve precedence over the state or a social group, while opposing external interference upon one's own interests by society or institutions such as the government. _____ is often defined in contrast to totalitarianism, collectivism, and more corporate social forms.

Exam Probability: **High**

35. *Answer choices:*

(see index for correct answer)

- a. hierarchical
- b. surface-level diversity
- c. Sarbanes-Oxley act of 2002
- d. Individualism

Guidance: level 1

:: Employment compensation ::

An _____ is an employee benefit program that assists employees with personal problems and/or work-related problems that may impact their job performance, health, mental and emotional well-being. EAPs generally offer free and confidential assessments, short-term counseling, referrals, and follow-up services for employees and their household members. EAP counselors also work in a consultative role with managers and supervisors to address employee and organizational challenges and needs. Many corporations, academic institution and/or government agencies are active in helping organizations prevent and cope with workplace violence, trauma, and other emergency response situations. There is a variety of support programs offered for employees. Even though EAPs are mainly aimed at work-related problems, there are a variety of programs that can assist with problems outside of the workplace. EAPs have grown over the years, and are more desirable economically and socially.

Exam Probability: **Medium**

36. *Answer choices:*

(see index for correct answer)

- a. WorkCover Authority of New South Wales
- b. Anderson v. Mt. Clemens Pottery Co.
- c. Workers Compensation Act 1987
- d. Living wage

Guidance: level 1

:: Offshoring ::

Outsourcing is an agreement in which one company hires another company to be responsible for a planned or existing activity that is or could be done internally.and sometimes involves transferring employees and assets from one firm to another.

Exam Probability: **Medium**

37. *Answer choices:*

(see index for correct answer)

- a. Global labor arbitrage
- b. Offshoring Research Network
- c. Programmers Guild
- d. Nearshoring

Guidance: level 1

:: ::

_____ is defined by sociologist John R. Schermerhorn as the "...degree to which the people affected by decision are treated by dignity and respect. The theory focuses on the interpersonal treatment people receive when procedures are implemented.

Exam Probability: **Medium**

38. *Answer choices:*

(see index for correct answer)

- a. process perspective
- b. Interactional justice
- c. deep-level diversity
- d. surface-level diversity

Guidance: level 1

:: ::

_____ is a form of development in which a person called a coach supports a learner or client in achieving a specific personal or professional goal by providing training and guidance. The learner is sometimes called a coachee. Occasionally, _____ may mean an informal relationship between two people, of whom one has more experience and expertise than the other and offers advice and guidance as the latter learns; but _____ differs from mentoring in focusing on specific tasks or objectives, as opposed to more general goals or overall development.

Exam Probability: **Medium**

39. *Answer choices:*
(see index for correct answer)

- a. interpersonal communication
- b. Coaching
- c. Sarbanes-Oxley act of 2002

- d. Character

Guidance: level 1

:: Financial terminology ::

_____ is the cost of maintaining a certain standard of living. Changes in the _____ over time are often operationalized in a cost-of-living index. _____ calculations are also used to compare the cost of maintaining a certain standard of living in different geographic areas. Differences in _____ between locations can also be measured in terms of purchasing power parity rates.

Exam Probability: **Medium**

40. *Answer choices:*

(see index for correct answer)

- a. Diagonal spread
- b. Dividend recapitalization
- c. Multi-currency pricing
- d. Custodial participant

Guidance: level 1

:: ::

In educational development, _____ provides a person, often a student, focus for selecting a career or subject to undertake in the future. Often educational institutions provide career counsellors to assist students with their educational development.

Exam Probability: **Low**

41. *Answer choices:*

(see index for correct answer)

- a. process perspective
- b. cultural
- c. empathy
- d. open system

Guidance: level 1

:: Financial accounting ::

_____ is the intangible value of a business, covering its people , the value relating to its relationships , and everything that is left when the employees go home , of which intellectual property is but one component. It is the sum of everything everybody in a company knows that gives it a competitive edge. The term is used in academia in an attempt to account for the value of intangible assets not listed explicitly on a company's balance sheets. On a national level _____ refers to national intangible capital, NIC.A second meaning that is used in academia and was adopted in large corporations is focused on the recycling of knowledge via knowledge management and _____ management . Creating, shaping and updating the stock of _____ requires the formulation of a strategic vision, which blends together all three dimensions of _____ within the organisational context through exploration, exploitation, measurement, and disclosure. _____ is used in the context of assessing the wealth of organizations. A metric for the value of _____ is the amount by which the enterprise value of a firm exceeds the value of its tangible assets. Directly visible on corporate books is capital embodied in its physical assets and financial capital; however all three make up the value of an enterprise. Measuring the real value and the total performance of _____'s components is a critical part of running a company in the knowledge economy and Information Age. Understanding the _____ in an enterprise allows leveraging of its intellectual assets. For a corporation, the result will optimize its stock price.

Exam Probability: **Low**

42. *Answer choices:*

(see index for correct answer)

- a. Floating capital
- b. Intellectual capital
- c. Convenience translation
- d. Accelerated depreciation

Guidance: level 1

:: Labour relations ::

A _____ , also known as a post-entry closed shop, is a form of a union security clause. Under this, the employer agrees to either only hire labor union members or to require that any new employees who are not already union members become members within a certain amount of time. Use of the _____ varies widely from nation to nation, depending on the level of protection given trade unions in general.

Exam Probability: **High**

43. *Answer choices:*

(see index for correct answer)

- a. Lockout
- b. Union representative
- c. Union shop
- d. Worker center

Guidance: level 1

:: Employment ::

Onboarding, also known as _____ , is management jargon first created in 1988 that refers to the mechanism through which new employees acquire the necessary knowledge, skills, and behaviors in order to become effective organizational members and insiders.

Exam Probability: **Medium**

44. *Answer choices:*

(see index for correct answer)

- a. Workgang
- b. Legal working age
- c. Organizational socialization
- d. Social VAT

Guidance: level 1

:: Ethically disputed business practices ::

An _____ in US labor law refers to certain actions taken by employers or unions that violate the National Labor Relations Act of 1935 29 U.S.C. § 151–169 and other legislation. Such acts are investigated by the National Labor Relations Board .

Exam Probability: **Medium**

45. *Answer choices:*

(see index for correct answer)

- a. Hollywood accounting
- b. Two sets of books
- c. False economy
- d. Persuasive technology

Guidance: level 1

:: Problem solving ::

A _____ is a unit or formation established to work on a single defined task or activity. Originally introduced by the United States Navy, the term has now caught on for general usage and is a standard part of NATO terminology. Many non-military organizations now create "_____ s" or task groups for temporary activities that might have once been performed by ad hoc committees.

Exam Probability: **Low**

46. *Answer choices:*

(see index for correct answer)

- a. Creative Education Foundation
- b. Task force
- c. Self-organising heuristic
- d. Project Euler

:: Industrial engineering ::

_____ is the formal process that sits alongside Requirements analysis and focuses on the human elements of the requirements.

Exam Probability: **Low**

47. *Answer choices:*

(see index for correct answer)

- a. Design of experiments
- b. H. Milton Stewart School of Industrial and Systems Engineering
- c. Bayesian experimental design
- d. Package testing

:: Organizational behavior ::

In organizational behavior and industrial and organizational psychology, _____ is an individual's psychological attachment to the organization. The basis behind many of these studies was to find ways to improve how workers feel about their jobs so that these workers would become more committed to their organizations. _____ predicts work variables such as turnover, organizational citizenship behavior, and job performance. Some of the factors such as role stress, empowerment, job insecurity and employability, and distribution of leadership have been shown to be connected to a worker's sense of _____ .

Exam Probability: **High**

48. *Answer choices:*

(see index for correct answer)

- a. Organizational justice
- b. Behavioral systems analysis
- c. Organizational Expedience
- d. Organizational commitment

Guidance: level 1

:: ::

_____ is a labor union representing almost 1.9 million workers in over 100 occupations in the United States and Canada. SEIU is focused on organizing workers in three sectors: health care , including hospital, home care and nursing home workers; public services ; and property services .

49. *Answer choices:*

(see index for correct answer)

- a. cultural
- b. Sarbanes-Oxley act of 2002
- c. Service Employees International Union
- d. hierarchical perspective

Guidance: level 1

:: Behavior ::

_____ refers to behavior-change procedures that were employed during the 1970s and early 1980s. Based on methodological behaviorism, overt behavior was modified with presumed consequences, including artificial positive and negative reinforcement contingencies to increase desirable behavior, or administering positive and negative punishment and/or extinction to reduce problematic behavior. For the treatment of phobias, habituation and punishment were the basic principles used in flooding, a subcategory of desensitization.

Exam Probability: **High**

50. *Answer choices:*

(see index for correct answer)

- a. theory of reasoned action

- b. Behavior modification

Guidance: level 1

:: Validity (statistics) ::

_____ is "the degree to which a test measures what it claims, or purports, to be measuring." In the classical model of test validity, _____ is one of three main types of validity evidence, alongside content validity and criterion validity. Modern validity theory defines _____ as the overarching concern of validity research, subsuming all other types of validity evidence.

Exam Probability: **High**

51. *Answer choices:*

(see index for correct answer)

- a. Validation
- b. Incremental validity
- c. Construct validity
- d. Criterion validity

Guidance: level 1

:: ::

A _____ , medical practitioner, medical doctor, or simply doctor, is a professional who practises medicine, which is concerned with promoting, maintaining, or restoring health through the study, diagnosis, prognosis and treatment of disease, injury, and other physical and mental impairments.

_____ s may focus their practice on certain disease categories, types of patients, and methods of treatment—known as specialities—or they may assume responsibility for the provision of continuing and comprehensive medical care to individuals, families, and communities—known as general practice. Medical practice properly requires both a detailed knowledge of the academic disciplines, such as anatomy and physiology, underlying diseases and their treatment—the science of medicine—and also a decent competence in its applied practice—the art or craft of medicine.

Exam Probability: **Medium**

52. *Answer choices:*

(see index for correct answer)

- a. hierarchical perspective
- b. interpersonal communication
- c. Physician
- d. surface-level diversity

Guidance: level 1

:: Parental leave ::

_____ is a type of employment discrimination that occurs when expectant women are fired, not hired, or otherwise discriminated against due to their pregnancy or intention to become pregnant. Common forms of _____ include not being hired due to visible pregnancy or likelihood of becoming pregnant, being fired after informing an employer of one's pregnancy, being fired after maternity leave, and receiving a pay dock due to pregnancy. Convention on the Elimination of All Forms of Discrimination against Women prohibits dismissal on the grounds of maternity or pregnancy and ensures right to maternity leave or comparable social benefits. The Maternity Protection Convention C 183 proclaims adequate protection for pregnancy as well. Though women have some protection in the United States because of the _____ Act of 1978, it has not completely curbed the incidence of _____ . The Equal Rights Amendment could ensure more robust sex equality ensuring that women and men could both work and have children at the same time.

Exam Probability: **High**

53. *Answer choices:*

(see index for correct answer)

- a. Sara Hlupekile Longwe
- b. Geduldig v. Aiello
- c. Pregnant Workers Directive
- d. Equal Opportunities Commission v Secretary of State for Trade and Industry

Guidance: level 1

:: ::

_____ medicine is an approach to medical practice intended to optimize decision-making by emphasizing the use of evidence from well-designed and well-conducted research. Although all medicine based on science has some degree of empirical support, EBM goes further, classifying evidence by its epistemologic strength and requiring that only the strongest types can yield strong recommendations; weaker types can yield only weak recommendations. The term was originally used to describe an approach to teaching the practice of medicine and improving decisions by individual physicians about individual patients. Use of the term rapidly expanded to include a previously described approach that emphasized the use of evidence in the design of guidelines and policies that apply to groups of patients and populations . It has subsequently spread to describe an approach to decision-making that is used at virtually every level of health care as well as other fields .

Exam Probability: **Medium**

54. *Answer choices:*

(see index for correct answer)

- a. similarity-attraction theory
- b. personal values
- c. Evidence-based
- d. Character

Guidance: level 1

:: Employment ::

_____ is measuring the output of a particular business process or procedure, then modifying the process or procedure to increase the output, increase efficiency, or increase the effectiveness of the process or procedure. _____ can be applied to either individual performance such as an athlete or organizational performance such as a racing team or a commercial business.

Exam Probability: **High**

55. *Answer choices:*

(see index for correct answer)

- a. Digital nomad
- b. Suspension
- c. Saudization
- d. Careers advisory service

Guidance: level 1

:: Packaging ::

In work place, _____ or job _____ means good ranking with the hypothesized conception of requirements of a role. There are two types of job _____ s: contextual and task. Task _____ is related to cognitive ability while contextual _____ is dependent upon personality. Task _____ are behavioral roles that are recognized in job descriptions and by remuneration systems, they are directly related to organizational _____ , whereas, contextual _____ are value based and additional behavioral roles that are not recognized in job descriptions and covered by compensation; they are extra roles that are indirectly related to organizational _____ . Citizenship _____ like contextual _____ means a set of individual activity/contribution that supports the organizational culture.

Exam Probability: **High**

56. *Answer choices:*

(see index for correct answer)

- a. Dangerous Preparations Directive
- b. Performance
- c. 463L master pallet
- d. Load securing

Guidance: level 1

:: Organizational structure ::

An _____ defines how activities such as task allocation, coordination, and supervision are directed toward the achievement of organizational aims.

57. *Answer choices:*

(see index for correct answer)

- a. The Starfish and the Spider
- b. Organization of the New York City Police Department
- c. Organizational structure
- d. Unorganisation

Guidance: level 1

:: Belief ::

_____ is the ability to acquire knowledge without proof, evidence, or conscious reasoning, or without understanding how the knowledge was acquired. Different writers give the word " _____ " a great variety of different meanings, ranging from direct access to unconscious knowledge, unconscious cognition, inner sensing, inner insight to unconscious pattern-recognition and the ability to understand something instinctively, without the need for conscious reasoning.

58. *Answer choices:*

(see index for correct answer)

- a. Intuition

- b. Belief-knowledge gap hypothesis
- c. Blind men and an elephant
- d. Urdoxa

Guidance: level 1

:: United States employment discrimination case law ::

_____ , 490 U.S. 228 , was an important decision by the United States Supreme Court on the issues of prescriptive sex discrimination and employer liability for sex discrimination. The employee, Ann Hopkins, sued her former employer, the accounting firm Price Waterhouse. She argued that the firm denied her partnership because she didn't fit the partners` idea of what a female employee should look like and act like. The employer failed to prove that it would have denied her partnership anyway, and the Court held that constituted sex discrimination under Title VII of the Civil Rights Act of 1964. The significance of the Supreme Court`s ruling was twofold. First, it established that gender stereotyping is actionable as sex discrimination. Second, it established the mixed-motive framework that enables employees to prove discrimination when other, lawful reasons for the adverse employment action exist alongside discriminatory motivations or reasons.

Exam Probability: **Low**

59. *Answer choices:*

(see index for correct answer)

- a. Griggs v. Duke Power Co.
- b. McDonnell Douglas Corp. v. Green
- c. Shyamala Rajender v. University of Minnesota

- d. Faragher v. City of Boca Raton

Guidance: level 1

Information systems

Information systems (IS) are formal, sociotechnical, organizational systems designed to collect, process, store, and distribute information. In a sociotechnical perspective Information Systems are composed by four components: technology, process, people and organizational structure.

:: ::

_____ is the fundamental facilities and systems serving a country, city, or other area, including the services and facilities necessary for its economy to function. _____ is composed of public and private physical improvements such as roads, bridges, tunnels, water supply, sewers, electrical grids, and telecommunications . In general, it has also been defined as "the physical components of interrelated systems providing commodities and services essential to enable, sustain, or enhance societal living conditions".

Exam Probability: **High**

1. *Answer choices:*

(see index for correct answer)

- a. deep-level diversity
- b. Character
- c. personal values
- d. interpersonal communication

Guidance: level 1

:: Data management ::

_____ s or data _____ s are computer languages used to make queries in databases and information systems.

Exam Probability: **Medium**

2. Answer choices:

(see index for correct answer)

- a. Grid-oriented storage
- b. Query language
- c. PerformancePoint
- d. SQL programming tool

Guidance: level 1

:: ::

A _____ is a published declaration of the intentions, motives, or views of the issuer, be it an individual, group, political party or government. A _____ usually accepts a previously published opinion or public consensus or promotes a new idea with prescriptive notions for carrying out changes the author believes should be made. It often is political or artistic in nature, but may present an individual's life stance. _____ s relating to religious belief are generally referred to as creeds.

Exam Probability: **Medium**

3. Answer choices:

(see index for correct answer)

- a. process perspective
- b. Manifesto
- c. Character

- d. hierarchical perspective

Guidance: level 1

:: Computer data ::

In computer science, _____ is the ability to access an arbitrary element of a sequence in equal time or any datum from a population of addressable elements roughly as easily and efficiently as any other, no matter how many elements may be in the set. It is typically contrasted to sequential access.

Exam Probability: **Medium**

4. *Answer choices:*

(see index for correct answer)

- a. Fuzzy backup
- b. Random access
- c. Persistent data
- d. Energy Logic

Guidance: level 1

:: Virtual economies ::

_____ Inc. is an American social game developer running social video game services founded in April 2007 and headquartered in San Francisco, California, United States. The company primarily focuses on mobile and social networking platforms. _____ states its mission as "connecting the world through games."

Exam Probability: **Medium**

5. *Answer choices:*

(see index for correct answer)

- a. Gaia Online
- b. Zynga
- c. Pioneer
- d. Evony

Guidance: level 1

:: Market structure and pricing ::

_____ is a term denoting that a product includes permission to use its source code, design documents, or content. It most commonly refers to the open-source model, in which open-source software or other products are released under an open-source license as part of the open-source-software movement. Use of the term originated with software, but has expanded beyond the software sector to cover other open content and forms of open collaboration.

Exam Probability: **Low**

6. *Answer choices:*

(see index for correct answer)

- a. Liberalization
- b. Open-source economics
- c. Market structure
- d. industry concentration

Guidance: level 1

:: ::

A database is an organized collection of data, generally stored and accessed electronically from a computer system. Where databases are more complex they are often developed using formal design and modeling techniques.

Exam Probability: **Medium**

7. *Answer choices:*

(see index for correct answer)

- a. Database management system
- b. levels of analysis
- c. functional perspective
- d. information systems assessment

Guidance: level 1

:: Industrial automation ::

_____ is the technology by which a process or procedure is performed with minimal human assistance. _____ or automatic control is the use of various control systems for operating equipment such as machinery, processes in factories, boilers and heat treating ovens, switching on telephone networks, steering and stabilization of ships, aircraft and other applications and vehicles with minimal or reduced human intervention.

Exam Probability: **High**

8. *Answer choices:*

(see index for correct answer)

- a. IODD
- b. RAPIEnet
- c. CODESYS
- d. Automation

Guidance: level 1

:: Remote administration software ::

_____ is a protocol used on the Internet or local area network to provide a bidirectional interactive text-oriented communication facility using a virtual terminal connection. User data is interspersed in-band with _____ control information in an 8-bit byte oriented data connection over the Transmission Control Protocol .

Exam Probability: **Low**

9. *Answer choices:*

(see index for correct answer)

- a. Apple Remote Desktop
- b. LogMeIn
- c. Rtelnet
- d. UltraVNC

Guidance: level 1

:: Web security exploits ::

A _____ is a baked or cooked food that is small, flat and sweet. It usually contains flour, sugar and some type of oil or fat. It may include other ingredients such as raisins, oats, chocolate chips, nuts, etc.

Exam Probability: **High**

10. *Answer choices:*

- a. Browser security
- b. XML external entity
- c. Referer spoofing
- d. Cookie

Guidance: level 1

:: Payment systems ::

A _____ is any system used to settle financial transactions through the transfer of monetary value. This includes the institutions, instruments, people, rules, procedures, standards, and technologies that make it exchange possible. A common type of _____ is called an operational network that links bank accounts and provides for monetary exchange using bank deposits. Some _____ s also include credit mechanisms, which are essentially a different aspect of payment.

Exam Probability: **High**

11. *Answer choices:*

- a. Single Euro Payments Area
- b. SuperRewards
- c. Payment system
- d. MoneyGram

:: Fraud ::

In law, _____ is intentional deception to secure unfair or unlawful gain, or to deprive a victim of a legal right. _____ can violate civil law , a criminal law , or it may cause no loss of money, property or legal right but still be an element of another civil or criminal wrong. The purpose of _____ may be monetary gain or other benefits, for example by obtaining a passport, travel document, or driver's license, or mortgage _____ , where the perpetrator may attempt to qualify for a mortgage by way of false statements.

Exam Probability: **High**

12. *Answer choices:*

(see index for correct answer)

- a. Money mule
- b. Faked death
- c. Essay mill
- d. Parcel mule scam

:: Digital rights management ::

_____ tools or technological protection measures are a set of access control technologies for restricting the use of proprietary hardware and copyrighted works. DRM technologies try to control the use, modification, and distribution of copyrighted works , as well as systems within devices that enforce these policies.

Exam Probability: **High**

13. *Answer choices:*

(see index for correct answer)

- a. Digital rights management
- b. ByteShield
- c. Secure Digital Music Initiative
- d. Smart cow problem

Guidance: level 1

:: Data management ::

An _____ is a term used in data warehousing to refer to a system that is used to process the day-to-day transactions of an organization. These systems are designed in a manner that processing of day-to-day transactions is performed efficiently and the integrity of the transactional data is preserved.

Exam Probability: **Medium**

14. *Answer choices:*

(see index for correct answer)

- a. ISO 8000
- b. Flat file database
- c. Concurrency control
- d. Storage block

Guidance: level 1

:: Knowledge engineering ::

The _____ is an extension of the World Wide Web through standards by the World Wide Web Consortium . The standards promote common data formats and exchange protocols on the Web, most fundamentally the Resource Description Framework . According to the W3C, "The _____ provides a common framework that allows data to be shared and reused across application, enterprise, and community boundaries". The _____ is therefore regarded as an integrator across different content, information applications and systems.

Exam Probability: **Medium**

15. *Answer choices:*

(see index for correct answer)

- a. DTRules
- b. Collaborative innovation network
- c. NetWeaver Developer

- d. Semantic Web

Guidance: level 1

:: ::

A web _____ or Internet _____ is a software system that is designed to carry out web search , which means to search the World Wide Web in a systematic way for particular information specified in a web search query. The search results are generally presented in a line of results, often referred to as _____ results pages . The information may be a mix of web pages, images, videos, infographics, articles, research papers and other types of files. Some _____ s also mine data available in databases or open directories. Unlike web directories, which are maintained only by human editors, _____ s also maintain real-time information by running an algorithm on a web crawler.Internet content that is not capable of being searched by a web _____ is generally described as the deep web.

Exam Probability: **High**

16. *Answer choices:*

(see index for correct answer)

- a. process perspective
- b. surface-level diversity
- c. empathy
- d. Sarbanes-Oxley act of 2002

Guidance: level 1

A _____ is a group of interacting or interrelated entities that form a unified whole. A _____ is delineated by its spatial and temporal boundaries, surrounded and influenced by its environment, described by its structure and purpose and expressed in its functioning.

Exam Probability: **High**

17. *Answer choices:*

(see index for correct answer)

- a. decentralized system
- b. process system
- c. System
- d. Viable System Model

Guidance: level 1

:: ::

_____ consists of tailoring a service or a product to accommodate specific individuals, sometimes tied to groups or segments of individuals. A wide variety of organizations use _____ to improve customer satisfaction, digital sales conversion, marketing results, branding, and improved website metrics as well as for advertising. _____ is a key element in social media and recommender systems.

Exam Probability: **High**

18. *Answer choices:*

(see index for correct answer)

- a. deep-level diversity
- b. hierarchical perspective
- c. cultural
- d. Personalization

Guidance: level 1

:: Database theory ::

_____ is the organisation of data according to a database model. The designer determines what data must be stored and how the data elements interrelate. With this information, they can begin to fit the data to the database model.

Exam Probability: **High**

19. *Answer choices:*

(see index for correct answer)

- a. Database design
- b. Transitive dependency
- c. Recursive join
- d. View

Guidance: level 1

:: Network performance ::

_____ is a distributed computing paradigm which brings computer data storage closer to the location where it is needed. Computation is largely or completely performed on distributed device nodes. _____ pushes applications, data and computing power away from centralized points to locations closer to the user. The target of _____ is any application or general functionality needing to be closer to the source of the action where distributed systems technology interacts with the physical world. _____ does not need contact with any centralized cloud, although it may interact with one. In contrast to cloud computing, _____ refers to decentralized data processing at the edge of the network.

Exam Probability: **High**

20. *Answer choices:*

(see index for correct answer)

- a. Edge computing

- b. Goodput
- c. Supernetwork
- d. Quality of service

Guidance: level 1

:: Data modeling languages ::

An entity–relationship model describes interrelated things of interest in a specific domain of knowledge. A basic ER model is composed of entity types and specifies relationships that can exist between entities .

Exam Probability: **High**

21. *Answer choices:*

(see index for correct answer)

- a. Entity-relationship
- b. TREX
- c. Text Encoding Initiative
- d. Binary Format Description language

Guidance: level 1

:: ::

The _____ of 1996 was enacted by the 104th United States Congress and signed by President Bill Clinton in 1996. It was created primarily to modernize the flow of healthcare information, stipulate how Personally Identifiable Information maintained by the healthcare and healthcare insurance industries should be protected from fraud and theft, and address limitations on healthcare insurance coverage.

Exam Probability: **Medium**

22. *Answer choices:*

(see index for correct answer)

- a. process perspective
- b. Character
- c. corporate values
- d. Health Insurance Portability and Accountability Act

Guidance: level 1

:: Data management ::

A _____ , or metadata repository, as defined in the IBM Dictionary of Computing, is a "centralized repository of information about data such as meaning, relationships to other data, origin, usage, and format". Oracle defines it as a collection of tables with metadata. The term can have one of several closely related meanings pertaining to databases and database management systems .

23. *Answer choices:*

(see index for correct answer)

- a. National Information Governance Board for Health and Social Care
- b. Data dictionary
- c. HyperLogLog
- d. Automatic data processing equipment

Guidance: level 1

:: Production economics ::

In microeconomics, _____ are the cost advantages that enterprises obtain due to their scale of operation , with cost per unit of output decreasing with increasing scale.

Exam Probability: **High**

24. *Answer choices:*

(see index for correct answer)

- a. Post-Fordism
- b. Constant elasticity of transformation
- c. Economies of scale
- d. Producer's risk

:: ::

A _____ is a control panel usually located directly ahead of a vehicle's driver, displaying instrumentation and controls for the vehicle's operation.

Exam Probability: **High**

25. *Answer choices:*

(see index for correct answer)

- a. surface-level diversity
- b. open system
- c. Dashboard
- d. empathy

:: Payment systems ::

_____ s are part of a payment system issued by financial institutions, such as a bank, to a customer that enables its owner to access the funds in the customer's designated bank accounts, or through a credit account and make payments by electronic funds transfer and access automated teller machines . Such cards are known by a variety of names including bank cards, ATM cards, MAC , client cards, key cards or cash cards.

Exam Probability: **High**

26. *Answer choices:*

(see index for correct answer)

- a. Freedompay
- b. BACHO record format
- c. Payment card
- d. Ebillz

Guidance: level 1

:: Database management systems ::

A _____ is a type of data model that determines the logical structure of a database and fundamentally determines in which manner data can be stored, organized and manipulated. The most popular example of a _____ is the relational model, which uses a table-based format.

Exam Probability: **High**

27. *Answer choices:*

(see index for correct answer)

- a. Cursor
- b. BigTable
- c. Database model
- d. The Third Manifesto

Guidance: level 1

:: Data management ::

" _____ " is a field that treats ways to analyze, systematically extract information from, or otherwise deal with data sets that are too large or complex to be dealt with by traditional data-processing application software. Data with many cases offer greater statistical power, while data with higher complexity may lead to a higher false discovery rate. _____ challenges include capturing data, data storage, data analysis, search, sharing, transfer, visualization, querying, updating, information privacy and data source. _____ was originally associated with three key concepts: volume, variety, and velocity. Other concepts later attributed with _____ are veracity and value.

Exam Probability: **High**

28. *Answer choices:*

(see index for correct answer)

- a. Machine-readable data

- b. Address space
- c. ISO/IEC JTC 1/SC 32
- d. Electronic lab notebook

Guidance: level 1

:: Strategic management ::

In marketing strategy, first-mover advantage is the advantage gained by the initial significant occupant of a market segment. First-mover advantage may be gained by technological leadership, or early purchase of resources.

Exam Probability: **Medium**

29. *Answer choices:*

(see index for correct answer)

- a. Rule of three
- b. Results-based management
- c. First mover advantage
- d. Functional Strategy

Guidance: level 1

:: Information systems ::

_____ is a process used in the life cycle area of the dynamic systems development method to collect business requirements while developing new information systems for a company. "The JAD process also includes approaches for enhancing user participation, expediting development, and improving the quality of specifications." It consists of a workshop where "knowledge workers and IT specialists meet, sometimes for several days, to define and review the business requirements for the system." The attendees include high level management officials who will ensure the product provides the needed reports and information at the end. This acts as "a management process which allows Corporate Information Services departments to work more effectively with users in a shorter time frame".

Exam Probability: **Low**

30. *Answer choices:*

(see index for correct answer)

- a. Connectionist expert system
- b. Joint application design
- c. Clinical decision support system
- d. Sales force management system

Guidance: level 1

:: E-commerce ::

_____ is a method of e-commerce where shoppers' friends become involved in the shopping experience. _____ attempts to use technology to mimic the social interactions found in physical malls and stores. With the rise of mobile devices, _____ is now extending beyond the online world and into the offline world of shopping.

Exam Probability: **High**

31. *Answer choices:*

(see index for correct answer)

- a. XBRL GL
- b. Social shopping
- c. AsiaPay
- d. AdsML

Guidance: level 1

:: E-commerce ::

_____ is the activity of buying or selling of products on online services or over the Internet. Electronic commerce draws on technologies such as mobile commerce, electronic funds transfer, supply chain management, Internet marketing, online transaction processing, electronic data interchange , inventory management systems, and automated data collection systems.

Exam Probability: **Medium**

32. *Answer choices:*

(see index for correct answer)

- a. E-commerce
- b. Cleaning card
- c. Smscoin
- d. Webcam Social Shopper

Guidance: level 1

:: Multi-agent systems ::

A _____ is a number of Internet-connected devices, each of which is running one or more bots. _____ s can be used to perform distributed denial-of-service attack , steal data, send spam, and allows the attacker to access the device and its connection. The owner can control the _____ using command and control software. The word " _____ " is a combination of the words "robot" and "network". The term is usually used with a negative or malicious connotation.

Exam Probability: **High**

33. *Answer choices:*

(see index for correct answer)

- a. Health Level 7
- b. Botnet
- c. Net-SNMP

- d. Kaseya Network Monitor

Guidance: level 1

:: Data analysis ::

_____ , also referred to as text data mining, roughly equivalent to text analytics, is the process of deriving high-quality information from text. High-quality information is typically derived through the devising of patterns and trends through means such as statistical pattern learning. _____ usually involves the process of structuring the input text , deriving patterns within the structured data, and finally evaluation and interpretation of the output. `High quality` in _____ usually refers to some combination of relevance, novelty, and interest. Typical _____ tasks include text categorization, text clustering, concept/entity extraction, production of granular taxonomies, sentiment analysis, document summarization, and entity relation modeling .

Exam Probability: **High**

34. *Answer choices:*

(see index for correct answer)

- a. Grouped data
- b. Missing data
- c. Natural Language Toolkit
- d. Multiple factor analysis

Guidance: level 1

:: Process management ::

When used in the context of communication networks, such as Ethernet or packet radio, _____ or network _____ is the rate of successful message delivery over a communication channel. The data these messages belong to may be delivered over a physical or logical link, or it can pass through a certain network node. _____ is usually measured in bits per second , and sometimes in data packets per second or data packets per time slot.

Exam Probability: **Medium**

35. *Answer choices:*

(see index for correct answer)

- a. Throughput
- b. Value grid
- c. YAWL
- d. Revenue assurance

Guidance: level 1

:: History of human–computer interaction ::

_____ is a line of motion sensing input devices produced by Microsoft. Initially, the _____ was developed as a gaming accessory for Xbox 360 and Xbox One video game consoles and Microsoft Windows PCs. Based around a webcam-style add-on peripheral, it enabled users to control and interact with their console/computer without the need for a game controller, through a natural user interface using gestures and spoken commands. While the gaming line did not gain much traction and eventually discontinued, third-party developers and researches found several after-market uses for _____ `s advanced low-cost sensor features, leading Microsoft to drive the product line towards more application-neutral uses, including integrating the device with Microsoft's cloud computing platform Azure.

Exam Probability: **High**

36. *Answer choices:*

(see index for correct answer)

- a. CICS
- b. IRCF360
- c. Trackball
- d. Touchpad

Guidance: level 1

:: ::

Within the Internet, _____ s are formed by the rules and procedures of the _____ System . Any name registered in the DNS is a _____ . _____ s are used in various networking contexts and for application-specific naming and addressing purposes. In general, a _____ represents an Internet Protocol resource, such as a personal computer used to access the Internet, a server computer hosting a web site, or the web site itself or any other service communicated via the Internet. In 2017, 330.6 million _____ s had been registered.

Exam Probability: **Medium**

37. *Answer choices:*

(see index for correct answer)

- a. cultural
- b. process perspective
- c. corporate values
- d. hierarchical

Guidance: level 1

:: ::

_____ is a free email service developed by Google. Users can access _____ on the web and using third-party programs that synchronize email content through POP or IMAP protocols. _____ started as a limited beta release on April 1, 2004 and ended its testing phase on July 7, 2009.

38. *Answer choices:*

(see index for correct answer)

- a. co-culture
- b. empathy
- c. imperative
- d. surface-level diversity

Guidance: level 1

:: ::

The _____ , commonly known as the Web, is an information system where documents and other web resources are identified by Uniform Resource Locators , which may be interlinked by hypertext, and are accessible over the Internet. The resources of the WWW may be accessed by users by a software application called a web browser.

Exam Probability: **Medium**

39. *Answer choices:*

(see index for correct answer)

- a. corporate values
- b. hierarchical perspective

- c. World Wide Web
- d. functional perspective

Guidance: level 1

:: ::

_____ is a brand name associated with the development of the _____ web browser. It is now owned by Verizon Media, a subsidiary of Verizon. The brand belonged to the _____ Communications Corporation , an independent American computer services company, whose headquarters were in Mountain View, California, and later Dulles, Virginia. The browser was once dominant but lost to Internet Explorer and other competitors after the so-called first browser war, its market share falling from more than 90 percent in the mid-1990s to less than 1 percent in 2006.

Exam Probability: **High**

40. *Answer choices:*

(see index for correct answer)

- a. hierarchical
- b. Sarbanes-Oxley act of 2002
- c. process perspective
- d. functional perspective

Guidance: level 1

:: Domain name system ::

The _____ is a hierarchical and decentralized naming system for computers, services, or other resources connected to the Internet or a private network. It associates various information with domain names assigned to each of the participating entities. Most prominently, it translates more readily memorized domain names to the numerical IP addresses needed for locating and identifying computer services and devices with the underlying network protocols. By providing a worldwide, distributed directory service, the _____ has been an essential component of the functionality of the Internet since 1985.

Exam Probability: **Medium**

41. *Answer choices:*

(see index for correct answer)

- a. Lame delegation
- b. Fully qualified domain name
- c. Domain Name System
- d. Planned Parenthood Federation of America, Inc. v. Bucci

Guidance: level 1

:: Data management ::

In computing, a _____ , also known as an enterprise _____ , is a system used for reporting and data analysis, and is considered a core component of business intelligence. DWs are central repositories of integrated data from one or more disparate sources. They store current and historical data in one single place that are used for creating analytical reports for workers throughout the enterprise.

Exam Probability: **High**

42. *Answer choices:*

(see index for correct answer)

- a. Big data
- b. Navigational database
- c. Long-running transaction
- d. Data warehouse

Guidance: level 1

:: Information technology ::

_____ is the reorientation of product and service designs to focus on the end user as an individual consumer, in contrast with an earlier era of only organization-oriented offerings . Technologies whose first commercialization was at the inter-organization level thus have potential for later _____ . The emergence of the individual consumer as the primary driver of product and service design is most commonly associated with the IT industry, as large business and government organizations dominated the early decades of computer usage and development. Thus the microcomputer revolution, in which electronic computing moved from exclusively enterprise and government use to include personal computing, is a cardinal example of _____ . But many technology-based products, such as calculators and mobile phones, have also had their origins in business markets, and only over time did they become dominated by high-volume consumer usage, as these products commoditized and prices fell. An example of enterprise software that became consumer software is optical character recognition software, which originated with banks and postal systems but eventually became personal productivity software.

Exam Probability: **Medium**

43. *Answer choices:*

(see index for correct answer)

- a. Software-based Storage
- b. Information and communications technology
- c. Information and communication technologies in education
- d. Antlabs

Guidance: level 1

:: Types of marketing ::

In microeconomics and management, _____ is an arrangement in which the supply chain of a company is owned by that company. Usually each member of the supply chain produces a different product or service, and the products combine to satisfy a common need. It is contrasted with horizontal integration, wherein a company produces several items which are related to one another. _____ has also described management styles that bring large portions of the supply chain not only under a common ownership, but also into one corporation .

Exam Probability: **Medium**

44. *Answer choices:*

(see index for correct answer)

- a. Vertical integration
- b. Customerization
- c. Evangelism marketing
- d. Megamarketing

Guidance: level 1

:: Infographics ::

A _____ is a symbolic representation of information according to visualization technique. _____ s have been used since ancient times, but became more prevalent during the Enlightenment. Sometimes, the technique uses a three-dimensional visualization which is then projected onto a two-dimensional surface. The word graph is sometimes used as a synonym for _____ .

45. *Answer choices:*

(see index for correct answer)

- a. Wigmore chart
- b. U.S. Route shield
- c. Chartjunk
- d. Diagram

Guidance: level 1

:: ::

_____ is an American video-sharing website headquartered in San Bruno, California. Three former PayPal employees—Chad Hurley, Steve Chen, and Jawed Karim—created the service in February 2005. Google bought the site in November 2006 for US$1.65 billion; _____ now operates as one of Google's subsidiaries.

Exam Probability: **Medium**

46. *Answer choices:*

(see index for correct answer)

- a. YouTube
- b. process perspective

- c. cultural
- d. Character

Guidance: level 1

:: Business ::

_____ is a sourcing model in which individuals or organizations obtain goods and services, including ideas and finances, from a large, relatively open and often rapidly-evolving group of internet users; it divides work between participants to achieve a cumulative result. The word _____ itself is a portmanteau of crowd and outsourcing, and was coined in 2005. As a mode of sourcing, _____ existed prior to the digital age .

Exam Probability: **High**

47. *Answer choices:*

(see index for correct answer)

- a. Legal governance, risk management, and compliance
- b. Crowdsourcing
- c. Atmospherics
- d. Professional conference organiser

Guidance: level 1

:: ::

A _____ is a structure / access pattern specific to data warehouse environments, used to retrieve client-facing data. The _____ is a subset of the data warehouse and is usually oriented to a specific business line or team. Whereas data warehouses have an enterprise-wide depth, the information in _____ s pertains to a single department. In some deployments, each department or business unit is considered the owner of its _____ including all the hardware, software and data. This enables each department to isolate the use, manipulation and development of their data. In other deployments where conformed dimensions are used, this business unit ownership will not hold true for shared dimensions like customer, product, etc.

Exam Probability: **High**

48. *Answer choices:*

(see index for correct answer)

- a. hierarchical
- b. process perspective
- c. hierarchical perspective
- d. Data mart

Guidance: level 1

:: ::

A _____ is a discussion or informational website published on the World Wide Web consisting of discrete, often informal diary-style text entries . Posts are typically displayed in reverse chronological order, so that the most recent post appears first, at the top of the web page. Until 2009, _____ s were usually the work of a single individual, occasionally of a small group, and often covered a single subject or topic. In the 2010s, "multi-author _____ s" emerged, featuring the writing of multiple authors and sometimes professionally edited. MABs from newspapers, other media outlets, universities, think tanks, advocacy groups, and similar institutions account for an increasing quantity of _____ traffic. The rise of Twitter and other "micro _____ ging" systems helps integrate MABs and single-author _____ s into the news media. _____ can also be used as a verb, meaning to maintain or add content to a _____ .

Exam Probability: **High**

49. *Answer choices:*

(see index for correct answer)

- a. personal values
- b. Sarbanes-Oxley act of 2002
- c. Blog
- d. open system

Guidance: level 1

:: Google services ::

_____ is a web mapping service developed by Google. It offers satellite imagery, aerial photography, street maps, 360° panoramic views of streets , real-time traffic conditions, and route planning for traveling by foot, car, bicycle and air , or public transportation.

Exam Probability: **Low**

50. *Answer choices:*

(see index for correct answer)

- a. Google Maps
- b. App Inventor for Android
- c. Google Cultural Institute
- d. Google APIs

Guidance: level 1

:: ::

Collaborative software or _____ is application software designed to help people involved in a common task to achieve their goals. One of the earliest definitions of collaborative software is "intentional group processes plus software to support them".

Exam Probability: **Low**

51. *Answer choices:*

(see index for correct answer)

- a. hierarchical
- b. open system
- c. Sarbanes-Oxley act of 2002
- d. surface-level diversity

Guidance: level 1

:: Network theory ::

A _____ is a social structure made up of a set of social actors , sets of dyadic ties, and other social interactions between actors. The _____ perspective provides a set of methods for analyzing the structure of whole social entities as well as a variety of theories explaining the patterns observed in these structures. The study of these structures uses _____ analysis to identify local and global patterns, locate influential entities, and examine network dynamics.

Exam Probability: **Low**

52. *Answer choices:*
(see index for correct answer)

- a. Assortative mixing
- b. Modularity
- c. Social network
- d. Shortest path problem

:: Data management ::

Given organizations' increasing dependency on information technology to run their operations, Business continuity planning covers the entire organization, and Disaster recovery focuses on IT.

Exam Probability: **High**

53. *Answer choices:*

(see index for correct answer)

- a. Learning object
- b. Data architecture
- c. Technical data management system
- d. Disaster recovery plan

Guidance: level 1

:: E-commerce ::

Electronic governance or e-governance is the application of information and communication technology for delivering government services, exchange of information, communication transactions, integration of various stand-alone systems and services between government-to-citizen , _____ , government-to-government , government-to-employees as well as back-office processes and interactions within the entire government framework. Through e-governance, government services are made available to citizens in a convenient, efficient, and transparent manner. The three main target groups that can be distinguished in governance concepts are government, citizens, andbusinesses/interest groups. In e-governance, there are no distinct boundaries.

Exam Probability: **High**

54. *Answer choices:*

(see index for correct answer)

- a. Standard Interchange Language
- b. Government-to-business
- c. CA/Browser Forum
- d. Digital currency

Guidance: level 1

:: Google services ::

A blog is a discussion or informational website published on the World Wide Web consisting of discrete, often informal diary-style text entries. Posts are typically displayed in reverse chronological order, so that the most recent post appears first, at the top of the web page. Until 2009, blogs were usually the work of a single individual, occasionally of a small group, and often covered a single subject or topic. In the 2010s, "multi-author blogs" emerged, featuring the writing of multiple authors and sometimes professionally edited. MABs from newspapers, other media outlets, universities, think tanks, advocacy groups, and similar institutions account for an increasing quantity of blog traffic. The rise of Twitter and other "microblogging" systems helps integrate MABs and single-author blogs into the news media. Blog can also be used as a verb, meaning to maintain or add content to a blog.

Exam Probability: **Medium**

55. *Answer choices:*

(see index for correct answer)

- a. AdWords
- b. Google Alerts
- c. Google Sync
- d. Google Contacts

Guidance: level 1

:: Intrusion detection systems ::

An _____ is a device or software application that monitors a network or systems for malicious activity or policy violations. Any malicious activity or violation is typically reported either to an administrator or collected centrally using a security information and event management system. A SIEM system combines outputs from multiple sources, and uses alarm filtering techniques to distinguish malicious activity from false alarms.

Exam Probability: **Medium**

56. *Answer choices:*

(see index for correct answer)

- a. Intrusion detection system
- b. Security Device Event Exchange
- c. Application protocol-based intrusion detection system
- d. Sucuri

Guidance: level 1

:: ::

In communications and information processing, _____ is a system of rules to convert information—such as a letter, word, sound, image, or gesture—into another form or representation, sometimes shortened or secret, for communication through a communication channel or storage in a storage medium. An early example is the invention of language, which enabled a person, through speech, to communicate what they saw, heard, felt, or thought to others. But speech limits the range of communication to the distance a voice can carry, and limits the audience to those present when the speech is uttered. The invention of writing, which converted spoken language into visual symbols, extended the range of communication across space and time.

Exam Probability: **Low**

57. *Answer choices:*

(see index for correct answer)

- a. Code
- b. Character
- c. deep-level diversity
- d. cultural

Guidance: level 1

:: Data quality ::

_____ or data cleaning is the process of detecting and correcting corrupt or inaccurate records from a record set, table, or database and refers to identifying incomplete, incorrect, inaccurate or irrelevant parts of the data and then replacing, modifying, or deleting the dirty or coarse data. _____ may be performed interactively with data wrangling tools, or as batch processing through scripting.

Exam Probability: **Low**

58. *Answer choices:*

(see index for correct answer)

- a. Data Quality Campaign
- b. Data degradation
- c. Data truncation
- d. Data Quality Firewall

Guidance: level 1

:: Information technology management ::

_____ within quality management systems and information technology systems is a process—either formal or informal—used to ensure that changes to a product or system are introduced in a controlled and coordinated manner. It reduces the possibility that unnecessary changes will be introduced to a system without forethought, introducing faults into the system or undoing changes made by other users of software. The goals of a _____ procedure usually include minimal disruption to services, reduction in back-out activities, and cost-effective utilization of resources involved in implementing change.

59. *Answer choices:*

(see index for correct answer)

- a. Production support
- b. Change control
- c. Software asset management
- d. ESCM

Guidance: level 1

Marketing

Marketing is the study and management of exchange relationships. Marketing is the business process of creating relationships with and satisfying customers. With its focus on the customer, marketing is one of the premier components of business management.

Marketing is defined by the American Marketing Association as "the activity, set of institutions, and processes for creating, communicating, delivering, and exchanging offerings that have value for customers, clients, partners, and society at large."

:: Brand management ::

In marketing, _____ is the analysis and planning on how a brand is perceived in the market. Developing a good relationship with the target market is essential for _____ . Tangible elements of _____ include the product itself; its look, price, and packaging, etc. The intangible elements are the experiences that the consumers share with the brand, and also the relationships they have with the brand. A brand manager would oversee all aspects of the consumer's brand association as well as relationships with members of the supply chain.

Exam Probability: **High**

1. *Answer choices:*

(see index for correct answer)

- a. Naming rights
- b. Brand strength analysis
- c. Brand preference
- d. Brand management

Guidance: level 1

:: Stochastic processes ::

_____ in its modern meaning is a "new idea, creative thoughts, new imaginations in form of device or method". _____ is often also viewed as the application of better solutions that meet new requirements, unarticulated needs, or existing market needs. Such _____ takes place through the provision of more-effective products, processes, services, technologies, or business models that are made available to markets, governments and society. An _____ is something original and more effective and, as a consequence, new, that "breaks into" the market or society. _____ is related to, but not the same as, invention, as _____ is more apt to involve the practical implementation of an invention to make a meaningful impact in the market or society, and not all _____ s require an invention. _____ often manifests itself via the engineering process, when the problem being solved is of a technical or scientific nature. The opposite of _____ is exnovation.

Exam Probability: **High**

2. *Answer choices:*

(see index for correct answer)

- a. numeraire
- b. File dynamics
- c. Multiscale decision-making
- d. Innovation

Guidance: level 1

:: ::

_____ is an abstract concept of management of complex systems according to a set of rules and trends. In systems theory, these types of rules exist in various fields of biology and society, but the term has slightly different meanings according to context. For example.

Exam Probability: **High**

3. *Answer choices:*

(see index for correct answer)

- a. surface-level diversity
- b. open system
- c. similarity-attraction theory
- d. Regulation

Guidance: level 1

:: ::

A _____ is a research instrument consisting of a series of questions for the purpose of gathering information from respondents. The _____ was invented by the Statistical Society of London in 1838.

Exam Probability: **Medium**

4. *Answer choices:*

(see index for correct answer)

- a. cultural
- b. interpersonal communication
- c. Questionnaire
- d. surface-level diversity

Guidance: level 1

:: Data management ::

_____ is a form of intellectual property that grants the creator of an original creative work an exclusive legal right to determine whether and under what conditions this original work may be copied and used by others, usually for a limited term of years. The exclusive rights are not absolute but limited by limitations and exceptions to _____ law, including fair use. A major limitation on _____ on ideas is that _____ protects only the original expression of ideas, and not the underlying ideas themselves.

Exam Probability: **Low**

5. *Answer choices:*

(see index for correct answer)

- a. ROOT
- b. Copyright
- c. Single customer view
- d. Data warehouse

:: Management ::

The term _____ refers to measures designed to increase the degree of autonomy and self-determination in people and in communities in order to enable them to represent their interests in a responsible and self-determined way, acting on their own authority. It is the process of becoming stronger and more confident, especially in controlling one's life and claiming one's rights.

_____ as action refers both to the process of self- _____ and to professional support of people, which enables them to overcome their sense of powerlessness and lack of influence, and to recognize and use their resources. To do work with power.

Exam Probability: **High**

6. *Answer choices:*

(see index for correct answer)

- a. Scenario planning
- b. Empowerment
- c. Risk appetite
- d. Duality

:: ::

_____ or commercialisation is the process of introducing a new product or production method into commerce—making it available on the market. The term often connotes especially entry into the mass market , but it also includes a move from the laboratory into commerce. Many technologies begin in a research and development laboratory or in an inventor's workshop and may not be practical for commercial use in their infancy . The "development" segment of the "research and development" spectrum requires time and money as systems are engineered with a view to making the product or method a paying commercial proposition. The product launch of a new product is the final stage of new product development - at this point advertising, sales promotion, and other marketing efforts encourage commercial adoption of the product or method. Beyond _____ can lie consumerization .

Exam Probability: **Low**

7. *Answer choices:*

(see index for correct answer)

- a. Sarbanes-Oxley act of 2002
- b. empathy
- c. open system
- d. cultural

Guidance: level 1

:: Marketing ::

_____ s are structured marketing strategies designed by merchants to encourage customers to continue to shop at or use the services of businesses associated with each program. These programs exist covering most types of commerce, each one having varying features and rewards-schemes.

Exam Probability: **Medium**

8. *Answer choices:*

(see index for correct answer)

- a. Intent scale translation
- b. Loyalty program
- c. Party plan
- d. Interruption marketing

Guidance: level 1

:: Income ::

_____ is a ratio between the net profit and cost of investment resulting from an investment of some resources. A high ROI means the investment's gains favorably to its cost. As a performance measure, ROI is used to evaluate the efficiency of an investment or to compare the efficiencies of several different investments. In purely economic terms, it is one way of relating profits to capital invested. _____ is a performance measure used by businesses to identify the efficiency of an investment or number of different investments.

9. *Answer choices:*

(see index for correct answer)

- a. Aggregate expenditure
- b. Return of investment
- c. Return on investment
- d. Income earner

Guidance: level 1

:: Network theory ::

A _____ is a social structure made up of a set of social actors , sets of dyadic ties, and other social interactions between actors. The _____ perspective provides a set of methods for analyzing the structure of whole social entities as well as a variety of theories explaining the patterns observed in these structures. The study of these structures uses _____ analysis to identify local and global patterns, locate influential entities, and examine network dynamics.

10. *Answer choices:*

(see index for correct answer)

- a. Top 100 historical figures of Wikipedia

- b. Longest path problem
- c. Average path length
- d. Social network

Guidance: level 1

:: Supply chain management terms ::

In business and finance, _____ is a system of organizations, people, activities, information, and resources involved in moving a product or service from supplier to customer. _____ activities involve the transformation of natural resources, raw materials, and components into a finished product that is delivered to the end customer. In sophisticated _____ systems, used products may re-enter the _____ at any point where residual value is recyclable. _____ s link value chains.

Exam Probability: **Medium**

11. *Answer choices:*

(see index for correct answer)

- a. Supply chain
- b. Last mile
- c. Final assembly schedule
- d. Stockout

Guidance: level 1

An _____ is a systematic and independent examination of books, accounts, statutory records, documents and vouchers of an organization to ascertain how far the financial statements as well as non-financial disclosures present a true and fair view of the concern. It also attempts to ensure that the books of accounts are properly maintained by the concern as required by law. _____ ing has become such a ubiquitous phenomenon in the corporate and the public sector that academics started identifying an " _____ Society". The _____ or perceives and recognises the propositions before them for examination, obtains evidence, evaluates the same and formulates an opinion on the basis of his judgement which is communicated through their _____ ing report.

Exam Probability: **Medium**

12. *Answer choices:*

(see index for correct answer)

- a. Audit
- b. empathy
- c. interpersonal communication
- d. open system

Guidance: level 1

Advertising is a marketing communication that employs an openly sponsored, non-personal message to promote or sell a product, service or idea. Sponsors of advertising are typically businesses wishing to promote their products or services. Advertising is differentiated from public relations in that an advertiser pays for and has control over the message. It differs from personal selling in that the message is non-personal, i.e., not directed to a particular individual.Advertising is communicated through various mass media, including traditional media such as newspapers, magazines, television, radio, outdoor advertising or direct mail; and new media such as search results, blogs, social media, websites or text messages. The actual presentation of the message in a medium is referred to as an _____ , or "ad" or advert for short.

Exam Probability: **Low**

13. *Answer choices:*

(see index for correct answer)

- a. surface-level diversity
- b. Character
- c. hierarchical perspective
- d. corporate values

Guidance: level 1

:: Consumer theory ::

_____ is the quantity of a good that consumers are willing and able to purchase at various prices during a given period of time.

14. *Answer choices:*

(see index for correct answer)

- a. Elasticity of substitution
- b. Consumer sovereignty
- c. Elasticity of intertemporal substitution
- d. Demand

Guidance: level 1

:: Marketing ::

The _____ is a foundation model for businesses. The _____ has been defined as the "set of marketing tools that the firm uses to pursue its marketing objectives in the target market". Thus the _____ refers to four broad levels of marketing decision, namely: product, price, place, and promotion. Marketing practice has been occurring for millennia, but marketing theory emerged in the early twentieth century. The contemporary _____ , or the 4 Ps, which has become the dominant framework for marketing management decisions, was first published in 1960. In services marketing, an extended _____ is used, typically comprising 7 Ps, made up of the original 4 Ps extended by process, people, and physical evidence. Occasionally service marketers will refer to 8 Ps, comprising these 7 Ps plus performance.

15. *Answer choices:*

- a. Consumer culture theory
- b. Price on application
- c. Gimmick
- d. Counteradvertising

Guidance: level 1

:: Product management ::

A _____ , trade mark, or trade-mark is a recognizable sign, design, or expression which identifies products or services of a particular source from those of others, although _____ s used to identify services are usually called service marks. The _____ owner can be an individual, business organization, or any legal entity. A _____ may be located on a package, a label, a voucher, or on the product itself. For the sake of corporate identity, _____ s are often displayed on company buildings. It is legally recognized as a type of intellectual property.

Exam Probability: **Low**

16. *Answer choices:*

- a. Trademark
- b. Product information
- c. Service life

- d. Trademark look

Guidance: level 1

:: Marketing ::

_____ or stock is the goods and materials that a business holds for the ultimate goal of resale .

Exam Probability: **Low**

17. *Answer choices:*
(see index for correct answer)

- a. Exploratory research
- b. Blind taste test
- c. MARC USA
- d. Inventory

Guidance: level 1

:: Monopoly (economics) ::

A _____ exists when a specific person or enterprise is the only supplier of a particular commodity. This contrasts with a monopsony which relates to a single entity's control of a market to purchase a good or service, and with oligopoly which consists of a few sellers dominating a market. Monopolies are thus characterized by a lack of economic competition to produce the good or service, a lack of viable substitute goods, and the possibility of a high _____ price well above the seller's marginal cost that leads to a high _____ profit. The verb monopolise or monopolize refers to the process by which a company gains the ability to raise prices or exclude competitors. In economics, a _____ is a single seller. In law, a _____ is a business entity that has significant market power, that is, the power to charge overly high prices. Although monopolies may be big businesses, size is not a characteristic of a _____ . A small business may still have the power to raise prices in a small industry .

Exam Probability: **High**

18. *Answer choices:*

(see index for correct answer)

- a. Contestable market
- b. Monopoly
- c. Sherman Antitrust Act
- d. Cost per procedure

Guidance: level 1

:: Management ::

A _____ describes the rationale of how an organization creates, delivers, and captures value, in economic, social, cultural or other contexts. The process of _____ construction and modification is also called _____ innovation and forms a part of business strategy.

Exam Probability: **Low**

19. *Answer choices:*

(see index for correct answer)

- a. Top development
- b. Quick response manufacturing
- c. Business model
- d. Best current practice

Guidance: level 1

:: Business law ::

A _____ is an arrangement where parties, known as partners, agree to cooperate to advance their mutual interests. The partners in a _____ may be individuals, businesses, interest-based organizations, schools, governments or combinations. Organizations may partner to increase the likelihood of each achieving their mission and to amplify their reach. A _____ may result in issuing and holding equity or may be only governed by a contract.

Exam Probability: **Low**

20. *Answer choices:*

(see index for correct answer)

- a. Partnership
- b. Teck Corp. Ltd. v. Millar
- c. Lien
- d. Lex mercatoria

Guidance: level 1

:: ::

The _____ is a U.S. business-focused, English-language international daily newspaper based in New York City. The Journal, along with its Asian and European editions, is published six days a week by Dow Jones & Company, a division of News Corp. The newspaper is published in the broadsheet format and online. The Journal has been printed continuously since its inception on July 8, 1889, by Charles Dow, Edward Jones, and Charles Bergstresser.

Exam Probability: **Low**

21. *Answer choices:*

(see index for correct answer)

- a. empathy
- b. corporate values
- c. Wall Street Journal
- d. Character

:: ::

_____ , known in Europe as research and technological development , refers to innovative activities undertaken by corporations or governments in developing new services or products, or improving existing services or products. _____ constitutes the first stage of development of a potential new service or the production process.

Exam Probability: **Low**

22. *Answer choices:*

(see index for correct answer)

- a. process perspective
- b. cultural
- c. Research and development
- d. information systems assessment

:: Television commercials ::

_____ is a phenomenon whereby something new and somehow valuable is formed. The created item may be intangible or a physical object .

Exam Probability: **High**

23. *Answer choices:*

(see index for correct answer)

- a. An American Revolution
- b. CM Yoko
- c. Knock-off Nigel
- d. Creativity

Guidance: level 1

:: ::

_____ Motor Company is an American multinational automaker that has its main headquarter in Dearborn, Michigan, a suburb of Detroit. It was founded by Henry _____ and incorporated on June 16, 1903. The company sells automobiles and commercial vehicles under the _____ brand and most luxury cars under the Lincoln brand. _____ also owns Brazilian SUV manufacturer Troller, an 8% stake in Aston Martin of the United Kingdom and a 32% stake in Jiangling Motors. It also has joint-ventures in China , Taiwan , Thailand , Turkey , and Russia . The company is listed on the New York Stock Exchange and is controlled by the _____ family; they have minority ownership but the majority of the voting power.

24. *Answer choices:*

(see index for correct answer)

- a. Ford
- b. levels of analysis
- c. imperative
- d. interpersonal communication

Guidance: level 1

:: Trade associations ::

A _____ , also known as an industry trade group, business association, sector association or industry body, is an organization founded and funded by businesses that operate in a specific industry. An industry _____ participates in public relations activities such as advertising, education, political donations, lobbying and publishing, but its focus is collaboration between companies. Associations may offer other services, such as producing conferences, networking or charitable events or offering classes or educational materials. Many associations are non-profit organizations governed by bylaws and directed by officers who are also members.

Exam Probability: **Medium**

25. *Answer choices:*

(see index for correct answer)

- a. Trade association
- b. Bromine Science and Environmental Forum
- c. Futures Industry Association
- d. Glass Packaging Institute

Guidance: level 1

:: ::

Consumer behaviour is the study of individuals, groups, or organizations and all the activities associated with the purchase, use and disposal of goods and services, including the consumer's emotional, mental and behavioural responses that precede or follow these activities. Consumer behaviour emerged in the 1940s and 50s as a distinct sub-discipline in the marketing area.

Exam Probability: **Medium**

26. *Answer choices:*

(see index for correct answer)

- a. corporate values
- b. surface-level diversity
- c. levels of analysis
- d. Consumer behavior

Guidance: level 1

:: Stock market ::

_____ is freedom from, or resilience against, potential harm caused by others. Beneficiaries of _____ may be of persons and social groups, objects and institutions, ecosystems or any other entity or phenomenon vulnerable to unwanted change by its environment.

Exam Probability: **Low**

27. *Answer choices:*

(see index for correct answer)

- a. NewConnect
- b. GXG Markets
- c. Rogue trader
- d. Security

Guidance: level 1

:: Marketing ::

_____ is based on a marketing concept which can be adopted by an organization as a strategy for business expansion. Where implemented, a franchisor licenses its know-how, procedures, intellectual property, use of its business model, brand, and rights to sell its branded products and services to a franchisee. In return the franchisee pays certain fees and agrees to comply with certain obligations, typically set out in a Franchise Agreement.

28. *Answer choices:*

(see index for correct answer)

- a. Private label
- b. Pitching engine
- c. Product literature
- d. Franchising

Guidance: level 1

:: Product development ::

In business and engineering, _____ covers the complete process of bringing a new product to market. A central aspect of NPD is product design, along with various business considerations. _____ is described broadly as the transformation of a market opportunity into a product available for sale. The product can be tangible or intangible , though sometimes services and other processes are distinguished from "products." NPD requires an understanding of customer needs and wants, the competitive environment, and the nature of the market.Cost, time and quality are the main variables that drive customer needs. Aiming at these three variables, innovative companies develop continuous practices and strategies to better satisfy customer requirements and to increase their own market share by a regular development of new products. There are many uncertainties and challenges which companies must face throughout the process. The use of best practices and the elimination of barriers to communication are the main concerns for the management of the NPD .

29. *Answer choices:*

(see index for correct answer)

- a. New product development
- b. Line extension
- c. Product design specification
- d. Front end innovation

Guidance: level 1

:: ::

_____ , or auditory perception, is the ability to perceive sounds by detecting vibrations, changes in the pressure of the surrounding medium through time, through an organ such as the ear. The academic field concerned with _____ is auditory science.

Exam Probability: **Medium**

30. *Answer choices:*

(see index for correct answer)

- a. Hearing
- b. functional perspective
- c. surface-level diversity
- d. cultural

:: Meetings ::

A _____ is a body of one or more persons that is subordinate to a deliberative assembly. Usually, the assembly sends matters into a _____ as a way to explore them more fully than would be possible if the assembly itself were considering them. _____ s may have different functions and their type of work differ depending on the type of the organization and its needs.

Exam Probability: **High**

31. *Answer choices:*

(see index for correct answer)

- a. Committee
- b. Awayday
- c. Prayer meeting
- d. Convocation

:: Market research ::

_____ , an acronym for Information through Disguised Experimentation is an annual market research fair conducted by the students of IIM-Lucknow. Students create games and use various other simulated environments to capture consumers' subconscious thoughts. This innovative method of market research removes the sensitization effect that might bias peoples answers to questions. This ensures that the most truthful answers are captured to research questions. The games are designed in such a way that the observers can elicit all the required information just by observing and noting down the behaviour and the responses of the participants.

Exam Probability: **Low**

32. *Answer choices:*

(see index for correct answer)

- a. Innovation game
- b. Competitor analysis
- c. INDEX
- d. LRMR

Guidance: level 1

:: ::

In the broadest sense, _____ is any practice which contributes to the sale of products to a retail consumer. At a retail in-store level, _____ refers to the variety of products available for sale and the display of those products in such a way that it stimulates interest and entices customers to make a purchase.

33. *Answer choices:*

(see index for correct answer)

- a. process perspective
- b. functional perspective
- c. levels of analysis
- d. Merchandising

Guidance: level 1

:: International trade ::

_____ or globalisation is the process of interaction and integration among people, companies, and governments worldwide. As a complex and multifaceted phenomenon, _____ is considered by some as a form of capitalist expansion which entails the integration of local and national economies into a global, unregulated market economy. _____ has grown due to advances in transportation and communication technology. With the increased global interactions comes the growth of international trade, ideas, and culture. _____ is primarily an economic process of interaction and integration that's associated with social and cultural aspects. However, conflicts and diplomacy are also large parts of the history of _____ , and modern _____ .

34. *Answer choices:*

- a. International Standards of Accounting and Reporting
- b. Home country control
- c. Globalization
- d. Plaza Accord

Guidance: level 1

:: Electronic feedback ::

_____ occurs when outputs of a system are routed back as inputs as part of a chain of cause-and-effect that forms a circuit or loop. The system can then be said to feed back into itself. The notion of cause-and-effect has to be handled carefully when applied to _____ systems.

Exam Probability: **Low**

35. *Answer choices:*

- a. feedback loop
- b. Positive feedback

Guidance: level 1

A _____ is a professional who provides expert advice in a particular area such as security , management, education, accountancy, law, human resources, marketing , finance, engineering, science or any of many other specialized fields.

Exam Probability: **Low**

36. *Answer choices:*

(see index for correct answer)

- a. Sarbanes-Oxley act of 2002
- b. Consultant
- c. open system
- d. functional perspective

Guidance: level 1

Retail is the process of selling consumer goods or services to customers through multiple channels of distribution to earn a profit. Retailers satisfy demand identified through a supply chain. The term "retailer" is typically applied where a service provider fills the small orders of a large number of individuals, who are end-users, rather than large orders of a small number of wholesale, corporate or government clientele. Shopping generally refers to the act of buying products. Sometimes this is done to obtain final goods, including necessities such as food and clothing; sometimes it takes place as a recreational activity. Recreational shopping often involves window shopping and browsing: it does not always result in a purchase.

Exam Probability: **High**

37. *Answer choices:*

(see index for correct answer)

- a. corporate values
- b. Retailing
- c. deep-level diversity
- d. information systems assessment

Guidance: level 1

:: Marketing ::

_____ is the percentage of a market accounted for by a specific entity. In a survey of nearly 200 senior marketing managers, 67% responded that they found the revenue- "dollar _____ " metric very useful, while 61% found "unit _____ " very useful.

38. *Answer choices:*

(see index for correct answer)

- a. Market share
- b. MaxDiff
- c. BEC
- d. Adobe Experience Manager

Guidance: level 1

:: ::

_____ are interactive computer-mediated technologies that facilitate the creation and sharing of information, ideas, career interests and other forms of expression via virtual communities and networks. The variety of stand-alone and built-in _____ services currently available introduces challenges of definition; however, there are some common features.

39. *Answer choices:*

(see index for correct answer)

- a. surface-level diversity
- b. similarity-attraction theory

- c. Social media
- d. personal values

Guidance: level 1

:: Retailing ::

A _____ is a self-service shop offering a wide variety of food, beverages and household products, organized into sections and shelves. It is larger and has a wider selection than earlier grocery stores, but is smaller and more limited in the range of merchandise than a hypermarket or big-box market.

Exam Probability: **Medium**

40. *Answer choices:*

(see index for correct answer)

- a. Selena Etc.
- b. Diffusion line
- c. Non-store retailing
- d. Supermarket

Guidance: level 1

:: ::

An _____ , often referred to as a creative agency or an ad agency, is a business dedicated to creating, planning, and handling advertising and sometimes other forms of promotion and marketing for its clients. An ad agency is generally independent from the client; it may be an internal department or agency that provides an outside point of view to the effort of selling the client's products or services, or an outside firm. An agency can also handle overall marketing and branding strategies promotions for its clients, which may include sales as well.

Exam Probability: **High**

41. *Answer choices:*

(see index for correct answer)

- a. Advertising agency
- b. corporate values
- c. empathy
- d. Sarbanes-Oxley act of 2002

Guidance: level 1

:: Direct selling ::

_____ consists of two main business models: single-level marketing, in which a direct seller makes money by buying products from a parent organization and selling them directly to customers, and multi-level marketing , in which the direct seller may earn money from both direct sales to customers and by sponsoring new direct sellers and potentially earning a commission from their efforts.

42. *Answer choices:*

(see index for correct answer)

- a. CVSL
- b. Direct Selling News
- c. Direct selling
- d. The Longaberger Company

Guidance: level 1

:: Management ::

A _____ is an idea of the future or desired result that a person or a group of people envisions, plans and commits to achieve. People endeavor to reach _____ s within a finite time by setting deadlines.

43. *Answer choices:*

(see index for correct answer)

- a. Purchasing management
- b. Goal
- c. Preparation
- d. Behavioral risk management

:: ::

_____ refers to a business or organization attempting to acquire goods or services to accomplish its goals. Although there are several organizations that attempt to set standards in the _____ process, processes can vary greatly between organizations. Typically the word " _____ " is not used interchangeably with the word "procurement", since procurement typically includes expediting, supplier quality, and transportation and logistics in addition to _____ .

Exam Probability: **High**

44. *Answer choices:*

(see index for correct answer)

- a. Purchasing
- b. hierarchical
- c. co-culture
- d. levels of analysis

:: ::

_____ consists of using generic or ad hoc methods in an orderly manner to find solutions to problems. Some of the problem-solving techniques developed and used in philosophy, artificial intelligence, computer science, engineering, mathematics, or medicine are related to mental problem-solving techniques studied in psychology.

Exam Probability: **High**

45. *Answer choices:*

(see index for correct answer)

- a. functional perspective
- b. similarity-attraction theory
- c. Problem Solving
- d. co-culture

Guidance: level 1

:: Internet privacy ::

An _____ is a private network accessible only to an organization's staff. Often, a wide range of information and services are available on an organization's internal _____ that are unavailable to the public, unlike the Internet. A company-wide _____ can constitute an important focal point of internal communication and collaboration, and provide a single starting point to access internal and external resources. In its simplest form, an _____ is established with the technologies for local area networks and wide area networks . Many modern _____ s have search engines, user profiles, blogs, mobile apps with notifications, and events planning within their infrastructure.

Exam Probability: **Medium**

46. *Answer choices:*

(see index for correct answer)

- a. Split tunneling
- b. Right to be forgotten
- c. 2010 Duke University faux sex thesis controversy
- d. Secure communication

Guidance: level 1

:: ::

A _____ is a discussion or informational website published on the World Wide Web consisting of discrete, often informal diary-style text entries . Posts are typically displayed in reverse chronological order, so that the most recent post appears first, at the top of the web page. Until 2009, _____ s were usually the work of a single individual, occasionally of a small group, and often covered a single subject or topic. In the 2010s, "multi-author _____ s" emerged, featuring the writing of multiple authors and sometimes professionally edited. MABs from newspapers, other media outlets, universities, think tanks, advocacy groups, and similar institutions account for an increasing quantity of _____ traffic. The rise of Twitter and other "micro _____ ging" systems helps integrate MABs and single-author _____ s into the news media. _____ can also be used as a verb, meaning to maintain or add content to a _____ .

Exam Probability: **Low**

47. *Answer choices:*

(see index for correct answer)

- a. Character
- b. Sarbanes-Oxley act of 2002
- c. process perspective
- d. Blog

Guidance: level 1

:: Business ::

The seller, or the provider of the goods or services, completes a sale in response to an acquisition, appropriation, requisition or a direct interaction with the buyer at the point of sale. There is a passing of title of the item, and the settlement of a price, in which agreement is reached on a price for which transfer of ownership of the item will occur. The seller, not the purchaser typically executes the sale and it may be completed prior to the obligation of payment. In the case of indirect interaction, a person who sells goods or service on behalf of the owner is known as a _____ man or _____ woman or _____ person, but this often refers to someone selling goods in a store/shop, in which case other terms are also common, including _____ clerk, shop assistant, and retail clerk.

Exam Probability: **Low**

48. *Answer choices:*

(see index for correct answer)

- a. Sales
- b. Business as usual
- c. Ha Van Tham
- d. Religion and business

Guidance: level 1

:: Promotion and marketing communications ::

_____ is one of the elements of the promotional mix. . _____ uses both media and non-media marketing communications for a pre-determined, limited time to increase consumer demand, stimulate market demand or improve product availability. Examples include contests, coupons, freebies, loss leaders, point of purchase displays, premiums, prizes, product samples, and rebates.

Exam Probability: **Medium**

49. *Answer choices:*

(see index for correct answer)

- a. Infoganda
- b. Event television
- c. Sales promotion
- d. One Club

Guidance: level 1

:: Market research ::

An _____ or lighthouse customer is an early customer of a given company, product, or technology. The term originates from Everett M. Rogers' Diffusion of Innovations .

Exam Probability: **Medium**

50. *Answer choices:*

(see index for correct answer)

- a. Early adopter
- b. Market research
- c. Innovation game
- d. Automated Measurement of Lineups

Guidance: level 1

:: ::

A _____ is a graphic mark, emblem, or symbol used to aid and promote public identification and recognition. It may be of an abstract or figurative design or include the text of the name it represents as in a wordmark.

Exam Probability: **Medium**

51. *Answer choices:*

(see index for correct answer)

- a. interpersonal communication
- b. Logo
- c. similarity-attraction theory
- d. Character

Guidance: level 1

:: Management ::

A _____ is a comprehensive document or blueprint that outlines the advertising and marketing efforts for the coming year. It describes business activities involved in accomplishing specific marketing objectives within a set time frame. A _____ also includes a description of the current marketing position of a business, a discussion of the target market and a description of the marketing mix that a business will use to achieve their marketing goals. A _____ has a formal structure, but can be used as a formal or informal document which makes it very flexible. It contains some historical data, future predictions, and methods or strategies to achieve the marketing objectives. _____ s start with the identification of customer needs through a market research and how the business can satisfy these needs while generating an acceptable return. This includes processes such as market situation analysis, action programs, budgets, sales forecasts, strategies and projected financial statements. A _____ can also be described as a technique that helps a business to decide on the best use of its resources to achieve corporate objectives. It can also contain a full analysis of the strengths and weaknesses of a company, its organization and its products.

Exam Probability: **Low**

52. *Answer choices:*

(see index for correct answer)

- a. Manager Tools Podcast
- b. Marketing plan
- c. Provectus IT Inc
- d. PhD in management

Guidance: level 1

:: Competition regulators ::

The _____ is an independent agency of the United States government, established in 1914 by the _____ Act. Its principal mission is the promotion of consumer protection and the elimination and prevention of anticompetitive business practices, such as coercive monopoly. It is headquartered in the _____ Building in Washington, D.C.

Exam Probability: **Medium**

53. *Answer choices:*

(see index for correct answer)

- a. Competition Appeal Tribunal
- b. Superintendency of Industry and Commerce
- c. Commerce Commission
- d. Directorate-General for Competition

Guidance: level 1

:: ::

_____ Corporation is an American multinational technology company with headquarters in Redmond, Washington. It develops, manufactures, licenses, supports and sells computer software, consumer electronics, personal computers, and related services. Its best known software products are the _____ Windows line of operating systems, the _____ Office suite, and the Internet Explorer and Edge Web browsers. Its flagship hardware products are the Xbox video game consoles and the _____ Surface lineup of touchscreen personal computers. As of 2016, it is the world's largest software maker by revenue, and one of the world's most valuable companies. The word "_____" is a portmanteau of "microcomputer" and "software". _____ is ranked No. 30 in the 2018 Fortune 500 rankings of the largest United States corporations by total revenue.

Exam Probability: **High**

54. *Answer choices:*

(see index for correct answer)

- a. information systems assessment
- b. hierarchical
- c. personal values
- d. Microsoft

Guidance: level 1

:: Market research ::

_____ refers to a collection of methods that managers use to analyze an organization's internal and external environment to understand the organization's capabilities, customers, and business environment. The _____ consists of several methods of analysis: The 5Cs Analysis, SWOT analysis and Porter five forces analysis. A Marketing Plan is created to guide businesses on how to communicate the benefits of their products to the needs of potential customer. The _____ is the second step in the marketing plan and is a critical step in establishing a long term relationship with customers.

Exam Probability: **High**

55. *Answer choices:*

(see index for correct answer)

- a. Central location test
- b. Situation analysis
- c. Confidence interval
- d. Voter News Service

Guidance: level 1

:: Marketing techniques ::

The _____ or unique selling point is a marketing concept first
proposed as a theory to explain a pattern in successful advertising campaigns
of the early 1940s. The USP states that such campaigns made unique propositions
to customers that convinced them to switch brands. The term was developed by
television advertising pioneer Rosser Reeves of Ted Bates & Company.
Theodore Levitt, a professor at Harvard Business School, suggested that,
"Differentiation is one of the most important strategic and tactical activities
in which companies must constantly engage." The term has been used to describe
one`s "personal brand" in the marketplace. Today, the term is used in other
fields or just casually to refer to any aspect of an object that differentiates
it from similar objects.

Exam Probability: **Low**

56. *Answer choices:*

(see index for correct answer)

- a. Virtual event
- b. Rebranding
- c. Angel dusting
- d. unique selling point

Guidance: level 1

:: International trade ::

In finance, an _____ is the rate at which one currency will be exchanged for another. It is also regarded as the value of one country's currency in relation to another currency. For example, an interbank _____ of 114 Japanese yen to the United States dollar means that ¥114 will be exchanged for each US$1 or that US$1 will be exchanged for each ¥114. In this case it is said that the price of a dollar in relation to yen is ¥114, or equivalently that the price of a yen in relation to dollars is $1/114.

Exam Probability: **Low**

57. *Answer choices:*

(see index for correct answer)

- a. Common Fund for Commodities
- b. Exchange rate
- c. Competitiveness
- d. The Product Space

Guidance: level 1

:: ::

_____ involves decision making. It can include judging the merits of multiple options and selecting one or more of them. One can make a _____ between imagined options or between real options followed by the corresponding action. For example, a traveler might choose a route for a journey based on the preference of arriving at a given destination as soon as possible. The preferred route can then follow from information such as the length of each of the possible routes, traffic conditions, etc. The arrival at a _____ can include more complex motivators such as cognition, instinct, and feeling.

Exam Probability: **Medium**

58. *Answer choices:*

(see index for correct answer)

- a. Sarbanes-Oxley act of 2002
- b. interpersonal communication
- c. Choice
- d. co-culture

Guidance: level 1

:: ::

Business is the activity of making one's living or making money by producing or buying and selling products . Simply put, it is "any activity or enterprise entered into for profit. It does not mean it is a company, a corporation, partnership, or have any such formal organization, but it can range from a street peddler to General Motors."

59. *Answer choices:*

- a. functional perspective
- b. personal values
- c. interpersonal communication
- d. Firm

Guidance: level 1

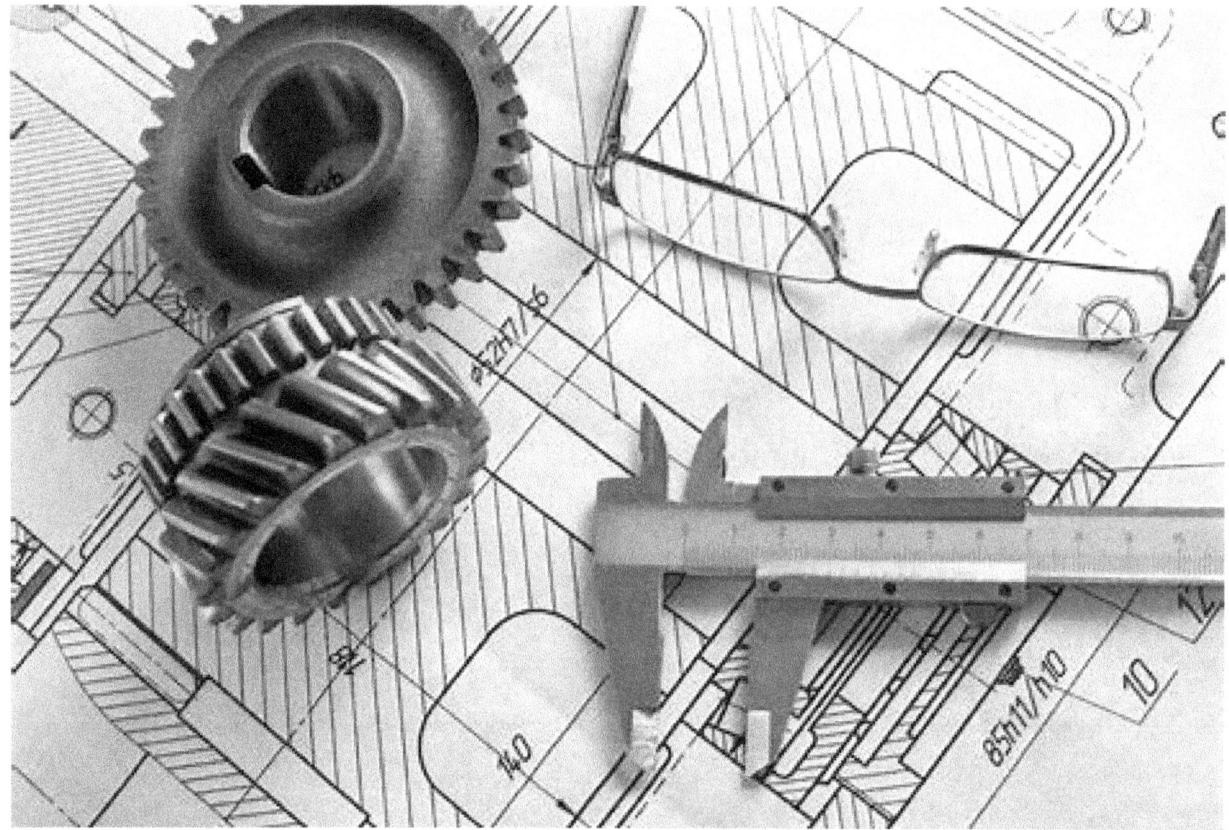

Manufacturing

Manufacturing is the production of merchandise for use or sale using labor and machines, tools, chemical and biological processing, or formulation. The term may refer to a range of human activity, from handicraft to high tech, but is most commonly applied to industrial design , in which raw materials are transformed into finished goods on a large scale. Such finished goods may be sold to other manufacturers for the production of other, more complex products, such as aircraft, household appliances, furniture, sports equipment or automobiles, or sold to wholesalers, who in turn sell them to retailers, who then sell them to end users and consumers.

:: Fault-tolerant computer systems ::

_____ decision-making is a group decision-making process in which group members develop, and agree to support a decision in the best interest of the whole group or common goal. _____ may be defined professionally as an acceptable resolution, one that can be supported, even if not the "favourite" of each individual. It has its origin in the Latin word consensus , which is from consentio meaning literally feel together. It is used to describe both the decision and the process of reaching a decision. _____ decision-making is thus concerned with the process of deliberating and finalizing a decision, and the social, economic, legal, environmental and political effects of applying this process.

Exam Probability: **High**

1. *Answer choices:*

(see index for correct answer)

- a. Consensus
- b. Uptime
- c. Disk mirroring
- d. Toric code

Guidance: level 1

:: Unit operations ::

_____ is the process of separating the components or substances from a liquid mixture by using selective boiling and condensation. _____ may result in essentially complete separation , or it may be a partial separation that increases the concentration of selected components in the mixture. In either case, the process exploits differences in the volatility of the mixture's components. In industrial chemistry, _____ is a unit operation of practically universal importance, but it is a physical separation process, not a chemical reaction.

Exam Probability: **Medium**

2. *Answer choices:*

(see index for correct answer)

- a. Theoretical plate
- b. Homogenization
- c. Distillation
- d. Heat transfer

Guidance: level 1

:: Production and manufacturing ::

A BOM can define products as they are designed , as they are ordered , as they are built , or as they are maintained . The different types of BOMs depend on the business need and use for which they are intended. In process industries, the BOM is also known as the formula, recipe, or ingredients list. The phrase "bill of material" is frequently used by engineers as an adjective to refer not to the literal bill, but to the current production configuration of a product, to distinguish it from modified or improved versions under study or in test.

Exam Probability: **High**

3. *Answer choices:*

(see index for correct answer)

- a. Nondestructive testing
- b. Countercurrent exchange
- c. DeviceNet
- d. Bill of materials

Guidance: level 1

:: E-commerce ::

_____ is the activity of buying or selling of products on online services or over the Internet. Electronic commerce draws on technologies such as mobile commerce, electronic funds transfer, supply chain management, Internet marketing, online transaction processing, electronic data interchange , inventory management systems, and automated data collection systems.

4. *Answer choices:*

(see index for correct answer)

- a. RSA
- b. BuildDirect
- c. E-commerce
- d. WePay

Guidance: level 1

:: Asset ::

In financial accounting, an _____ is any resource owned by the business. Anything tangible or intangible that can be owned or controlled to produce value and that is held by a company to produce positive economic value is an _____ . Simply stated, _____ s represent value of ownership that can be converted into cash . The balance sheet of a firm records the monetary value of the _____ s owned by that firm. It covers money and other valuables belonging to an individual or to a business.

Exam Probability: **High**

5. *Answer choices:*

(see index for correct answer)

- a. Fixed asset

- b. Asset

Guidance: level 1

:: Production and manufacturing ::

_____ is a systematic method to improve the "value" of goods or products and services by using an examination of function. Value, as defined, is the ratio of function to cost. Value can therefore be manipulated by either improving the function or reducing the cost. It is a primary tenet of _____ that basic functions be preserved and not be reduced as a consequence of pursuing value improvements.

Exam Probability: **Medium**

6. *Answer choices:*

(see index for correct answer)

- a. Production part approval process
- b. Craft production
- c. Value engineering
- d. Hydrosila

Guidance: level 1

:: Industrial processes ::

_____ is a technique involving the condensation of vapors and the return of this condensate to the system from which it originated. It is used in industrial and laboratory distillations. It is also used in chemistry to supply energy to reactions over a long period of time.

Exam Probability: **High**

7. *Answer choices:*

(see index for correct answer)

- a. Sol-gel
- b. Basic oxygen steelmaking
- c. Grainer evaporation process
- d. Reflux

Guidance: level 1

:: ::

In a supply chain, a _____ , or a seller, is an enterprise that contributes goods or services. Generally, a supply chain _____ manufactures inventory/stock items and sells them to the next link in the chain. Today, these terms refer to a supplier of any good or service.

Exam Probability: **Low**

8. *Answer choices:*

(see index for correct answer)

- a. empathy
- b. process perspective
- c. interpersonal communication
- d. hierarchical perspective

Guidance: level 1

:: Industrial engineering ::

_____ , in its contemporary conceptualisation, is a comparison of perceived expectations of a service with perceived performance , giving rise to the equation SQ=P-E. This conceptualistion of _____ has its origins in the expectancy-disconfirmation paradigm.

Exam Probability: **High**

9. *Answer choices:*

(see index for correct answer)

- a. Service quality
- b. Design of experiments
- c. Systematic layout planning
- d. Worker-machine activity chart

Guidance: level 1

:: Quality management ::

_____ is a not-for-profit membership foundation in Brussels, established in 1989 to increase the competitiveness of the European economy. The initial impetus for forming _____ was a response to the work of W. Edwards Deming and the development of the concepts of Total Quality Management.

Exam Probability: **Medium**

10. *Answer choices:*

(see index for correct answer)

- a. China Quality Course
- b. QC Reporting
- c. Quality management
- d. Quality Management Maturity Grid

Guidance: level 1

:: ::

_____ refers to the confirmation of certain characteristics of an object, person, or organization. This confirmation is often, but not always, provided by some form of external review, education, assessment, or audit. Accreditation is a specific organization's process of _____ . According to the National Council on Measurement in Education, a _____ test is a credentialing test used to determine whether individuals are knowledgeable enough in a given occupational area to be labeled "competent to practice" in that area.

Exam Probability: **Low**

11. *Answer choices:*

(see index for correct answer)

- a. hierarchical perspective
- b. similarity-attraction theory
- c. levels of analysis
- d. Certification

Guidance: level 1

:: Chemical processes ::

_____ is the understanding and application of the fundamental principles and laws of nature that allow us to transform raw material and energy into products that are useful to society, at an industrial level. By taking advantage of the driving forces of nature such as pressure, temperature and concentration gradients, as well as the law of conservation of mass, process engineers can develop methods to synthesize and purify large quantities of desired chemical products. _____ focuses on the design, operation, control, optimization and intensification of chemical, physical, and biological processes. _____ encompasses a vast range of industries, such as agriculture, automotive, biotechnical, chemical, food, material development, mining, nuclear, petrochemical, pharmaceutical, and software development. The application of systematic computer-based methods to _____ is "process systems engineering".

Exam Probability: **High**

12. *Answer choices:*

(see index for correct answer)

- a. SNOX process
- b. Process engineering
- c. FFC Cambridge process
- d. Sulfite process

Guidance: level 1

:: Sampling (statistics) ::

_____ uses statistical sampling to determine whether to accept or reject a production lot of material. It has been a common quality control technique used in industry. It is usually done as products leaves the factory, or in some cases even within the factory. Most often a producer supplies a consumer a number of items and a decision to accept or reject the items is made by determining the number of defective items in a sample from the lot. The lot is accepted if the number of defects falls below where the acceptance number or otherwise the lot is rejected.

Exam Probability: **Low**

13. *Answer choices:*

(see index for correct answer)

- a. Acceptance sampling
- b. Sampling frame
- c. Sampling risk
- d. Correct sampling

Guidance: level 1

:: Quality ::

The _____ , formerly the _____ Control , is a knowledge-based global community of quality professionals, with nearly 80,000 members dedicated to promoting and advancing quality tools, principles, and practices in their workplaces and communities.

14. *Answer choices:*

(see index for correct answer)

- a. Ringtest
- b. American Society for Quality
- c. European Practice Assessment
- d. Root cause

Guidance: level 1

:: Distribution, retailing, and wholesaling ::

_____ measures the performance of a system. Certain goals are defined and the _____ gives the percentage to which those goals should be achieved. Fill rate is different from _____ .

Exam Probability: **Low**

15. *Answer choices:*

(see index for correct answer)

- a. Cost to serve
- b. Chicago Review Press
- c. Service level
- d. Teleflorist

:: Production and manufacturing ::

Automatic _____ in continuous production processes is a combination of control engineering and chemical engineering disciplines that uses industrial control systems to achieve a production level of consistency, economy and safety which could not be achieved purely by human manual control. It is implemented widely in industries such as oil refining, pulp and paper manufacturing, chemical processing and power generating plants.

Exam Probability: **Low**

16. *Answer choices:*

(see index for correct answer)

- a. Process control
- b. Verband der Automobilindustrie
- c. Job shop
- d. Traditional engineering

:: Infographics ::

The _____ is a form used to collect data in real time at the location where the data is generated. The data it captures can be quantitative or qualitative. When the information is quantitative, the _____ is sometimes called a tally sheet.

Exam Probability: **Medium**

17. *Answer choices:*

(see index for correct answer)

- a. Treemapping
- b. Archaeological plan
- c. Glyph
- d. Check sheet

Guidance: level 1

:: Software testing ::

_____ 1 was the first artificial Earth satellite. The Soviet Union launched it into an elliptical low Earth orbit on 4 October 1957, orbiting for three weeks before its batteries died, then silently for two more months before falling back into the atmosphere. It was a 58 cm diameter polished metal sphere, with four external radio antennas to broadcast radio pulses. Its radio signal was easily detectable even by radio amateurs, and the 65° inclination and duration of its orbit made its flight path cover virtually the entire inhabited Earth. This surprise success precipitated the American _____ crisis and triggered the Space Race, a part of the Cold War. The launch was the beginning of a new era of political, military, technological, and scientific developments.

Exam Probability: **High**

18. *Answer choices:*

(see index for correct answer)

- a. Equivalence partitioning
- b. Transformation Priority Premise
- c. Test data
- d. Sputnik

Guidance: level 1

:: Monopoly (economics) ::

_____ are "efficiencies formed by variety, not volume" . For example, a gas station that sells gasoline can sell soda, milk, baked goods, etc through their customer service representatives and thus achieve gasoline companies _____ .

19. *Answer choices:*

(see index for correct answer)

- a. Economies of scope
- b. Ownership unbundling
- c. Government monopoly
- d. Tesco Town

Guidance: level 1

:: Project management ::

_____ is a work methodology emphasizing the parallelisation of tasks , which is sometimes called simultaneous engineering or integrated product development using an integrated product team approach. It refers to an approach used in product development in which functions of design engineering, manufacturing engineering, and other functions are integrated to reduce the time required to bring a new product to market.

20. *Answer choices:*

(see index for correct answer)

- a. Stakeholder analysis
- b. Concurrent engineering
- c. Risk management plan
- d. Budgeted cost of work performed

Guidance: level 1

:: Lean manufacturing ::

_____ is a Japanese term that means "mistake-proofing" or "inadvertent error prevention". A _____ is any mechanism in any process that helps an equipment operator avoid mistakes . Its purpose is to eliminate product defects by preventing, correcting, or drawing attention to human errors as they occur. The concept was formalised, and the term adopted, by Shigeo Shingo as part of the Toyota Production System. It was originally described as baka-yoke, but as this means "fool-proofing" the name was changed to the milder

_____ .

Exam Probability: **Medium**

21. *Answer choices:*

(see index for correct answer)

- a. Lean CFP driven
- b. Continuous improvement

- c. Value stream mapping
- d. Lean enterprise

Guidance: level 1

:: Quality management ::

_____ ensures that an organization, product or service is consistent. It has four main components: quality planning, quality assurance, quality control and quality improvement. _____ is focused not only on product and service quality, but also on the means to achieve it. _____ , therefore, uses quality assurance and control of processes as well as products to achieve more consistent quality. What a customer wants and is willing to pay for it determines quality. It is written or unwritten commitment to a known or unknown consumer in the market . Thus, quality can be defined as fitness for intended use or, in other words, how well the product performs its intended function

Exam Probability: **Low**

22. *Answer choices:*

(see index for correct answer)

- a. Quality Management Maturity Grid
- b. Det Norske Veritas
- c. Regulatory translation
- d. Quality policy

Guidance: level 1

:: Supply chain management ::

_____ is a core supply chain function and includes supply chain planning and supply chain execution capabilities. Specifically, _____ is the capability firms use to plan total material requirements. The material requirements are communicated to procurement and other functions for sourcing. _____ is also responsible for determining the amount of material to be deployed at each stocking location across the supply chain, establishing material replenishment plans, determining inventory levels to hold for each type of inventory , and communicating information regarding material needs throughout the extended supply chain.

Exam Probability: **Low**

23. *Answer choices:*

(see index for correct answer)

- a. Delayed differentiation
- b. Supply chain surplus
- c. Materials management
- d. Design for logistics

Guidance: level 1

:: Process management ::

_____ is a statistics package developed at the Pennsylvania State University by researchers Barbara F. Ryan, Thomas A. Ryan, Jr., and Brian L. Joiner in 1972. It began as a light version of OMNITAB 80, a statistical analysis program by NIST. Statistical analysis software such as _____ automates calculations and the creation of graphs, allowing the user to focus more on the analysis of data and the interpretation of results. It is compatible with other _____ , Inc. software.

Exam Probability: **Medium**

24. *Answer choices:*

(see index for correct answer)

- a. business process re-engineering
- b. Modular process skid
- c. Business process orientation
- d. Minitab

Guidance: level 1

:: Production and manufacturing ::

In industry, _____ is a system of maintaining and improving the integrity of production and quality systems through the machines, equipment, processes, and employees that add business value to an organization.

Exam Probability: **Medium**

25. *Answer choices:*

- a. Total productive maintenance
- b. Licensed production
- c. Alarm fatigue
- d. Total quality management

Guidance: level 1

:: ::

_____ is a kind of action that occur as two or more objects have an effect upon one another. The idea of a two-way effect is essential in the concept of _____ , as opposed to a one-way causal effect. A closely related term is interconnectivity, which deals with the _____ s of _____ s within systems: combinations of many simple _____ s can lead to surprising emergent phenomena. _____ has different tailored meanings in various sciences. Changes can also involve _____ .

Exam Probability: **Low**

26. *Answer choices:*

- a. open system
- b. corporate values
- c. process perspective

- d. Interaction

Guidance: level 1

:: Management ::

A _____ is an idea of the future or desired result that a person or a group of people envisions, plans and commits to achieve. People endeavor to reach _____ s within a finite time by setting deadlines.

Exam Probability: **Medium**

27. *Answer choices:*

(see index for correct answer)

- a. Goal
- b. Management fad
- c. Change advisory board
- d. Project team builder

Guidance: level 1

:: Commerce ::

A _____ is an employee within a company, business or other organization who is responsible at some level for buying or approving the acquisition of goods and services needed by the company. Responsible for buying the best quality products, goods and services for their company at the most competitive prices, _____ s work in a wide range of sectors for many different organizations. The position responsibilities may be the same as that of a buyer or purchasing agent, or may include wider supervisory or managerial responsibilities. A _____ may oversee the acquisition of materials needed for production, general supplies for offices and facilities, equipment, or construction contracts. A _____ often supervises purchasing agents and buyers, but in small companies the _____ may also be the purchasing agent or buyer. The _____ position may also carry the title "Procurement Manager" or in the public sector, "Procurement Officer". He or she can come from both an Engineering or Economics background.

Exam Probability: **Low**

28. *Answer choices:*

(see index for correct answer)

- a. Customs broking
- b. Deal transaction
- c. Purchasing manager
- d. Statutory holdback

Guidance: level 1

:: Promotion and marketing communications ::

The _____ of American Manufacturers, now ThomasNet, is an online platform for supplier discovery and product sourcing in the US and Canada. It was once known as the "big green books" and "Thomas Registry", and was a multi-volume directory of industrial product information covering 650,000 distributors, manufacturers and service companies within 67,000-plus industrial categories that is now published on ThomasNet.

Exam Probability: **Medium**

29. *Answer choices:*

(see index for correct answer)

- a. Pakistan Electronic Media Regulatory Authority
- b. Video news release
- c. Thomas Register
- d. Flashpoint Studios

Guidance: level 1

:: Insulators ::

A _____ is a piece of soft cloth large enough either to cover or to enfold a great portion of the user's body, usually when sleeping or otherwise at rest, thereby trapping radiant bodily heat that otherwise would be lost through convection, and so keeping the body warm.

Exam Probability: **High**

30. *Answer choices:*

(see index for correct answer)

- a. Blanket
- b. Pipe insulation
- c. Sleeping bag
- d. Vacuum insulated panel

Guidance: level 1

:: Project management ::

Contemporary business and science treat as a _____ any undertaking, carried out individually or collaboratively and possibly involving research or design, that is carefully planned to achieve a particular aim.

Exam Probability: **High**

31. *Answer choices:*

(see index for correct answer)

- a. Project
- b. Project management process
- c. Critical path drag
- d. P3M3

Guidance: level 1

:: Consortia ::

A _____ is an association of two or more individuals, companies, organizations or governments with the objective of participating in a common activity or pooling their resources for achieving a common goal.

Exam Probability: **High**

32. *Answer choices:*

(see index for correct answer)

- a. Consortium
- b. TranSys
- c. Digital Living Network Alliance
- d. National Center for Manufacturing Sciences

Guidance: level 1

:: Information technology management ::

_____ within quality management systems and information technology systems is a process—either formal or informal—used to ensure that changes to a product or system are introduced in a controlled and coordinated manner. It reduces the possibility that unnecessary changes will be introduced to a system without forethought, introducing faults into the system or undoing changes made by other users of software. The goals of a _____ procedure usually include minimal disruption to services, reduction in back-out activities, and cost-effective utilization of resources involved in implementing change.

Exam Probability: **High**

33. *Answer choices:*

- a. Library Review
- b. Building lifecycle management
- c. Change control
- d. Professional Petroleum Data Management Association

Guidance: level 1

:: Process management ::

When used in the context of communication networks, such as Ethernet or packet radio, _____ or network _____ is the rate of successful message delivery over a communication channel. The data these messages belong to may be delivered over a physical or logical link, or it can pass through a certain network node. _____ is usually measured in bits per second , and sometimes in data packets per second or data packets per time slot.

34. *Answer choices:*

(see index for correct answer)

- a. Process
- b. President%27s Quality Award
- c. Throughput
- d. SREDIM

Guidance: level 1

:: Quality ::

A _____ is an initiating cause of either a condition or a causal chain that leads to an outcome or effect of interest. The term denotes the earliest, most basic, `deepest`, cause for a given behavior; most often a fault. The idea is that you can only see an error by its manifest signs. Those signs can be widespread, multitudinous, and convoluted, whereas the _____ leading to them often is a lot simpler.

35. *Answer choices:*

(see index for correct answer)

- a. Quality by Design
- b. Root cause

- c. Society for Software Quality
- d. Robustification

Guidance: level 1

:: Business process ::

_____ is the value to an enterprise which is derived from the techniques, procedures, and programs that implement and enhance the delivery of goods and services. _____ is one of the three components of structural capital, itself a component of intellectual capital. _____ can be seen as the value of processes to any entity, whether for profit or not-for profit, but is most commonly used in reference to for-profit entities.

Exam Probability: **Medium**

36. *Answer choices:*

(see index for correct answer)

- a. IDS Scheer
- b. International business development
- c. Process capital
- d. Direct store delivery

Guidance: level 1

:: Management ::

In economics and marketing, _____ is the process of distinguishing a product or service from others, to make it more attractive to a particular target market. This involves differentiating it from competitors' products as well as a firm's own products. The concept was proposed by Edward Chamberlin in his 1933 The Theory of Monopolistic Competition.

Exam Probability: **Medium**

37. *Answer choices:*

(see index for correct answer)

- a. Product differentiation
- b. Responsible autonomy
- c. Planning fallacy
- d. Porter five forces analysis

Guidance: level 1

:: Metalworking ::

A _____ is a round object with various uses. It is used in _____ games, where the play of the game follows the state of the _____ as it is hit, kicked or thrown by players. _____ s can also be used for simpler activities, such as catch or juggling. _____ s made from hard-wearing materials are used in engineering applications to provide very low friction bearings, known as _____ bearings. Black-powder weapons use stone and metal _____ s as projectiles.

38. *Answer choices:*

(see index for correct answer)

- a. Tension control bolt
- b. Low plasticity burnishing
- c. Ball
- d. Semi-solid metal casting

Guidance: level 1

:: Management ::

A supply-chain network is an evolution of the basic supply chain. Due to rapid technological advancement, organisations with a basic supply chain can develop this chain into a more complex structure involving a higher level of interdependence and connectivity between more organisations, this constitutes a supply-chain network.

Exam Probability: **Medium**

39. *Answer choices:*

(see index for correct answer)

- a. Six phases of a big project
- b. Double linking

- c. Supply chain network
- d. Overtime rate

Guidance: level 1

:: Retailing ::

_____ is the process of selling consumer goods or services to customers through multiple channels of distribution to earn a profit. _____ ers satisfy demand identified through a supply chain. The term " _____ er" is typically applied where a service provider fills the small orders of a large number of individuals, who are end-users, rather than large orders of a small number of wholesale, corporate or government clientele. Shopping generally refers to the act of buying products. Sometimes this is done to obtain final goods, including necessities such as food and clothing; sometimes it takes place as a recreational activity. Recreational shopping often involves window shopping and browsing: it does not always result in a purchase.

Exam Probability: **High**

40. *Answer choices:*

(see index for correct answer)

- a. Variety store
- b. Retail
- c. Automated retail
- d. Endcap

Guidance: level 1

:: Business ::

The seller, or the provider of the goods or services, completes a sale in response to an acquisition, appropriation, requisition or a direct interaction with the buyer at the point of sale. There is a passing of title of the item, and the settlement of a price, in which agreement is reached on a price for which transfer of ownership of the item will occur. The seller, not the purchaser typically executes the sale and it may be completed prior to the obligation of payment. In the case of indirect interaction, a person who sells goods or service on behalf of the owner is known as a _____ man or _____ woman or _____ person, but this often refers to someone selling goods in a store/shop, in which case other terms are also common, including _____ clerk, shop assistant, and retail clerk.

Exam Probability: **Medium**

41. *Answer choices:*

(see index for correct answer)

- a. Sales
- b. Vendor screening
- c. Policy capturing
- d. Business interoperability interface

Guidance: level 1

:: Industrial equipment ::

_____ s are heat exchangers typically used to provide heat to the bottom of industrial distillation columns. They boil the liquid from the bottom of a distillation column to generate vapors which are returned to the column to drive the distillation separation. The heat supplied to the column by the _____ at the bottom of the column is removed by the condenser at the top of the column.

Exam Probability: **High**

42. *Answer choices:*

(see index for correct answer)

- a. Buell dryer
- b. Wheel washing system
- c. Whirlwind mill
- d. Reboiler

Guidance: level 1

:: Management ::

Business _____ is a discipline in operations management in which people use various methods to discover, model, analyze, measure, improve, optimize, and automate business processes. BPM focuses on improving corporate performance by managing business processes. Any combination of methods used to manage a company's business processes is BPM. Processes can be structured and repeatable or unstructured and variable. Though not required, enabling technologies are often used with BPM.

43. *Answer choices:*

(see index for correct answer)

- a. Corporate recovery
- b. Event chain methodology
- c. Process management
- d. Libertarian management

Guidance: level 1

:: Metals ::

A _____ is a material that, when freshly prepared, polished, or fractured, shows a lustrous appearance, and conducts electricity and heat relatively well. _____ s are typically malleable or ductile . A _____ may be a chemical element such as iron, or an alloy such as stainless steel.

Exam Probability: **High**

44. *Answer choices:*

(see index for correct answer)

- a. Metal
- b. Telluric iron

- c. Light metal
- d. Silver overlay

Guidance: level 1

:: ::

_____ is the process of making predictions of the future based on past and present data and most commonly by analysis of trends. A commonplace example might be estimation of some variable of interest at some specified future date. Prediction is a similar, but more general term. Both might refer to formal statistical methods employing time series, cross-sectional or longitudinal data, or alternatively to less formal judgmental methods. Usage can differ between areas of application: for example, in hydrology the terms "forecast" and "_____" are sometimes reserved for estimates of values at certain specific future times, while the term "prediction" is used for more general estimates, such as the number of times floods will occur over a long period.

Exam Probability: **High**

45. *Answer choices:*

(see index for correct answer)

- a. deep-level diversity
- b. Sarbanes-Oxley act of 2002
- c. co-culture
- d. imperative

Guidance: level 1

A _____ or business method is a collection of related, structured activities or tasks by people or equipment which in a specific sequence produce a service or product for a particular customer or customers. _____ es occur at all organizational levels and may or may not be visible to the customers. A _____ may often be visualized as a flowchart of a sequence of activities with interleaving decision points or as a process matrix of a sequence of activities with relevance rules based on data in the process. The benefits of using _____ es include improved customer satisfaction and improved agility for reacting to rapid market change. Process-oriented organizations break down the barriers of structural departments and try to avoid functional silos.

Exam Probability: **High**

46. *Answer choices:*

(see index for correct answer)

- a. Business communication
- b. Business process
- c. Process-centered design
- d. Process capital

Guidance: level 1

_____ is an iterative four-step management method used in business for the control and continuous improvement of processes and products. It is also known as the Deming circle/cycle/wheel, the Shewhart cycle, the control circle/cycle, or plan–do–study–act . Another version of this _____ cycle is O _____ . The added "O" stands for observation or as some versions say: "Observe the current condition." This emphasis on observation and current condition has currency with the literature on lean manufacturing and the Toyota Production System. The _____ cycle, with Ishikawa's changes, can be traced back to S. Mizuno of the Tokyo Institute of Technology in 1959.

Exam Probability: **Medium**

47. *Answer choices:*

(see index for correct answer)

- a. PDCA
- b. Continuous-flow manufacturing
- c. Project management information system
- d. Law practice management

Guidance: level 1

:: ::

An _____ is, most an organized examination or formal evaluation exercise. In engineering activities _____ involves the measurements, tests, and gauges applied to certain characteristics in regard to an object or activity. The results are usually compared to specified requirements and standards for determining whether the item or activity is in line with these targets, often with a Standard _____ Procedure in place to ensure consistent checking. _____ s are usually non-destructive.

Exam Probability: **Low**

48. *Answer choices:*

(see index for correct answer)

- a. personal values
- b. interpersonal communication
- c. Inspection
- d. corporate values

Guidance: level 1

:: Data management ::

_____ is the ability of a physical product to remain functional, without requiring excessive maintenance or repair, when faced with the challenges of normal operation over its design lifetime. There are several measures of _____ in use, including years of life, hours of use, and number of operational cycles. In economics, goods with a long usable life are referred to as durable goods.

49. *Answer choices:*

(see index for correct answer)

- a. Durability
- b. Data profiling
- c. Dynamic knowledge repository
- d. Two-phase commit protocol

Guidance: level 1

:: Production economics ::

In economics and related disciplines, a _____ is a cost in making any economic trade when participating in a market.

50. *Answer choices:*

(see index for correct answer)

- a. Producer's risk
- b. Transaction cost
- c. Marginal product of labor
- d. Specialization

:: Production and manufacturing ::

_____ is the process of determining the production capacity needed by an organization to meet changing demands for its products. In the context of _____ , design capacity is the maximum amount of work that an organization is capable of completing in a given period. Effective capacity is the maximum amount of work that an organization is capable of completing in a given period due to constraints such as quality problems, delays, material handling, etc.

Exam Probability: **High**

51. *Answer choices:*

(see index for correct answer)

- a. Resource Breakdown
- b. Capacity planning
- c. Hydrosila
- d. Changeover

:: Distribution, retailing, and wholesaling ::

The _____ is a distribution channel phenomenon in which forecasts yield supply chain inefficiencies. It refers to increasing swings in inventory in response to shifts in customer demand as one moves further up the supply chain. The concept first appeared in Jay Forrester's Industrial Dynamics and thus it is also known as the Forrester effect. The _____ was named for the way the amplitude of a whip increases down its length. The further from the originating signal, the greater the distortion of the wave pattern. In a similar manner, forecast accuracy decreases as one moves upstream along the supply chain. For example, many consumer goods have fairly consistent consumption at retail but this signal becomes more chaotic and unpredictable as the focus moves away from consumer purchasing behavior.

Exam Probability: **Medium**

52. *Answer choices:*

(see index for correct answer)

- a. Bullwhip effect
- b. Bridgewater House, Manchester
- c. Silenzio Music
- d. Open Payment Initiative

Guidance: level 1

:: Project management ::

In economics, _____ is the assignment of available resources to various uses. In the context of an entire economy, resources can be allocated by various means, such as markets or central planning.

53. *Answer choices:*

(see index for correct answer)

- a. Drag cost
- b. Resource allocation
- c. PM Declaration of Interdependence
- d. Product-based planning

Guidance: level 1

:: Quality awards ::

The _____ recognizes U.S. organizations in the business, health care, education, and nonprofit sectors for performance excellence. The Baldrige Award is the only formal recognition of the performance excellence of both public and private U.S. organizations given by the President of the United States. It is administered by the Baldrige Performance Excellence Program, which is based at and managed by the National Institute of Standards and Technology , an agency of the U.S. Department of Commerce.

Exam Probability: **Medium**

54. *Answer choices:*

(see index for correct answer)

- a. The Deming Cup

- b. Canada Awards for Excellence
- c. Malcolm Baldrige National Quality Award
- d. Rajiv Gandhi National Quality Award

Guidance: level 1

:: Computer memory companies ::

_____ Corporation is a Japanese multinational conglomerate headquartered in Tokyo, Japan. Its diversified products and services include information technology and communications equipment and systems, electronic components and materials, power systems, industrial and social infrastructure systems, consumer electronics, household appliances, medical equipment, office equipment, as well as lighting and logistics.

Exam Probability: **Low**

55. *Answer choices:*

(see index for correct answer)

- a. G.Skill
- b. Winbond
- c. SanDisk
- d. Corsair Memory

Guidance: level 1

:: Knowledge representation ::

_____ s are causal diagrams created by Kaoru Ishikawa that show the causes of a specific event.

Exam Probability: **High**

56. *Answer choices:*

(see index for correct answer)

- a. Enactive interfaces
- b. Region connection calculus
- c. UMBEL
- d. Ishikawa diagram

Guidance: level 1

:: Production and manufacturing ::

_____ is a production planning, scheduling, and inventory control system used to manage manufacturing processes. Most MRP systems are software-based, but it is possible to conduct MRP by hand as well.

Exam Probability: **Low**

57. *Answer choices:*

(see index for correct answer)

- a. Contract manufacturer
- b. Profibus
- c. MAPICS
- d. Product layout

Guidance: level 1

:: Lean manufacturing ::

_____ is the Sino-Japanese word for "improvement". In business, _____ refers to activities that continuously improve all functions and involve all employees from the CEO to the assembly line workers. It also applies to processes, such as purchasing and logistics, that cross organizational boundaries into the supply chain. It has been applied in healthcare, psychotherapy, life-coaching, government, and banking.

Exam Probability: **Medium**

58. *Answer choices:*

(see index for correct answer)

- a. Just in sequence
- b. Agent-assisted automation
- c. Supply chain responsiveness matrix
- d. Lean Government

:: Management ::

_____ is a process by which entities review the quality of all factors involved in production. ISO 9000 defines _____ as "A part of quality management focused on fulfilling quality requirements".

Exam Probability: **Low**

59. *Answer choices:*

(see index for correct answer)

- a. Backsourcing
- b. Quality control
- c. Public sector consulting
- d. Certified Energy Manager

Commerce

Commerce relates to "the exchange of goods and services, especially on a large scale." It includes legal, economic, political, social, cultural and technological systems that operate in any country or internationally.

:: Production economics ::

In microeconomics, _____ are the cost advantages that enterprises obtain due to their scale of operation , with cost per unit of output decreasing with increasing scale.

Exam Probability: **Medium**

1. *Answer choices:*

- a. Partial productivity
- b. Diseconomies of scale
- c. Split-off point
- d. Economies of scale

Guidance: level 1

:: Commercial item transport and distribution ::

Wholesaling or distributing is the sale of goods or merchandise to retailers; to industrial, commercial, institutional, or other professional business users; or to other _____ rs and related subordinated services. In general, it is the sale of goods to anyone other than a standard consumer.

Exam Probability: **High**

2. *Answer choices:*

- a. Dock
- b. Containerlift
- c. Inland navigation
- d. Heavy lift

:: ::

A _____ is an organization, usually a group of people or a company, authorized to act as a single entity and recognized as such in law. Early incorporated entities were established by charter . Most jurisdictions now allow the creation of new _____ s through registration.

Exam Probability: **High**

3. *Answer choices:*

(see index for correct answer)

- a. personal values
- b. levels of analysis
- c. Corporation
- d. co-culture

:: Securities (finance) ::

A _____ is a container that is traditionally constructed from stiff fibers, and can be made from a range of materials, including wood splints, runners, and cane. While most _____ s are made from plant materials, other materials such as horsehair, baleen, or metal wire can be used. _____ s are generally woven by hand. Some _____ s are fitted with a lid, while others are left open on top.

Exam Probability: **Medium**

4. *Answer choices:*

(see index for correct answer)

- a. Principal at risk notes
- b. Basket
- c. Look-through approach
- d. New York Institute of Finance

Guidance: level 1

:: ::

The _____ is a U.S. business-focused, English-language international daily newspaper based in New York City. The Journal, along with its Asian and European editions, is published six days a week by Dow Jones & Company, a division of News Corp. The newspaper is published in the broadsheet format and online. The Journal has been printed continuously since its inception on July 8, 1889, by Charles Dow, Edward Jones, and Charles Bergstresser.

5. *Answer choices:*

(see index for correct answer)

- a. information systems assessment
- b. Sarbanes-Oxley act of 2002
- c. Wall Street Journal
- d. process perspective

Guidance: level 1

:: ::

The _____ of 1990 is a civil rights law that prohibits discrimination based on disability. It affords similar protections against discrimination to Americans with disabilities as the Civil Rights Act of 1964, which made discrimination based on race, religion, sex, national origin, and other characteristics illegal. In addition, unlike the Civil Rights Act, the ADA also requires covered employers to provide reasonable accommodations to employees with disabilities, and imposes accessibility requirements on public accommodations.

6. *Answer choices:*

(see index for correct answer)

- a. personal values
- b. Americans with Disabilities Act
- c. deep-level diversity
- d. corporate values

Guidance: level 1

:: ::

A _____ is a sworn body of people convened to render an impartial verdict officially submitted to them by a court, or to set a penalty or judgment. Modern juries tend to be found in courts to ascertain the guilt or lack thereof in a crime. In Anglophone jurisdictions, the verdict may be guilty or not guilty . The old institution of grand juries still exists in some places, particularly the United States, to investigate whether enough evidence of a crime exists to bring someone to trial.

Exam Probability: **Medium**

7. *Answer choices:*

(see index for correct answer)

- a. Sarbanes-Oxley act of 2002
- b. cultural
- c. Jury
- d. levels of analysis

Guidance: level 1

:: Management ::

The term _____ refers to measures designed to increase the degree of autonomy and self-determination in people and in communities in order to enable them to represent their interests in a responsible and self-determined way, acting on their own authority. It is the process of becoming stronger and more confident, especially in controlling one`s life and claiming one`s rights. _____ as action refers both to the process of self- _____ and to professional support of people, which enables them to overcome their sense of powerlessness and lack of influence, and to recognize and use their resources. To do work with power.

Exam Probability: **Medium**

8. *Answer choices:*

(see index for correct answer)

- a. Supply chain optimization
- b. Empowerment
- c. Meeting
- d. Six phases of a big project

Guidance: level 1

:: Management ::

_____ is the identification, evaluation, and prioritization of risks followed by coordinated and economical application of resources to minimize, monitor, and control the probability or impact of unfortunate events or to maximize the realization of opportunities.

Exam Probability: **Low**

9. *Answer choices:*

(see index for correct answer)

- a. Automated decision support
- b. Risk management
- c. Organizational hologram
- d. Vorstand

Guidance: level 1

:: Credit cards ::

The _____ Company, also known as Amex, is an American multinational financial services corporation headquartered in Three World Financial Center in New York City. The company was founded in 1850 and is one of the 30 components of the Dow Jones Industrial Average. The company is best known for its charge card, credit card, and traveler's cheque businesses.

Exam Probability: **High**

10. *Answer choices:*

- a. Kisan Credit Card
- b. Universal Air Travel Plan
- c. Netbanx
- d. China UnionPay

Guidance: level 1

:: Economic globalization ::

_____ is an agreement in which one company hires another company to be responsible for a planned or existing activity that is or could be done internally,and sometimes involves transferring employees and assets from one firm to another.

Exam Probability: **Medium**

11. *Answer choices:*

- a. global financial
- b. Outsourcing

Guidance: level 1

:: ::

Regulatory economics is the economics of regulation. It is the application of law by government or independent administrative agencies for various purposes, including remedying market failure, protecting the environment, centrally-planning an economy, enriching well-connected firms, or benefiting politicians.

Exam Probability: **High**

12. *Answer choices:*

(see index for correct answer)

- a. surface-level diversity
- b. corporate values
- c. Economic regulation
- d. interpersonal communication

Guidance: level 1

:: Human resource management ::

_____ are the people who make up the workforce of an organization, business sector, or economy. "Human capital" is sometimes used synonymously with " _____ ", although human capital typically refers to a narrower effect . Likewise, other terms sometimes used include manpower, talent, labor, personnel, or simply people.

13. *Answer choices:*

(see index for correct answer)

- a. Competency-based management
- b. Human resources
- c. Workplace mentoring
- d. IDS HR in Practice

Guidance: level 1

:: ::

In economics _____ is a theoretical concept where all markets are in equilibrium, and all prices and quantities have fully adjusted and are in equilibrium. The _____ contrasts with the short run where there are some constraints and markets are not fully in equilibrium.

Exam Probability: **High**

14. *Answer choices:*

(see index for correct answer)

- a. co-culture
- b. cultural
- c. hierarchical

- d. surface-level diversity

Guidance: level 1

:: Auctioneering ::

A _____ is a type of sealed-bid auction. Bidders submit written bids without knowing the bid of the other people in the auction. The highest bidder wins but the price paid is the second-highest bid. This type of auction is strategically similar to an English auction and gives bidders an incentive to bid their true value. The auction was first described academically by Columbia University professor William Vickrey in 1961 though it had been used by stamp collectors since 1893. In 1797 Johann Wolfgang von Goethe sold a manuscript using a sealed-bid, second-price auction.

Exam Probability: **High**

15. *Answer choices:*

(see index for correct answer)

- a. English auction
- b. Vickrey auction
- c. Auction catalog
- d. Art auction

Guidance: level 1

:: Payments ::

A _____ or government incentive is a form of financial aid or support extended to an economic sector generally with the aim of promoting economic and social policy. Although commonly extended from government, the term _____ can relate to any type of support – for example from NGOs or as implicit subsidies. Subsidies come in various forms including: direct and indirect .

Exam Probability: **Medium**

16. *Answer choices:*

(see index for correct answer)

- a. Subsidy
- b. Direct Payments
- c. Deficiency payments
- d. Thirty pieces of silver

Guidance: level 1

:: Commerce ::

A _____ is an employee within a company, business or other organization who is responsible at some level for buying or approving the acquisition of goods and services needed by the company. Responsible for buying the best quality products, goods and services for their company at the most competitive prices, _____ s work in a wide range of sectors for many different organizations. The position responsibilities may be the same as that of a buyer or purchasing agent, or may include wider supervisory or managerial responsibilities. A _____ may oversee the acquisition of materials needed for production, general supplies for offices and facilities, equipment, or construction contracts. A _____ often supervises purchasing agents and buyers, but in small companies the _____ may also be the purchasing agent or buyer. The _____ position may also carry the title "Procurement Manager" or in the public sector, "Procurement Officer". He or she can come from both an Engineering or Economics background.

Exam Probability: **High**

17. *Answer choices:*

(see index for correct answer)

- a. Card association
- b. Car boot sale
- c. Global Commerce Initiative
- d. Purchasing manager

Guidance: level 1

:: ::

An _____ is a systematic and independent examination of books, accounts, statutory records, documents and vouchers of an organization to ascertain how far the financial statements as well as non-financial disclosures present a true and fair view of the concern. It also attempts to ensure that the books of accounts are properly maintained by the concern as required by law. _____ ing has become such a ubiquitous phenomenon in the corporate and the public sector that academics started identifying an " _____ Society". The _____ or perceives and recognises the propositions before them for examination, obtains evidence, evaluates the same and formulates an opinion on the basis of his judgement which is communicated through their _____ ing report.

Exam Probability: **Medium**

18. *Answer choices:*

(see index for correct answer)

- a. Audit
- b. empathy
- c. information systems assessment
- d. functional perspective

Guidance: level 1

:: ::

_____ are electronic transfer of money from one bank account to another, either within a single financial institution or across multiple institutions, via computer-based systems, without the direct intervention of bank staff.

Exam Probability: **High**

19. *Answer choices:*

(see index for correct answer)

- a. hierarchical perspective
- b. imperative
- c. co-culture
- d. deep-level diversity

Guidance: level 1

:: Information retrieval ::

_____ is a technique used by recommender systems. _____ has two senses, a narrow one and a more general one.

Exam Probability: **Low**

20. *Answer choices:*

(see index for correct answer)

- a. Stop words
- b. DtSearch
- c. Collaborative filtering
- d. Collaborative search engine

Guidance: level 1

:: Debt ::

_____ , in finance and economics, is payment from a borrower or deposit-taking financial institution to a lender or depositor of an amount above repayment of the principal sum , at a particular rate. It is distinct from a fee which the borrower may pay the lender or some third party. It is also distinct from dividend which is paid by a company to its shareholders from its profit or reserve, but not at a particular rate decided beforehand, rather on a pro rata basis as a share in the reward gained by risk taking entrepreneurs when the revenue earned exceeds the total costs.

Exam Probability: **Low**

21. *Answer choices:*

(see index for correct answer)

- a. Interest
- b. Sum certain
- c. Debtors Anonymous
- d. Debt-lag

:: ::

In Christian denominations that practice infant baptism, confirmation is seen as the sealing of Christianity created in baptism. Those being _____ are known as confirmands. In some denominations, such as the Anglican Communion and Methodist Churches, confirmation bestows full membership in a local congregation upon the recipient. In others, such as the Roman Catholic Church, Confirmation "renders the bond with the Church more perfect", because, while a baptized person is already a member, "reception of the sacrament of Confirmation is necessary for the completion of baptismal grace".

Exam Probability: **Low**

22. *Answer choices:*

(see index for correct answer)

- a. co-culture
- b. similarity-attraction theory
- c. Confirmed
- d. hierarchical perspective

:: Investment ::

In finance, the benefit from an _____ is called a return. The return may consist of a gain realised from the sale of property or an _____ , unrealised capital appreciation , or _____ income such as dividends, interest, rental income etc., or a combination of capital gain and income. The return may also include currency gains or losses due to changes in foreign currency exchange rates.

Exam Probability: **Low**

23. *Answer choices:*

(see index for correct answer)

- a. Low Exercise Price Option
- b. Investing online
- c. Market exposure
- d. Investment

Guidance: level 1

:: Management occupations ::

_____ ship is the process of designing, launching and running a new business, which is often initially a small business. The people who create these businesses are called _____ s.

Exam Probability: **Low**

24. *Answer choices:*

- a. Legislator
- b. Chief sustainability officer
- c. Vorstandsassistent
- d. Entrepreneur

Guidance: level 1

:: ::

The _____ or just chief executive , is the most senior corporate, executive, or administrative officer in charge of managing an organization especially an independent legal entity such as a company or nonprofit institution. CEOs lead a range of organizations, including public and private corporations, non-profit organizations and even some government organizations . The CEO of a corporation or company typically reports to the board of directors and is charged with maximizing the value of the entity, which may include maximizing the share price, market share, revenues or another element. In the non-profit and government sector, CEOs typically aim at achieving outcomes related to the organization's mission, such as reducing poverty, increasing literacy, etc.

Exam Probability: **Low**

25. *Answer choices:*

- a. deep-level diversity
- b. Sarbanes-Oxley act of 2002
- c. hierarchical
- d. open system

Guidance: level 1

:: Meetings ::

A _____ is a body of one or more persons that is subordinate to a deliberative assembly. Usually, the assembly sends matters into a _____ as a way to explore them more fully than would be possible if the assembly itself were considering them. _____ s may have different functions and their type of work differ depending on the type of the organization and its needs.

Exam Probability: **Medium**

26. *Answer choices:*
(see index for correct answer)

- a. Committee
- b. Meeting point
- c. Colloquy
- d. Future workshop

Guidance: level 1

:: Scientific method ::

In the social sciences and life sciences, a _____ is a research method involving an up-close, in-depth, and detailed examination of a subject of study , as well as its related contextual conditions.

Exam Probability: **Medium**

27. *Answer choices:*

(see index for correct answer)

- a. Case study
- b. explanatory research
- c. Causal research
- d. pilot project

Guidance: level 1

:: Marketing analytics ::

_____ is a long-term, forward-looking approach to planning with the fundamental goal of achieving a sustainable competitive advantage. Strategic planning involves an analysis of the company's strategic initial situation prior to the formulation, evaluation and selection of market-oriented competitive position that contributes to the company's goals and marketing objectives.

28. *Answer choices:*

(see index for correct answer)

- a. Marketing strategy
- b. Marketing mix modeling
- c. Mission-driven marketing
- d. Perceptual map

Guidance: level 1

:: ::

_____ is the extraction of valuable minerals or other geological materials from the earth, usually from an ore body, lode, vein, seam, reef or placer deposit. These deposits form a mineralized package that is of economic interest to the miner.

Exam Probability: **High**

29. *Answer choices:*

(see index for correct answer)

- a. cultural
- b. information systems assessment
- c. Sarbanes-Oxley act of 2002

- d. hierarchical perspective

Guidance: level 1

:: ::

_____ is "property consisting of land and the buildings on it, along with its natural resources such as crops, minerals or water; immovable property of this nature; an interest vested in this an item of real property, buildings or housing in general. Also: the business of _____ ; the profession of buying, selling, or renting land, buildings, or housing." It is a legal term used in jurisdictions whose legal system is derived from English common law, such as India, England, Wales, Northern Ireland, United States, Canada, Pakistan, Australia, and New Zealand.

Exam Probability: **Medium**

30. *Answer choices:*

(see index for correct answer)

- a. levels of analysis
- b. personal values
- c. information systems assessment
- d. Real estate

Guidance: level 1

:: Costs ::

In economics, _____ is the total economic cost of production and is made up of variable cost, which varies according to the quantity of a good produced and includes inputs such as labour and raw materials, plus fixed cost, which is independent of the quantity of a good produced and includes inputs that cannot be varied in the short term: fixed costs such as buildings and machinery, including sunk costs if any. Since cost is measured per unit of time, it is a flow variable.

Exam Probability: **Low**

31. *Answer choices:*

(see index for correct answer)

- a. Economic cost
- b. Search cost
- c. Further processing cost
- d. Explicit cost

Guidance: level 1

:: Marketing ::

_____ or stock control can be broadly defined as "the activity of checking a shop's stock." However, a more focused definition takes into account the more science-based, methodical practice of not only verifying a business' inventory but also focusing on the many related facets of inventory management "within an organisation to meet the demand placed upon that business economically." Other facets of _____ include supply chain management, production control, financial flexibility, and customer satisfaction. At the root of _____ , however, is the _____ problem, which involves determining when to order, how much to order, and the logistics of those decisions.

Exam Probability: **High**

32. *Answer choices:*

(see index for correct answer)

- a. Alpha consumer
- b. Consumer-to-business
- c. Gatefold
- d. Online ethnography

Guidance: level 1

:: ::

_____ is an American restaurant chain and international franchise which was founded in 1958 by Dan and Frank Carney. The company is known for its Italian-American cuisine menu, including pizza and pasta, as well as side dishes and desserts. _____ has 18,431 restaurants worldwide as of December 31, 2018, making it the world's largest pizza chain in terms of locations. It is a subsidiary of Yum! Brands, Inc., one of the world's largest restaurant companies.

Exam Probability: **Medium**

33. *Answer choices:*

(see index for correct answer)

- a. Pizza Hut
- b. surface-level diversity
- c. functional perspective
- d. open system

Guidance: level 1

:: Business law ::

A _____ is a business entity created by two or more parties, generally characterized by shared ownership, shared returns and risks, and shared governance. Companies typically pursue _____ s for one of four reasons: to access a new market, particularly emerging markets; to gain scale efficiencies by combining assets and operations; to share risk for major investments or projects; or to access skills and capabilities.

34. *Answer choices:*

(see index for correct answer)

- a. Retroactive overtime
- b. Consignment agreement
- c. Partnership
- d. Joint venture

Guidance: level 1

:: E-commerce ::

_____ is the activity of buying or selling of products on online services or over the Internet. Electronic commerce draws on technologies such as mobile commerce, electronic funds transfer, supply chain management, Internet marketing, online transaction processing, electronic data interchange , inventory management systems, and automated data collection systems.

Exam Probability: **Low**

35. *Answer choices:*

(see index for correct answer)

- a. E-commerce
- b. AsiaPay

- c. Mobilpenge
- d. Travel website

Guidance: level 1

:: E-commerce ::

The phrase _____ was originally coined in 1997 by Kevin Duffey at the launch of the Global _____ Forum, to mean "the delivery of electronic commerce capabilities directly into the consumer's hand, anywhere, via wireless technology." Many choose to think of _____ as meaning "a retail outlet in your customer's pocket."

Exam Probability: **Low**

36. *Answer choices:*

(see index for correct answer)

- a. Mobile commerce
- b. Virtual currency
- c. Transport Layer Security
- d. Government-to-government

Guidance: level 1

:: ::

A _____ manages, commands, directs, or regulates the behavior of other devices or systems using control loops. It can range from a single home heating controller using a thermostat controlling a domestic boiler to large Industrial _____ s which are used for controlling processes or machines.

Exam Probability: **Low**

37. *Answer choices:*

(see index for correct answer)

- a. Character
- b. Control system
- c. hierarchical perspective
- d. similarity-attraction theory

Guidance: level 1

:: Quality management ::

_____ ensures that an organization, product or service is consistent. It has four main components: quality planning, quality assurance, quality control and quality improvement. _____ is focused not only on product and service quality, but also on the means to achieve it. _____ , therefore, uses quality assurance and control of processes as well as products to achieve more consistent quality. What a customer wants and is willing to pay for it determines quality. It is written or unwritten commitment to a known or unknown consumer in the market . Thus, quality can be defined as fitness for intended use or, in other words, how well the product performs its intended function

38. *Answer choices:*

(see index for correct answer)

- a. Quality circle
- b. ISO 9000
- c. Quality management system
- d. Quality management

Guidance: level 1

:: E-commerce ::

_____ is a type of performance-based marketing in which a business rewards one or more affiliates for each visitor or customer brought by the affiliate's own marketing efforts.

Exam Probability: **Medium**

39. *Answer choices:*

(see index for correct answer)

- a. Cart32
- b. Feefighters
- c. Affiliate marketing
- d. Inventory Information Approval System

:: Business models ::

A _____ is "an autonomous association of persons united voluntarily to meet their common economic, social, and cultural needs and aspirations through a jointly-owned and democratically-controlled enterprise". _____ s may include.

Exam Probability: **High**

40. *Answer choices:*

(see index for correct answer)

- a. Interactive contract manufacturing
- b. Subscription business model
- c. Free-to-play
- d. Cooperative

:: ::

_____ is the collection of techniques, skills, methods, and processes used in the production of goods or services or in the accomplishment of objectives, such as scientific investigation. _____ can be the knowledge of techniques, processes, and the like, or it can be embedded in machines to allow for operation without detailed knowledge of their workings. Systems applying _____ by taking an input, changing it according to the system's use, and then producing an outcome are referred to as _____ systems or technological systems.

Exam Probability: **Medium**

41. *Answer choices:*

(see index for correct answer)

- a. Technology
- b. deep-level diversity
- c. corporate values
- d. open system

Guidance: level 1

:: Minimum wage ::

A _____ is the lowest remuneration that employers can legally pay their workers—the price floor below which workers may not sell their labor. Most countries had introduced _____ legislation by the end of the 20th century.

42. *Answer choices:*

(see index for correct answer)

- a. Minimum wage in Taiwan
- b. Minimum wage
- c. Minimum wage in the United States
- d. Guaranteed minimum income

Guidance: level 1

:: ::

A trade fair is an exhibition organized so that companies in a specific industry can showcase and demonstrate their latest products and services, meet with industry partners and customers, study activities of rivals, and examine recent market trends and opportunities. In contrast to consumer fairs, only some trade fairs are open to the public, while others can only be attended by company representatives and members of the press, therefore _____ s are classified as either "public" or "trade only". A few fairs are hybrids of the two; one example is the Frankfurt Book Fair, which is trade only for its first three days and open to the general public on its final two days. They are held on a continuing basis in virtually all markets and normally attract companies from around the globe. For example, in the U.S., there are currently over 10,000 _____ s held every year, and several online directories have been established to help organizers, attendees, and marketers identify appropriate events.

43. *Answer choices:*

(see index for correct answer)

- a. Trade show
- b. surface-level diversity
- c. open system
- d. hierarchical perspective

Guidance: level 1

:: E-commerce ::

Customer to customer markets provide an innovative way to allow customers to interact with each other. Traditional markets require business to customer relationships, in which a customer goes to the business in order to purchase a product or service. In customer to customer markets, the business facilitates an environment where customers can sell goods or services to each other. Other types of markets include business to business and business to customer .

Exam Probability: **Low**

44. *Answer choices:*

(see index for correct answer)

- a. PagSeguro
- b. Government-to-government
- c. Cyberservices
- d. Free Shipping Day

:: Contract law ::

A _____ is a legally-binding agreement which recognises and governs the rights and duties of the parties to the agreement. A _____ is legally enforceable because it meets the requirements and approval of the law. An agreement typically involves the exchange of goods, services, money, or promises of any of those. In the event of breach of _____ , the law awards the injured party access to legal remedies such as damages and cancellation.

Exam Probability: **Low**

45. *Answer choices:*

(see index for correct answer)

- a. Redhibition
- b. Performance Based Contracting
- c. Posting rule
- d. Contract

:: ::

_____ is an emotion involving pleasure, , or anxiety in considering or awaiting an expected event.

Exam Probability: **Low**

46. *Answer choices:*

(see index for correct answer)

- a. information systems assessment
- b. functional perspective
- c. Anticipation
- d. hierarchical

Guidance: level 1

:: Information technology management ::

_____ s or pop-ups are forms of online advertising on the World Wide Web. A pop-up is a graphical user interface display area, usually a small window, that suddenly appears in the foreground of the visual interface. The pop-up window containing an advertisement is usually generated by JavaScript that uses cross-site scripting , sometimes with a secondary payload that uses Adobe Flash. They can also be generated by other vulnerabilities/security holes in browser security.

Exam Probability: **Medium**

47. *Answer choices:*

(see index for correct answer)

- a. Battle command knowledge system
- b. ODMA
- c. Pop-up ad
- d. Electronic document and records management system

Guidance: level 1

:: Management ::

_____ is the process of thinking about the activities required to achieve a desired goal. It is the first and foremost activity to achieve desired results. It involves the creation and maintenance of a plan, such as psychological aspects that require conceptual skills. There are even a couple of tests to measure someone's capability of _____ well. As such, _____ is a fundamental property of intelligent behavior An important further meaning, often just called " _____ " is the legal context of permitted building developments.

Exam Probability: **High**

48. *Answer choices:*

(see index for correct answer)

- a. Iterative and incremental development
- b. Matrix management

- c. Production flow analysis
- d. Planning

Guidance: level 1

:: Business law ::

The _____ , first published in 1952, is one of a number of Uniform Acts that have been established as law with the goal of harmonizing the laws of sales and other commercial transactions across the United States of America through UCC adoption by all 50 states, the District of Columbia, and the Territories of the United States.

Exam Probability: **High**

49. *Answer choices:*

(see index for correct answer)

- a. Lessor
- b. Equity of redemption
- c. Uniform Commercial Code
- d. Free agent

Guidance: level 1

:: Statutory law ::

_____ or statute law is written law set down by a body of legislature or by a singular legislator . This is as opposed to oral or customary law; or regulatory law promulgated by the executive or common law of the judiciary. Statutes may originate with national, state legislatures or local municipalities.

Exam Probability: **Medium**

50. *Answer choices:*

(see index for correct answer)

- a. statute law
- b. incorporation by reference
- c. ratification
- d. Statute of repose

Guidance: level 1

:: Dot-com bubble ::

_____ was an online grocery business that filed bankruptcy in 2001 after 3 years of operation and was later folded into Amazon.com. It was headquartered in Foster City, California, United States. It delivered products to customers' homes within a 30-minute window of their choosing. At its peak, it offered service in ten US markets: the San Francisco Bay Area; Dallas; Sacramento; San Diego; Los Angeles; Orange County, California; Chicago; Seattle; Portland, Oregon; and Atlanta, Georgia. The company had hoped to expand to 26 cities by 2001.

51. *Answer choices:*

(see index for correct answer)

- a. Lycos
- b. Pay to surf
- c. GeoCities
- d. AllAdvantage

Guidance: level 1

:: E-commerce ::

_____ is a method of e-commerce where shoppers' friends become involved in the shopping experience. _____ attempts to use technology to mimic the social interactions found in physical malls and stores. With the rise of mobile devices, _____ is now extending beyond the online world and into the offline world of shopping.

Exam Probability: **Low**

52. *Answer choices:*

(see index for correct answer)

- a. Foodie.fm
- b. Braintree

- c. Interactive Financial Exchange
- d. Social shopping

Guidance: level 1

:: Retailing ::

A _____ or trolley , also known by a variety of other names, is a cart supplied by a shop, especially supermarkets, for use by customers inside the shop for transport of merchandise to the checkout counter during shopping. In many cases customers can then also use the cart to transport their purchased goods to their vehicles, but some carts are designed to prevent them from leaving the shop.

Exam Probability: **Low**

53. *Answer choices:*

(see index for correct answer)

- a. Shopping concierge
- b. Warehouse store
- c. Chain store
- d. Vermaport

Guidance: level 1

:: Basic financial concepts ::

_____ is a sustained increase in the general price level of goods and services in an economy over a period of time. When the general price level rises, each unit of currency buys fewer goods and services; consequently, _____ reflects a reduction in the purchasing power per unit of money a loss of real value in the medium of exchange and unit of account within the economy. The measure of _____ is the _____ rate, the annualized percentage change in a general price index, usually the consumer price index, over time. The opposite of _____ is deflation.

Exam Probability: **Low**

54. *Answer choices:*

(see index for correct answer)

- a. balloon payment
- b. Inflation
- c. Forward guidance
- d. Leverage cycle

Guidance: level 1

:: Commerce ::

_____ , Inc. is an American media-services provider headquartered in Los Gatos, California, founded in 1997 by Reed Hastings and Marc Randolph in Scotts Valley, California. The company's primary business is its subscription-based streaming OTT service which offers online streaming of a library of films and television programs, including those produced in-house. As of April 2019, _____ had over 148 million paid subscriptions worldwide, including 60 million in the United States, and over 154 million subscriptions total including free trials. It is available almost worldwide except in mainland China as well as Syria, North Korea, and Crimea . The company also has offices in the Netherlands, Brazil, India, Japan, and South Korea. _____ is a member of the Motion Picture Association of America .

Exam Probability: **Medium**

55. *Answer choices:*

(see index for correct answer)

- a. RFM
- b. Netflix
- c. Recommerce
- d. Sales quote

Guidance: level 1

:: Theories ::

A _____ union is a type of multinational political union where negotiated power is delegated to an authority by governments of member states.

56. *Answer choices:*

(see index for correct answer)

- a. Taylorism
- b. Supranational

Guidance: level 1

:: International trade ::

In finance, an _____ is the rate at which one currency will be exchanged for another. It is also regarded as the value of one country's currency in relation to another currency. For example, an interbank _____ of 114 Japanese yen to the United States dollar means that ¥114 will be exchanged for each US$1 or that US$1 will be exchanged for each ¥114. In this case it is said that the price of a dollar in relation to yen is ¥114, or equivalently that the price of a yen in relation to dollars is $1/114.

Exam Probability: **High**

57. *Answer choices:*

(see index for correct answer)

- a. Exchange rate
- b. Balassa index
- c. Nordic Innovation

- d. Special drawing rights

Guidance: level 1

:: Export and import control ::

" _____ " means the Government Service which is responsible for the administration of _____ law and the collection of duties and taxes and which also has the responsibility for the application of other laws and regulations relating to the importation, exportation, movement or storage of goods.

Exam Probability: **High**

58. *Answer choices:*
(see index for correct answer)

- a. Canadian Export and Import Controls Bureau
- b. Customs valuation
- c. Riding officer
- d. Customs

Guidance: level 1

:: Marketing ::

The _____ is a foundation model for businesses. The _____ has been defined as the "set of marketing tools that the firm uses to pursue its marketing objectives in the target market". Thus the _____ refers to four broad levels of marketing decision, namely: product, price, place, and promotion. Marketing practice has been occurring for millennia, but marketing theory emerged in the early twentieth century. The contemporary _____ , or the 4 Ps, which has become the dominant framework for marketing management decisions, was first published in 1960. In services marketing, an extended _____ is used, typically comprising 7 Ps, made up of the original 4 Ps extended by process, people, and physical evidence. Occasionally service marketers will refer to 8 Ps, comprising these 7 Ps plus performance.

Exam Probability: **Medium**

59. *Answer choices:*

(see index for correct answer)

- a. Marketing mix
- b. Hype cycle
- c. Product category volume
- d. Movie packaging

Guidance: level 1

Business ethics

Business ethics (also known as corporate ethics) is a form of applied ethics or professional ethics, that examines ethical principles and moral or ethical problems that can arise in a business environment. It applies to all aspects of business conduct and is relevant to the conduct of individuals and entire organizations. These ethics originate from individuals, organizational statements or from the legal system. These norms, values, ethical, and unethical practices are what is used to guide business. They help those businesses maintain a better connection with their stakeholders.

:: ::

_____ or accountancy is the measurement, processing, and communication of financial information about economic entities such as businesses and corporations. The modern field was established by the Italian mathematician Luca Pacioli in 1494. _____ , which has been called the "language of business", measures the results of an organization`s economic activities and conveys this information to a variety of users, including investors, creditors, management, and regulators. Practitioners of _____ are known as accountants. The terms " _____ " and "financial reporting" are often used as synonyms.

Exam Probability: **Medium**

1. *Answer choices:*

(see index for correct answer)

- a. cultural
- b. functional perspective
- c. Accounting
- d. Sarbanes-Oxley act of 2002

Guidance: level 1

:: ::

The _____ was a severe worldwide economic depression that took place mostly during the 1930s, beginning in the United States. The timing of the _____ varied across nations; in most countries it started in 1929 and lasted until the late-1930s. It was the longest, deepest, and most widespread depression of the 20th century. In the 21st century, the _____ is commonly used as an example of how intensely the world's economy can decline.

Exam Probability: Low

2. *Answer choices:*

(see index for correct answer)

- a. imperative
- b. process perspective
- c. cultural
- d. Great Depression

Guidance: level 1

:: Minimum wage ::

The _____ are working people whose incomes fall below a given poverty line due to lack of work hours and/or low wages.Largely because they are earning such low wages, the _____ face numerous obstacles that make it difficult for many of them to find and keep a job, save up money, and maintain a sense of self-worth.

Exam Probability: Low

3. *Answer choices:*

(see index for correct answer)

- a. Guaranteed minimum income
- b. National Anti-Sweating League
- c. Minimum wage in Taiwan
- d. Working poor

Guidance: level 1

:: ::

_____ in the United States is a federal and state program that helps with medical costs for some people with limited income and resources. _____ also offers benefits not normally covered by Medicare, including nursing home care and personal care services. The Health Insurance Association of America describes _____ as "a government insurance program for persons of all ages whose income and resources are insufficient to pay for health care." _____ is the largest source of funding for medical and health-related services for people with low income in the United States, providing free health insurance to 74 million low-income and disabled people as of 2017. It is a means-tested program that is jointly funded by the state and federal governments and managed by the states, with each state currently having broad leeway to determine who is eligible for its implementation of the program. States are not required to participate in the program, although all have since 1982. _____ recipients must be U.S. citizens or qualified non-citizens, and may include low-income adults, their children, and people with certain disabilities. Poverty alone does not necessarily qualify someone for _____ .

Exam Probability: **Low**

4. *Answer choices:*

(see index for correct answer)

- a. functional perspective
- b. empathy
- c. imperative
- d. similarity-attraction theory

Guidance: level 1

:: Water law ::

The _____ is the primary federal law in the United States governing water pollution. Its objective is to restore and maintain the chemical, physical, and biological integrity of the nation's waters; recognizing the responsibilities of the states in addressing pollution and providing assistance to states to do so, including funding for publicly owned treatment works for the improvement of wastewater treatment; and maintaining the integrity of wetlands. It is one of the United States' first and most influential modern environmental laws. As with many other major U.S. federal environmental statutes, it is administered by the U.S. Environmental Protection Agency , in coordination with state governments. Its implementing regulations are codified at 40 C.F.R. Subchapters D, N, and O .

Exam Probability: **High**

5. *Answer choices:*

(see index for correct answer)

- a. The Helsinki Rules on the Uses of the Waters of International Rivers
- b. Berlin Rules on Water Resources
- c. Water right
- d. Clean Water Act

Guidance: level 1

:: Anti-capitalism ::

_____ is a range of economic and social systems characterised by social ownership of the means of production and workers' self-management, as well as the political theories and movements associated with them. Social ownership can be public, collective or cooperative ownership, or citizen ownership of equity. There are many varieties of _____ and there is no single definition encapsulating all of them, with social ownership being the common element shared by its various forms.

Exam Probability: **Low**

6. *Answer choices:*
(see index for correct answer)

- a. Social anarchism
- b. No War but the Class War
- c. Socialism
- d. Left anarchism

Guidance: level 1

:: False advertising law ::

The Lanham Act is the primary federal trademark statute of law in the United States. The Act prohibits a number of activities, including trademark infringement, trademark dilution, and false advertising.

Exam Probability: **Low**

7. *Answer choices:*

(see index for correct answer)

- a. POM Wonderful LLC v. Coca-Cola Co.
- b. Lanham Act

Guidance: level 1

:: Product certification ::

_____ is food produced by methods that comply with the standards of organic farming. Standards vary worldwide, but organic farming features practices that cycle resources, promote ecological balance, and conserve biodiversity. Organizations regulating organic products may restrict the use of certain pesticides and fertilizers in the farming methods used to produce such products. _____ s typically are not processed using irradiation, industrial solvents, or synthetic food additives.

8. *Answer choices:*

(see index for correct answer)

- a. NEMKO
- b. Type approval
- c. British Approvals Board for Telecommunications
- d. Organic food

Guidance: level 1

:: Culture ::

_____ is a society which is characterized by individualism, which is the prioritization or emphasis, of the individual over the entire group. _____ s are oriented around the self, being independent instead of identifying with a group mentality. They see each other as only loosely linked, and value personal goals over group interests. _____ s tend to have a more diverse population and are characterized with emphasis on personal achievements, and a rational assessment of both the beneficial and detrimental aspects of relationships with others. _____ s have such unique aspects of communication as being a low power-distance culture and having a low-context communication style. The United States, Australia, Great Britain, Canada, the Netherlands, and New Zealand have been identified as highly _____ s.

9. *Answer choices:*

(see index for correct answer)

- a. Low-context culture
- b. cultural framework
- c. Individualistic culture
- d. High-context

Guidance: level 1

:: Hazard analysis ::

Broadly speaking, a _____ is the combined effort of 1. identifying and analyzing potential events that may negatively impact individuals, assets, and/or the environment ; and 2. making judgments "on the tolerability of the risk on the basis of a risk analysis" while considering influencing factors . Put in simpler terms, a _____ analyzes what can go wrong, how likely it is to happen, what the potential consequences are, and how tolerable the identified risk is. As part of this process, the resulting determination of risk may be expressed in a quantitative or qualitative fashion. The _____ is an inherent part of an overall risk management strategy, which attempts to, after a _____ , "introduce control measures to eliminate or reduce" any potential risk-related consequences.

Exam Probability: **High**

10. *Answer choices:*

(see index for correct answer)

- a. Risk assessment

- b. Swiss cheese model
- c. Hazardous Materials Identification System

Guidance: level 1

:: United States federal defense and national security legislation ::

The USA _____ is an Act of the U.S. Congress that was signed into law by President George W. Bush on October 26, 2001. The title of the Act is a contrived three letter initialism preceding a seven letter acronym , which in combination stand for Uniting and Strengthening America by Providing Appropriate Tools Required to Intercept and Obstruct Terrorism Act of 2001. The acronym was created by a 23 year old Congressional staffer, Chris Kyle.

Exam Probability: **Medium**

11. *Answer choices:*

(see index for correct answer)

- a. Export Administration Act
- b. Patriot Act

Guidance: level 1

:: ::

_____ is a non-governmental environmental organization with offices in over 39 countries and an international coordinating body in Amsterdam, the Netherlands. _____ was founded in 1971 by Irving Stowe, and Dorothy Stowe, Canadian and US ex-pat environmental activists. _____ states its goal is to "ensure the ability of the Earth to nurture life in all its diversity" and focuses its campaigning on worldwide issues such as climate change, deforestation, overfishing, commercial whaling, genetic engineering, and anti-nuclear issues. It uses direct action, lobbying, research, and ecotage to achieve its goals. The global organization does not accept funding from governments, corporations, or political parties, relying on three million individual supporters and foundation grants. _____ has a general consultative status with the United Nations Economic and Social Council and is a founding member of the INGO Accountability Charter, an international non-governmental organization that intends to foster accountability and transparency of non-governmental organizations.

Exam Probability: **Medium**

12. *Answer choices:*

(see index for correct answer)

- a. levels of analysis
- b. similarity-attraction theory
- c. interpersonal communication
- d. deep-level diversity

Guidance: level 1

:: Progressive Era in the United States ::

The Clayton Antitrust Act of 1914 , was a part of United States antitrust law .
with the goal of adding further substance to the U.S. antitrust law regime; the
_____ sought to prevent anticompetitive practices in their incipiency.
That regime started with the Sherman Antitrust Act of 1890, the first Federal
law outlawing practices considered harmful to consumers . The _____
specified particular prohibited conduct, the three-level enforcement scheme,
the exemptions, and the remedial measures.

Exam Probability: **Low**

13. *Answer choices:*

(see index for correct answer)

- a. pragmatism
- b. Clayton Act
- c. Clayton Antitrust Act

Guidance: level 1

:: Professional ethics ::

In the mental health field, a _____ is a situation where multiple roles exist between a therapist, or other mental health practitioner, and a client. _____ s are also referred to as multiple relationships, and these two terms are used interchangeably in the research literature. The American Psychological Association Ethical Principles of Psychologists and Code of Conduct is a resource that outlines ethical standards and principles to which practitioners are expected to adhere. Standard 3.05 of the APA ethics code outlines the definition of multiple relationships. Dual or multiple relationships occur when.

Exam Probability: **Low**

14. *Answer choices:*

(see index for correct answer)

- a. Continuous professional development
- b. ethical code
- c. Dual relationship

Guidance: level 1

:: Statutory law ::

_____ or statute law is written law set down by a body of legislature or by a singular legislator . This is as opposed to oral or customary law; or regulatory law promulgated by the executive or common law of the judiciary. Statutes may originate with national, state legislatures or local municipalities.

15. *Answer choices:*

(see index for correct answer)

- a. Statute of repose
- b. statute law
- c. ratification
- d. Statutory law

Guidance: level 1

:: Monopoly (economics) ::

A _____ is a form of intellectual property that gives its owner the legal right to exclude others from making, using, selling, and importing an invention for a limited period of years, in exchange for publishing an enabling public disclosure of the invention. In most countries _____ rights fall under civil law and the _____ holder needs to sue someone infringing the _____ in order to enforce his or her rights. In some industries _____ s are an essential form of competitive advantage; in others they are irrelevant.

Exam Probability: **High**

16. *Answer choices:*

(see index for correct answer)

- a. Patent
- b. Average cost pricing
- c. Competition Commission
- d. Ownership unbundling

Guidance: level 1

:: Socialism ::

_____ is a label used to define the first currents of modern socialist thought as exemplified by the work of Henri de Saint-Simon, Charles Fourier, Étienne Cabet and Robert Owen.

Exam Probability: **High**

17. *Answer choices:*

(see index for correct answer)

- a. Pinko
- b. 1917 Club
- c. Champagne socialist
- d. Utopian socialism

Guidance: level 1

:: Market-based policy instruments ::

Cause marketing is defined as a type of corporate social responsibility, in which a company's promotional campaign has the dual purpose of increasing profitability while bettering society.

Exam Probability: **Medium**

18. *Answer choices:*

(see index for correct answer)

- a. Cause-related marketing
- b. Fiscal localism
- c. Regional Clean Air Incentives Market
- d. Public choice

Guidance: level 1

:: ::

_____ , O.S.A. was a German professor of theology, composer, priest, monk, and a seminal figure in the Protestant Reformation.

Exam Probability: **Medium**

19. *Answer choices:*

(see index for correct answer)

- a. interpersonal communication
- b. process perspective
- c. Martin Luther
- d. functional perspective

Guidance: level 1

:: ::

MCI, Inc. was an American telecommunication corporation, currently a subsidiary of Verizon Communications, with its main office in Ashburn, Virginia. The corporation was formed originally as a result of the merger of _____ and MCI Communications corporations, and used the name MCI _____ , succeeded by _____ , before changing its name to the present version on April 12, 2003, as part of the corporation's ending of its bankruptcy status. The company traded on NASDAQ as WCOM and MCIP . The corporation was purchased by Verizon Communications with the deal finalizing on January 6, 2006, and is now identified as that company's Verizon Enterprise Solutions division with the local residential divisions being integrated slowly into local Verizon subsidiaries.

Exam Probability: **Low**

20. *Answer choices:*

(see index for correct answer)

- a. process perspective
- b. WorldCom
- c. functional perspective

- d. empathy

Guidance: level 1

:: Electronic waste ::

_____ or e-waste describes discarded electrical or electronic devices. Used electronics which are destined for refurbishment, reuse, resale, salvage, recycling through material recovery, or disposal are also considered e-waste. Informal processing of e-waste in developing countries can lead to adverse human health effects and environmental pollution.

Exam Probability: **High**

21. *Answer choices:*

(see index for correct answer)

- a. Computer liquidator
- b. Digger gold
- c. Electronic waste
- d. Solving the E-waste Problem

Guidance: level 1

:: Corporate scandals ::

Exxon Mobil Corporation, doing business as _____ , is an American multinational oil and gas corporation headquartered in Irving, Texas. It is the largest direct descendant of John D. Rockefeller's Standard Oil Company, and was formed on November 30, 1999 by the merger of Exxon and Mobil . _____ 's primary brands are Exxon, Mobil, Esso, and _____ Chemical.

Exam Probability: **Low**

22. *Answer choices:*

(see index for correct answer)

- a. ExxonMobil
- b. Cash for comment affair
- c. Overseas Trust Bank
- d. Great Phenol Plot

Guidance: level 1

:: Business ethics ::

A _____ is a person who exposes any kind of information or activity that is deemed illegal, unethical, or not correct within an organization that is either private or public. The information of alleged wrongdoing can be classified in many ways: violation of company policy/rules, law, regulation, or threat to public interest/national security, as well as fraud, and corruption. Those who become _____ s can choose to bring information or allegations to surface either internally or externally. Internally, a _____ can bring his/her accusations to the attention of other people within the accused organization such as an immediate supervisor. Externally, a _____ can bring allegations to light by contacting a third party outside of an accused organization such as the media, government, law enforcement, or those who are concerned. _____ s, however, take the risk of facing stiff reprisal and retaliation from those who are accused or alleged of wrongdoing.

Exam Probability: **High**

23. *Answer choices:*
(see index for correct answer)

- a. Society of Corporate Compliance and Ethics
- b. CUC International
- c. Corporate Knights
- d. Creative destruction

Guidance: level 1

:: ::

The _____ to Fight AIDS, Tuberculosis and Malaria is an international financing organization that aims to "attract, leverage and invest additional resources to end the epidemics of HIV/AIDS, tuberculosis and malaria to support attainment of the Sustainable Development Goals established by the United Nations." A public-private partnership, the organization maintains its secretariat in Geneva, Switzerland. The organization began operations in January 2002. Microsoft founder Bill Gates was one of the first private foundations among many bilateral donors to provide seed money for the partnership.

Exam Probability: **High**

24. *Answer choices:*

(see index for correct answer)

- a. Global Fund
- b. surface-level diversity
- c. personal values
- d. information systems assessment

Guidance: level 1

:: Business law ::

A _____ is an arrangement where parties, known as partners, agree to cooperate to advance their mutual interests. The partners in a _____ may be individuals, businesses, interest-based organizations, schools, governments or combinations. Organizations may partner to increase the likelihood of each achieving their mission and to amplify their reach. A _____ may result in issuing and holding equity or may be only governed by a contract.

Exam Probability: **Low**

25. *Answer choices:*

(see index for correct answer)

- a. Statutory liability
- b. Perfection
- c. Partnership
- d. Court auction

Guidance: level 1

:: Corporate scandals ::

_____ was a bank based in the Caribbean, which operated from 1986 to 2009 when it went into receivership. It was an affiliate of the Stanford Financial Group and failed when the its parent was seized by United States authorities in early 2009 as part of the investigation into Allen Stanford.

Exam Probability: **High**

26. *Answer choices:*

(see index for correct answer)

- a. Stanford International Bank
- b. Barings Bank
- c. Patent encumbrance of large automotive NiMH batteries
- d. Crawford Texas Peace House

Guidance: level 1

:: Financial markets ::

The _____ is a United States federal government organization, established by Title I of the Dodd–Frank Wall Street Reform and Consumer Protection Act, which was signed into law by President Barack Obama on July 21, 2010. The Office of Financial Research is intended to provide support to the council.

Exam Probability: **Medium**

27. *Answer choices:*

(see index for correct answer)

- a. Floor broker
- b. Odd lot
- c. Exchange of futures for physicals
- d. Time-weighted average price

:: ::

_____ is a naturally occurring, yellowish-black liquid found in geological formations beneath the Earth's surface. It is commonly refined into various types of fuels. Components of _____ are separated using a technique called fractional distillation, i.e. separation of a liquid mixture into fractions differing in boiling point by means of distillation, typically using a fractionating column.

Exam Probability: **Medium**

28. *Answer choices:*

(see index for correct answer)

- a. deep-level diversity
- b. co-culture
- c. levels of analysis
- d. personal values

Guidance: level 1

:: Anti-competitive behaviour ::

_____ is a secret cooperation or deceitful agreement in order to deceive others, although not necessarily illegal, as a conspiracy. A secret agreement between two or more parties to limit open competition by deceiving, misleading, or defrauding others of their legal rights, or to obtain an objective forbidden by law typically by defrauding or gaining an unfair market advantage is an example of _____ . It is an agreement among firms or individuals to divide a market, set prices, limit production or limit opportunities.It can involve "unions, wage fixing, kickbacks, or misrepresenting the independence of the relationship between the colluding parties". In legal terms, all acts effected by _____ are considered void.

Exam Probability: **High**

29. *Answer choices:*

(see index for correct answer)

- a. Collusion
- b. Killer bees
- c. price maintenance
- d. Institute for Consumer Antitrust Studies

Guidance: level 1

:: Mortgage ::

In finance, _____ means making loans to people who may have difficulty maintaining the repayment schedule, sometimes reflecting setbacks, such as unemployment, divorce, medical emergencies, etc. Historically, subprime borrowers were defined as having FICO scores below 600, although "this has varied over time and circumstances."

Exam Probability: **High**

30. *Answer choices:*

(see index for correct answer)

- a. Subprime lending
- b. Ship mortgage
- c. Tracker mortgage
- d. Cash out

Guidance: level 1

:: ::

Oriental Nicety, formerly _____ , Exxon Mediterranean, SeaRiver
Mediterranean, S/R Mediterranean, Mediterranean, and Dong Fang Ocean, was an
oil tanker that gained notoriety after running aground in Prince William Sound
spilling hundreds of thousands of barrels of crude oil in Alaska. On March 24,
1989, while owned by the former Exxon Shipping Company, and captained by Joseph
Hazelwood and First Mate James Kunkel bound for Long Beach, California, the
vessel ran aground on the Bligh Reef resulting in the second largest oil spill
in United States history. The size of the spill is estimated to have been
40,900 to 120,000 m3 , or 257,000 to 750,000 barrels. In 1989, the _____
oil spill was listed as the 54th largest spill in history.

Exam Probability: **Medium**

31. *Answer choices:*

(see index for correct answer)

- a. corporate values
- b. personal values
- c. information systems assessment
- d. Exxon Valdez

Guidance: level 1

:: Nepotism ::

_____ is the granting of favour to relatives in various fields, including business, politics, entertainment, sports, religion and other activities. The term originated with the assignment of nephews to important positions by Catholic popes and bishops. Trading parliamentary employment for favors is a modern-day example of _____ . Criticism of _____ , however, can be found in ancient Indian texts such as the Kural literature.

Exam Probability: **Medium**

32. *Answer choices:*

(see index for correct answer)

- a. Ethnic nepotism
- b. Crachach
- c. Cardinal-nephew
- d. Nepotism

Guidance: level 1

:: Fraud ::

In law, _____ is intentional deception to secure unfair or unlawful gain, or to deprive a victim of a legal right. _____ can violate civil law , a criminal law , or it may cause no loss of money, property or legal right but still be an element of another civil or criminal wrong. The purpose of _____ may be monetary gain or other benefits, for example by obtaining a passport, travel document, or driver's license, or mortgage _____ , where the perpetrator may attempt to qualify for a mortgage by way of false statements.

33. *Answer choices:*

(see index for correct answer)

- a. Customer not present
- b. Fraud
- c. Accreditation mill
- d. Missing trader fraud

Guidance: level 1

:: ::

_____ ism is a form of government characterized by strong central power and limited political freedoms. Individual freedoms are subordinate to the state and there is no constitutional accountability and rule of law under an _____ regime. _____ regimes can be autocratic with power concentrated in one person or it can be more spread out between multiple officials and government institutions. Juan Linz's influential 1964 description of _____ ism characterized _____ political systems by four qualities.

Exam Probability: **High**

34. *Answer choices:*

(see index for correct answer)

- a. Authoritarian
- b. imperative
- c. empathy
- d. hierarchical perspective

Guidance: level 1

:: ::

An _____ is the release of a liquid petroleum hydrocarbon into the environment, especially the marine ecosystem, due to human activity, and is a form of pollution. The term is usually given to marine _____ s, where oil is released into the ocean or coastal waters, but spills may also occur on land. _____ s may be due to releases of crude oil from tankers, offshore platforms, drilling rigs and wells, as well as spills of refined petroleum products and their by-products, heavier fuels used by large ships such as bunker fuel, or the spill of any oily refuse or waste oil.

Exam Probability: **Low**

35. *Answer choices:*

(see index for correct answer)

- a. Character
- b. similarity-attraction theory
- c. surface-level diversity
- d. open system

:: Public relations terminology ::

_____ , also called "green sheen", is a form of spin in which green PR or green marketing is deceptively used to promote the perception that an organization's products, aims or policies are environmentally friendly. Evidence that an organization is _____ often comes from pointing out the spending differences: when significantly more money or time has been spent advertising being "green" , than is actually spent on environmentally sound practices. _____ efforts can range from changing the name or label of a product to evoke the natural environment on a product that contains harmful chemicals to multimillion-dollar marketing campaigns portraying highly polluting energy companies as eco-friendly.Publicized accusations of _____ have contributed to the term's increasing use.

Exam Probability: **Low**

36. *Answer choices:*

(see index for correct answer)

- a. PR Gallery
- b. Junk science
- c. Greenwashing
- d. Corporate pathos

:: Management ::

The term _____ refers to measures designed to increase the degree of autonomy and self-determination in people and in communities in order to enable them to represent their interests in a responsible and self-determined way, acting on their own authority. It is the process of becoming stronger and more confident, especially in controlling one's life and claiming one's rights. _____ as action refers both to the process of self-_____ and to professional support of people, which enables them to overcome their sense of powerlessness and lack of influence, and to recognize and use their resources. To do work with power.

Exam Probability: **High**

37. *Answer choices:*

(see index for correct answer)

- a. Association management company
- b. Adhocracy
- c. Quality control
- d. Empowerment

Guidance: level 1

:: ::

The _____ , founded in 1912, is a private, nonprofit organization whose self-described mission is to focus on advancing marketplace trust, consisting of 106 independently incorporated local BBB organizations in the United States and Canada, coordinated under the Council of _____ s in Arlington, Virginia.

Exam Probability: **High**

38. *Answer choices:*

(see index for correct answer)

- a. surface-level diversity
- b. empathy
- c. Better Business Bureau
- d. similarity-attraction theory

Guidance: level 1

:: Decentralization ::

_____ or sub _____ mainly refers to the unrestricted growth in many urban areas of housing, commercial development, and roads over large expanses of land, with little concern for urban planning. In addition to describing a particular form of urbanization, the term also relates to the social and environmental consequences associated with this development. In Continental Europe the term "peri-urbanisation" is often used to denote similar dynamics and phenomena, although the term _____ is currently being used by the European Environment Agency. There is widespread disagreement about what constitutes sprawl and how to quantify it. For example, some commentators measure sprawl only with the average number of residential units per acre in a given area. But others associate it with decentralization , discontinuity , segregation of uses, and so forth.

Exam Probability: **High**

39. *Answer choices:*

(see index for correct answer)

- a. Appropriate technology
- b. Regional state
- c. Ziyad Baroud
- d. Middlebury Institute

Guidance: level 1

:: Cultural appropriation ::

_____ is a social and economic order that encourages the acquisition of goods and services in ever-increasing amounts. With the industrial revolution, but particularly in the 20th century, mass production led to an economic crisis: there was overproduction—the supply of goods would grow beyond consumer demand, and so manufacturers turned to planned obsolescence and advertising to manipulate consumer spending. In 1899, a book on _____ published by Thorstein Veblen, called The Theory of the Leisure Class, examined the widespread values and economic institutions emerging along with the widespread "leisure time" in the beginning of the 20th century. In it Veblen "views the activities and spending habits of this leisure class in terms of conspicuous and vicarious consumption and waste. Both are related to the display of status and not to functionality or usefulness."

Exam Probability: **Medium**

40. *Answer choices:*

(see index for correct answer)

- a. Aunt Jemima
- b. Washington Redskins
- c. California Indian Song
- d. Consumerism

Guidance: level 1

:: Cognitive biases ::

In personality psychology, _____ is the degree to which people believe that they have control over the outcome of events in their lives, as opposed to external forces beyond their control. Understanding of the concept was developed by Julian B. Rotter in 1954, and has since become an aspect of personality studies. A person's "locus" is conceptualized as internal or external .

Exam Probability: **High**

41. *Answer choices:*

(see index for correct answer)

- a. Base rate fallacy
- b. Out-group homogeneity
- c. Extension neglect
- d. Mistakes Were Made

Guidance: level 1

:: Real estate ::

_____ s serve several societal needs – primarily as shelter from weather, security, living space, privacy, to store belongings, and to comfortably live and work. A _____ as a shelter represents a physical division of the human habitat and the outside .

Exam Probability: **Low**

42. *Answer choices:*

(see index for correct answer)

- a. EcoBroker
- b. Golf property
- c. ReOS
- d. Lease administration

Guidance: level 1

:: Auditing ::

_____ is a general term that can reflect various types of evaluations intended to identify environmental compliance and management system implementation gaps, along with related corrective actions. In this way they perform an analogous function to financial audits. There are generally two different types of _____ s: compliance audits and management systems audits. Compliance audits tend to be the primary type in the US or within US-based multinationals.

Exam Probability: **Medium**

43. *Answer choices:*

(see index for correct answer)

- a. International Federation of Audit Bureaux of Circulations
- b. Software licensing audit
- c. Utility bill audit

- d. Environmental audit

Guidance: level 1

:: Patent law ::

A _____ is generally any statement intended to specify or delimit the scope of rights and obligations that may be exercised and enforced by parties in a legally recognized relationship. In contrast to other terms for legally operative language, the term _____ usually implies situations that involve some level of uncertainty, waiver, or risk.

Exam Probability: **Medium**

44. *Answer choices:*

(see index for correct answer)

- a. Defensive publication
- b. Disclaimer
- c. Backlog of unexamined patent applications
- d. Claim

Guidance: level 1

:: Majority–minority relations ::

_____ , also known as reservation in India and Nepal, positive discrimination / action in the United Kingdom, and employment equity in Canada and South Africa, is the policy of promoting the education and employment of members of groups that are known to have previously suffered from discrimination. Historically and internationally, support for _____ has sought to achieve goals such as bridging inequalities in employment and pay, increasing access to education, promoting diversity, and redressing apparent past wrongs, harms, or hindrances.

Exam Probability: **Low**

45. *Answer choices:*

(see index for correct answer)

- a. cultural Relativism
- b. cultural dissonance
- c. Affirmative action

Guidance: level 1

:: Management ::

_____ is the identification, evaluation, and prioritization of risks followed by coordinated and economical application of resources to minimize, monitor, and control the probability or impact of unfortunate events or to maximize the realization of opportunities.

Exam Probability: **High**

46. *Answer choices:*

(see index for correct answer)

- a. Risk management
- b. Millennium software
- c. Line management
- d. Critical path method

Guidance: level 1

:: ::

A _____ is an organization, usually a group of people or a company, authorized to act as a single entity and recognized as such in law. Early incorporated entities were established by charter . Most jurisdictions now allow the creation of new _____ s through registration.

Exam Probability: **High**

47. *Answer choices:*

(see index for correct answer)

- a. hierarchical perspective
- b. Corporation
- c. process perspective
- d. interpersonal communication

:: Power (social and political) ::

_____ is a form of reverence gained by a leader who has strong interpersonal relationship skills. _____ , as an aspect of personal power, becomes particularly important as organizational leadership becomes increasingly about collaboration and influence, rather than command and control.

Exam Probability: **Low**

48. *Answer choices:*

(see index for correct answer)

- a. Referent power
- b. need for power
- c. Expert power

:: Business ethics ::

_____ is a type of international private business self-regulation. While once it was possible to describe CSR as an internal organisational policy or a corporate ethic strategy, that time has passed as various international laws have been developed and various organisations have used their authority to push it beyond individual or even industry-wide initiatives. While it has been considered a form of corporate self-regulation for some time, over the last decade or so it has moved considerably from voluntary decisions at the level of individual organisations, to mandatory schemes at regional, national and even transnational levels.

Exam Probability: **High**

49. *Answer choices:*

(see index for correct answer)

- a. Society of Corporate Compliance and Ethics
- b. Accounting scandals
- c. Corporate social responsibility
- d. Financial privacy

Guidance: level 1

:: Workplace ::

In business management, _____ is a management style whereby a manager closely observes and/or controls the work of his/her subordinates or employees.

50. *Answer choices:*

(see index for correct answer)

- a. Workplace harassment
- b. Workplace listening
- c. Performance appraisal
- d. Workplace violence

Guidance: level 1

:: Writs ::

In common law, a writ of _____ is a writ whereby a private individual who assists a prosecution can receive all or part of any penalty imposed. Its name is an abbreviation of the Latin phrase _____ pro domino rege quam pro se ipso in hac parte sequitur, meaning "[he] who sues in this matter for the king as well as for himself."

Exam Probability: **Low**

51. *Answer choices:*

(see index for correct answer)

- a. Writ of assistance
- b. Writ of execution

:: ::

A _____ is the ability to carry out a task with determined results often within a given amount of time, energy, or both. _____ s can often be divided into domain-general and domain-specific _____ s. For example, in the domain of work, some general _____ s would include time management, teamwork and leadership, self-motivation and others, whereas domain-specific _____ s would be used only for a certain job. _____ usually requires certain environmental stimuli and situations to assess the level of _____ being shown and used.

Exam Probability: **High**

52. *Answer choices:*

(see index for correct answer)

- a. corporate values
- b. Skill
- c. hierarchical perspective
- d. information systems assessment

:: Labour law ::

An _____ is special or specified circumstances that partially or fully exempt a person or organization from performance of a legal obligation so as to avoid an unreasonable or disproportionate burden or obstacle.

Exam Probability: **Medium**

53. *Answer choices:*

(see index for correct answer)

- a. Unreported employment
- b. Principles of Labor Legislation
- c. Non-compete clause
- d. Undue hardship

Guidance: level 1

:: ::

In ecology, a _____ is the type of natural environment in which a particular species of organism lives. It is characterized by both physical and biological features. A species' _____ is those places where it can find food, shelter, protection and mates for reproduction.

Exam Probability: **Low**

54. *Answer choices:*

(see index for correct answer)

- a. information systems assessment
- b. open system
- c. hierarchical perspective
- d. Habitat

Guidance: level 1

:: ::

The _____ is an 1848 political pamphlet by the German philosophers Karl Marx and Friedrich Engels. Commissioned by the Communist League and originally published in London just as the Revolutions of 1848 began to erupt, the Manifesto was later recognised as one of the world's most influential political documents. It presents an analytical approach to the class struggle and the conflicts of capitalism and the capitalist mode of production, rather than a prediction of communism's potential future forms.

Exam Probability: **High**

55. *Answer choices:*
(see index for correct answer)

- a. Communist Manifesto
- b. co-culture
- c. interpersonal communication
- d. cultural

:: ::

_____ is the study and management of exchange relationships. _____ is the business process of creating relationships with and satisfying customers. With its focus on the customer, _____ is one of the premier components of business management.

Exam Probability: **High**

56. *Answer choices:*

(see index for correct answer)

- a. Sarbanes-Oxley act of 2002
- b. hierarchical perspective
- c. Character
- d. Marketing

:: Monopoly (economics) ::

The _____ of 1890 was a United States antitrust law that regulates competition among enterprises, which was passed by Congress under the presidency of Benjamin Harrison.

Exam Probability: **High**

57. *Answer choices:*

(see index for correct answer)

- a. Sherman Antitrust Act
- b. Monopoly
- c. Government-granted monopoly
- d. Coercive monopoly

Guidance: level 1

:: ::

A _____ is a proceeding by a party or parties against another in the civil court of law. The archaic term "suit in law" is found in only a small number of laws still in effect today. The term "_____" is used in reference to a civil action brought in a court of law in which a plaintiff, a party who claims to have incurred loss as a result of a defendant's actions, demands a legal or equitable remedy. The defendant is required to respond to the plaintiff's complaint. If the plaintiff is successful, judgment is in the plaintiff's favor, and a variety of court orders may be issued to enforce a right, award damages, or impose a temporary or permanent injunction to prevent an act or compel an act. A declaratory judgment may be issued to prevent future legal disputes.

Exam Probability: **High**

58. *Answer choices:*

(see index for correct answer)

- a. cultural
- b. Lawsuit
- c. functional perspective
- d. co-culture

Guidance: level 1

:: Employment compensation ::

A _____ is the minimum income necessary for a worker to meet their basic needs. Needs are defined to include food, housing, and other essential needs such as clothing. The goal of a _____ is to allow a worker to afford a basic but decent standard of living. Due to the flexible nature of the term "needs", there is not one universally accepted measure of what a _____ is and as such it varies by location and household type.

Exam Probability: **Medium**

59. *Answer choices:*

(see index for correct answer)

- a. Living wage
- b. Paid Educational Leave Convention, 1974

- c. Wage payment systems
- d. Pay-for-Performance

Guidance: level 1

Accounting

Accounting or accountancy is the measurement, processing, and communication of financial information about economic entities such as businesses and corporations. The modern field was established by the Italian mathematician Luca Pacioli in 1494. Accounting, which has been called the "language of business", measures the results of an organization's economic activities and conveys this information to a variety of users, including investors, creditors, management, and regulators.

:: Auditing ::

_____ , as defined by accounting and auditing, is a process for assuring of an organization's objectives in operational effectiveness and efficiency, reliable financial reporting, and compliance with laws, regulations and policies. A broad concept, _____ involves everything that controls risks to an organization.

Exam Probability: **High**

1. *Answer choices:*

(see index for correct answer)

- a. Audit storm
- b. International Register of Certificated Auditors
- c. Utility bill audit
- d. Internal control

Guidance: level 1

:: Commercial crimes ::

_____ is the act of withholding assets for the purpose of conversion of such assets, by one or more persons to whom the assets were entrusted, either to be held or to be used for specific purposes. _____ is a type of financial fraud. For example, a lawyer might embezzle funds from the trust accounts of their clients; a financial advisor might embezzle the funds of investors; and a husband or a wife might embezzle funds from a bank account jointly held with the spouse.

2. *Answer choices:*

(see index for correct answer)

- a. Pranknet
- b. Monopolization
- c. Embezzlement
- d. Price gouging

Guidance: level 1

:: Generally Accepted Accounting Principles ::

_____ is a small amount of discretionary funds in the form of cash used for expenditures where it is not sensible to make any disbursement by cheque, because of the inconvenience and costs of writing, signing, and then cashing the cheque.

Exam Probability: **Medium**

3. *Answer choices:*

(see index for correct answer)

- a. Generally accepted accounting principles
- b. Trial balance
- c. Operating profit

- d. Petty cash

Guidance: level 1

:: ::

_____ or accountancy is the measurement, processing, and communication of financial information about economic entities such as businesses and corporations. The modern field was established by the Italian mathematician Luca Pacioli in 1494. _____ , which has been called the "language of business", measures the results of an organization`s economic activities and conveys this information to a variety of users, including investors, creditors, management, and regulators. Practitioners of _____ are known as accountants. The terms " _____ " and "financial reporting" are often used as synonyms.

Exam Probability: **Medium**

4. *Answer choices:*

(see index for correct answer)

- a. similarity-attraction theory
- b. functional perspective
- c. Accounting
- d. open system

Guidance: level 1

:: ::

The _____ of 1934 is a law governing the secondary trading of
securities in the United States of America. A landmark of wide-ranging
legislation, the Act of '34 and related statutes form the basis of regulation
of the financial markets and their participants in the United States. The 1934
Act also established the Securities and Exchange Commission , the agency
primarily responsible for enforcement of United States federal securities law.

Exam Probability: **Medium**

5. *Answer choices:*

(see index for correct answer)

- a. process perspective
- b. levels of analysis
- c. empathy
- d. Securities Exchange Act

Guidance: level 1

:: Valuation (finance) ::

The _____ is one of three major groups of methodologies, called valuation approaches, used by appraisers. It is particularly common in commercial real estate appraisal and in business appraisal. The fundamental math is similar to the methods used for financial valuation, securities analysis, or bond pricing. However, there are some significant and important modifications when used in real estate or business valuation.

Exam Probability: **High**

6. *Answer choices:*

(see index for correct answer)

- a. Quantitative analyst
- b. Cyclically adjusted price-to-earnings ratio
- c. Graham number
- d. Income approach

Guidance: level 1

:: ::

The _____ or just chief executive , is the most senior corporate, executive, or administrative officer in charge of managing an organization especially an independent legal entity such as a company or nonprofit institution. CEOs lead a range of organizations, including public and private corporations, non-profit organizations and even some government organizations . The CEO of a corporation or company typically reports to the board of directors and is charged with maximizing the value of the entity, which may include maximizing the share price, market share, revenues or another element. In the non-profit and government sector, CEOs typically aim at achieving outcomes related to the organization's mission, such as reducing poverty, increasing literacy, etc.

Exam Probability: **Medium**

7. *Answer choices:*

(see index for correct answer)

- a. interpersonal communication
- b. imperative
- c. corporate values
- d. Chief executive officer

Guidance: level 1

:: ::

The U.S. _____ is an independent agency of the United States federal government. The SEC holds primary responsibility for enforcing the federal securities laws, proposing securities rules, and regulating the securities industry, the nation's stock and options exchanges, and other activities and organizations, including the electronic securities markets in the United States.

Exam Probability: **High**

8. *Answer choices:*

(see index for correct answer)

- a. process perspective
- b. deep-level diversity
- c. functional perspective
- d. co-culture

Guidance: level 1

:: Accounting ::

It is the period for which books are balanced and the financial statements are prepared. Generally, the _____ consists of 12 months. However the beginning of the _____ differs according to the jurisdiction. For example, one entity may follow the regular calendar year, i.e. January to December as the accounting year, while another entity may follow April to March as the _____.

9. *Answer choices:*

(see index for correct answer)

- a. Profit model
- b. CPA Site Solutions
- c. Cost allocation
- d. INPACT International

Guidance: level 1

:: Generally Accepted Accounting Principles ::

Financial statements prepared and presented by a company typically follow an external standard that specifically guides their preparation. These standards vary across the globe and are typically overseen by some combination of the private accounting profession in that specific nation and the various government regulators. Variations across countries may be considerable, making cross-country evaluation of financial data challenging.

Exam Probability: **Medium**

10. *Answer choices:*

(see index for correct answer)

- a. Earnings before interest, taxes, depreciation, and amortization
- b. Completed-contract method

- c. Generally Accepted Accounting Principles
- d. Fin 48

Guidance: level 1

:: Accounting systems ::

In accounting, the _____ is an account in the general ledger for which a corresponding subsidiary ledger has been created. The subsidiary ledger allows for tracking transactions within the _____ in more detail. Individual transactions are posted both to the _____ and the corresponding subsidiary ledger, and the totals for both are compared when preparing a trial balance to ensure accuracy.

Exam Probability: **Low**

11. *Answer choices:*

(see index for correct answer)

- a. control account
- b. Accounting practice
- c. Purchase ledger
- d. Controlling account

Guidance: level 1

:: Shareholders ::

A _____ is a payment made by a corporation to its shareholders, usually as a distribution of profits. When a corporation earns a profit or surplus, the corporation is able to re-invest the profit in the business and pay a proportion of the profit as a _____ to shareholders. Distribution to shareholders may be in cash or, if the corporation has a _____ reinvestment plan, the amount can be paid by the issue of further shares or share repurchase. When _____ s are paid, shareholders typically must pay income taxes, and the corporation does not receive a corporate income tax deduction for the _____ payments.

Exam Probability: **High**

12. *Answer choices:*

(see index for correct answer)

- a. Dividend
- b. Total shareholder return
- c. non-controlling interest
- d. Institutional Shareholder Services

Guidance: level 1

:: Accounting in the United States ::

_____ is the title of qualified accountants in numerous countries in the English-speaking world. In the United States, the CPA is a license to provide accounting services to the public. It is awarded by each of the 50 states for practice in that state. Additionally, almost every state has passed mobility laws to allow CPAs from other states to practice in their state. State licensing requirements vary, but the minimum standard requirements include passing the Uniform _____ Examination, 150 semester units of college education, and one year of accounting related experience.

Exam Probability: **Low**

13. *Answer choices:*

(see index for correct answer)

- a. Adjusted basis
- b. National Association of State Boards of Accountancy
- c. Financial Accounting Foundation
- d. Comprehensive Performance Assessment

Guidance: level 1

:: United States Generally Accepted Accounting Principles ::

In the United States, the _____ , Subpart F of the OMB Uniform Guidance, is a rigorous, organization-wide audit or examination of an entity that expends $750,000 or more of federal assistance received for its operations. Usually performed annually, the _____ 's objective is to provide assurance to the US federal government as to the management and use of such funds by recipients such as states, cities, universities, non-profit organizations, and Indian Tribes. The audit is typically performed by an independent certified public accountant and encompasses both financial and compliance components. The _____ s must be submitted to the Federal Audit Clearinghouse along with a data collection form, Form SF-SAC.

Exam Probability: **High**

14. *Answer choices:*

(see index for correct answer)

- a. Impaired asset
- b. Comprehensive annual financial report
- c. Available for sale
- d. Single Audit

Guidance: level 1

:: Management accounting ::

A _____ is an organizational unit headed by a manager, who is responsible for its activities and results. In responsibility accounting, revenues and cost information are collected and reported on by _____ s.

15. *Answer choices:*

(see index for correct answer)

- a. Construction accounting
- b. Responsibility center
- c. Hedge accounting
- d. Variable cost

Guidance: level 1

:: Accounting in the United States ::

The _____ is located in Norwalk, Connecticut, United States. It was organized in 1972 as a non-stock, Delaware Corporation. It is an independent organization in the private sector, operating with the goal of ensuring objectivity and integrity in financial reporting standards.

Exam Probability: **Low**

16. *Answer choices:*

(see index for correct answer)

- a. Financial Accounting Foundation
- b. Other postemployment benefits
- c. Positive assurance

- d. Accounting Today

Guidance: level 1

:: ::

A _____ is a fund into which a sum of money is added during an employee's employment years, and from which payments are drawn to support the person's retirement from work in the form of periodic payments. A _____ may be a "defined benefit plan" where a fixed sum is paid regularly to a person, or a "defined contribution plan" under which a fixed sum is invested and then becomes available at retirement age. _____ s should not be confused with severance pay; the former is usually paid in regular installments for life after retirement, while the latter is typically paid as a fixed amount after involuntary termination of employment prior to retirement.

Exam Probability: **Low**

17. *Answer choices:*

(see index for correct answer)

- a. Character
- b. process perspective
- c. Pension
- d. corporate values

Guidance: level 1

:: Options (finance) ::

A _____ bond is a type of bond that allows the issuer of the bond to retain the privilege of redeeming the bond at some point before the bond reaches its date of maturity. In other words, on the call date, the issuer has the right, but not the obligation, to buy back the bonds from the bond holders at a defined call price. Technically speaking, the bonds are not really bought and held by the issuer but are instead cancelled immediately.

Exam Probability: **Low**

18. *Answer choices:*

(see index for correct answer)

- a. Barrier option
- b. Warrant
- c. Call option
- d. Ascot

Guidance: level 1

:: Taxation ::

A _____ is a person or organization subject to pay a tax. _____ s have an Identification Number, a reference number issued by a government to its citizens.

19. *Answer choices:*

(see index for correct answer)

- a. Taxpayer
- b. Language tax
- c. Tax cap
- d. African Tax Administration Forum

Guidance: level 1

:: Labor terms ::

_____ , often called DI or disability income insurance, or income protection, is a form of insurance that insures the beneficiary's earned income against the risk that a disability creates a barrier for a worker to complete the core functions of their work. For example, the worker may suffer from an inability to maintain composure in the case of psychological disorders or an injury, illness or condition that causes physical impairment or incapacity to work. It encompasses paid sick leave, short-term disability benefits , and long-term disability benefits . Statistics show that in the US a disabling accident occurs, on average, once every second. In fact, nearly 18.5% of Americans are currently living with a disability, and 1 out of every 4 persons in the US workforce will suffer a disabling injury before retirement.

20. *Answer choices:*

(see index for correct answer)

- a. Capital services
- b. Disability insurance
- c. Benefit incidence
- d. Civilian noninstitutional population

Guidance: level 1

:: Types of business entity ::

A _____ is a partnership in which some or all partners have limited liabilities. It therefore can exhibit elements of partnerships and corporations. In a LLP, each partner is not responsible or liable for another partner's misconduct or negligence. This is an important difference from the traditional partnership under the UK Partnership Act 1890, in which each partner has joint and several liability. In a LLP, some or all partners have a form of limited liability similar to that of the shareholders of a corporation. Unlike corporate shareholders, the partners have the right to manage the business directly. In contrast, corporate shareholders must elect a board of directors under the laws of various state charters. The board organizes itself and hires corporate officers who then have as "corporate" individuals the legal responsibility to manage the corporation in the corporation's best interest. A LLP also contains a different level of tax liability from that of a corporation.

Exam Probability: **High**

21. *Answer choices:*

(see index for correct answer)

- a. Limited liability partnership
- b. Public development authority
- c. Svenskt utlandsregistrerat f%C3%B6retag
- d. General partnership

:: Generally Accepted Accounting Principles ::

In accrual accounting, the revenue recognition principle states that expenses should be recorded during the period in which they are incurred, regardless of when the transfer of cash occurs. Conversely, cash basis accounting calls for the recognition of an expense when the cash is paid, regardless of when the expense was actually incurred.

Exam Probability: **High**

22. *Answer choices:*

(see index for correct answer)

- a. Fixed investment
- b. French generally accepted accounting principles
- c. Petty cash
- d. Matching principle

:: Basic financial concepts ::

In finance, maturity or _____ refers to the final payment date of a loan or other financial instrument, at which point the principal is due to be paid.

23. *Answer choices:*

(see index for correct answer)

- a. Tax shield
- b. Eurodollar
- c. Maturity date
- d. Short interest

Guidance: level 1

:: Taxation ::

In a tax system, the _____ is the ratio at which a business or person is taxed. There are several methods used to present a _____ : statutory, average, marginal, and effective. These rates can also be presented using different definitions applied to a tax base: inclusive and exclusive.

24. *Answer choices:*

(see index for correct answer)

- a. Max Planck Institute for Tax Law and Public Finance
- b. Fiscal memory devices
- c. Benefit principle
- d. Privatized tax collection

Guidance: level 1

:: Business law ::

A _____ , also known as the sole trader, individual entrepreneurship or proprietorship, is a type of enterprise that is owned and run by one person and in which there is no legal distinction between the owner and the business entity. A sole trader does not necessarily work `alone`—it is possible for the sole trader to employ other people.

Exam Probability: **Medium**

25. *Answer choices:*

(see index for correct answer)

- a. Consumer privacy
- b. Sole proprietorship
- c. Bulk sale
- d. Whitewash waiver

:: Management accounting ::

_____ is the profit the firm makes from serving a customer or customer group over a specified period of time, specifically the difference between the revenues earned from and the costs associated with the customer relationship in a specified period. According to Philip Kotler,"a profitable customer is a person, household or a company that overtime, yields a revenue stream that exceeds by an acceptable amount the company's cost stream of attracting, selling and servicing the customer."

Exam Probability: **High**

26. *Answer choices:*

(see index for correct answer)

- a. Customer profitability
- b. Certified Management Accountants of Canada
- c. Overhead
- d. Target income sales

:: Auditing ::

A _____ , also called "Internal _____ ", is a term of financial audit, internal audit and Enterprise Risk Management. It means the overall attitude, awareness and actions of directors and management regarding the internal control system and its importance to the entity. They express it in management style, corporate culture, values, philosophy and operating style, the organisational structure, and human resources policies and procedures.

Exam Probability: **Medium**

27. *Answer choices:*

(see index for correct answer)

- a. Analytical procedures
- b. audit log
- c. Continuous auditing
- d. Control environment

Guidance: level 1

:: Land value taxation ::

_____ , sometimes referred to as dry _____ , is the solid surface of Earth that is not permanently covered by water. The vast majority of human activity throughout history has occurred in _____ areas that support agriculture, habitat, and various natural resources. Some life forms have developed from predecessor species that lived in bodies of water.

Exam Probability: **Low**

28. *Answer choices:*

- a. Georgism
- b. Land
- c. Harry Gunnison Brown
- d. Prosper Australia

Guidance: level 1

:: Valuation (finance) ::

_____ refers to an assessment of the viability, stability, and profitability of a business, sub-business or project.

Exam Probability: **Medium**

29. *Answer choices:*

- a. Turnaround stock
- b. Financial analysis
- c. Value-in-use
- d. Investment value

Guidance: level 1

:: Quality control tools ::

A _____ is a type of diagram that represents an algorithm, workflow or process. _____ can also be defined as a diagramatic representation of an algorithm .

Exam Probability: **Medium**

30. *Answer choices:*

(see index for correct answer)

- a. Flowchart
- b. EVOP
- c. Fishbone diagram
- d. C-chart

Guidance: level 1

:: Management accounting ::

_____ is a method of identifying and evaluating activities that a business performs, using activity-based costing to carry out a value chain analysis or a re-engineering initiative to improve strategic and operational decisions in an organization.

31. *Answer choices:*

(see index for correct answer)

- a. Variable cost
- b. Activity-based management
- c. Constraints accounting
- d. RCA open-source application

Guidance: level 1

:: Project management ::

_____ is the widespread practice of collecting information and attempting to spot a pattern. In some fields of study, the term " _____ " has more formally defined meanings.

Exam Probability: **Low**

32. *Answer choices:*

(see index for correct answer)

- a. Trend analysis
- b. Code name
- c. Budgeted cost of work performed
- d. Dependency

:: Legal terms ::

_____ is a state of prolonged public dispute or debate, usually concerning a matter of conflicting opinion or point of view. The word was coined from the Latin controversia, as a composite of controversus – "turned in an opposite direction," from contra – "against" – and vertere – to turn, or versus , hence, "to turn against."

Exam Probability: **Medium**

33. *Answer choices:*

(see index for correct answer)

- a. Generally recognized as safe and effective
- b. Controversy
- c. European Authorized Representative
- d. Further and better particulars

:: Finance ::

A _____ , publicly-traded company, publicly-held company, publicly-listed company, or public limited company is a corporation whose ownership is dispersed among the general public in many shares of stock which are freely traded on a stock exchange or in over-the-counter markets. In some jurisdictions, public companies over a certain size must be listed on an exchange. A _____ can be listed or unlisted .

Exam Probability: **Medium**

34. *Answer choices:*

(see index for correct answer)

- a. Z-spread
- b. Volatility risk
- c. BIOFIN
- d. Public company

Guidance: level 1

:: Financial accounting ::

In macroeconomics and international finance, the _____ is one of two primary components of the balance of payments, the other being the current account. Whereas the current account reflects a nation's net income, the _____ reflects net change in ownership of national assets.

Exam Probability: **High**

35. *Answer choices:*

(see index for correct answer)

- a. Floating capital
- b. Deferred Acquisition Costs
- c. Commuted cash value
- d. Capital account

Guidance: level 1

:: Banking ::

A _____ is a financial institution that accepts deposits from the public and creates credit. Lending activities can be performed either directly or indirectly through capital markets. Due to their importance in the financial stability of a country, _____ s are highly regulated in most countries. Most nations have institutionalized a system known as fractional reserve _____ ing under which _____ s hold liquid assets equal to only a portion of their current liabilities. In addition to other regulations intended to ensure liquidity, _____ s are generally subject to minimum capital requirements based on an international set of capital standards, known as the Basel Accords.

Exam Probability: **High**

36. *Answer choices:*

(see index for correct answer)

- a. Full-reserve banking

- b. Sales and trading
- c. Bank
- d. Bank secrecy

Guidance: level 1

:: Stock market ::

_____ is a form of corporate equity ownership, a type of security. The terms voting share and ordinary share are also used frequently in other parts of the world; "_____" being primarily used in the United States. They are known as Equity shares or Ordinary shares in the UK and other Commonwealth realms. This type of share gives the stockholder the right to share in the profits of the company, and to vote on matters of corporate policy and the composition of the members of the board of directors.

Exam Probability: **Low**

37. *Answer choices:*
(see index for correct answer)

- a. Common stock
- b. PLUS Markets Group
- c. Chi-X Global
- d. Secondary market offering

Guidance: level 1

:: Banking ::

A _____ is a financial account maintained by a bank for a customer. A _____ can be a deposit account, a credit card account, a current account, or any other type of account offered by a financial institution, and represents the funds that a customer has entrusted to the financial institution and from which the customer can make withdrawals. Alternatively, accounts may be loan accounts in which case the customer owes money to the financial institution.

Exam Probability: **Medium**

38. *Answer choices:*

(see index for correct answer)

- a. Representative APR
- b. Wholesale banking
- c. Numbered bank account
- d. Bank account

Guidance: level 1

:: Taxation in the United States ::

The Modified Accelerated Cost Recovery System is the current tax depreciation system in the United States. Under this system, the capitalized cost of tangible property is recovered over a specified life by annual deductions for depreciation. The lives are specified broadly in the Internal Revenue Code. The Internal Revenue Service publishes detailed tables of lives by classes of assets. The deduction for depreciation is computed under one of two methods at the election of the taxpayer, with limitations. See IRS Publication 946 for a 120-page guide to _____ .

Exam Probability: **High**

39. *Answer choices:*

(see index for correct answer)

- a. Taxpayer Identification Number
- b. Carryover basis
- c. Applicable convention
- d. MACRS

Guidance: level 1

:: Management accounting ::

_____ is a managerial accounting cost concept. Under this method, manufacturing overhead is incurred in the period that a product is produced. This addresses the issue of absorption costing that allows income to rise as production rises. Under an absorption cost method, management can push forward costs to the next period when products are sold. This artificially inflates profits in the period of production by incurring less cost than would be incurred under a _____ system. _____ is generally not used for external reporting purposes. Under the Tax Reform Act of 1986, income statements must use absorption costing to comply with GAAP.

Exam Probability: **High**

40. *Answer choices:*

(see index for correct answer)

- a. Job costing
- b. Certified Management Accountants of Canada
- c. Variable Costing
- d. Hedge accounting

Guidance: level 1

:: Management accounting ::

_____ accounting is a traditional cost accounting method introduced in the 1920s, as an alternative for the traditional cost accounting method based on historical costs.

41. *Answer choices:*

(see index for correct answer)

- a. Bridge life-cycle cost analysis
- b. Average per-bit delivery cost
- c. Institute of Management Accountants
- d. Standard cost

Guidance: level 1

:: Credit cards ::

The _____ Company, also known as Amex, is an American multinational financial services corporation headquartered in Three World Financial Center in New York City. The company was founded in 1850 and is one of the 30 components of the Dow Jones Industrial Average. The company is best known for its charge card, credit card, and traveler's cheque businesses.

Exam Probability: **Medium**

42. *Answer choices:*

(see index for correct answer)

- a. China UnionPay
- b. American Express

- c. Credit card debt
- d. Gravity Payments

Guidance: level 1

:: Tax reform ::

_____ is the process of changing the way taxes are collected or managed by the government and is usually undertaken to improve tax administration or to provide economic or social benefits. _____ can include reducing the level of taxation of all people by the government, making the tax system more progressive or less progressive, or simplifying the tax system and making the system more understandable or more accountable.

Exam Probability: **Medium**

43. *Answer choices:*

(see index for correct answer)

- a. 2006 Puerto Rico budget crisis
- b. Enterprise Value Tax
- c. Tax reform
- d. Joseph A. Pechman

Guidance: level 1

:: Stock market ::

_____ is a form of stock which may have any combination of features not possessed by common stock including properties of both an equity and a debt instrument, and is generally considered a hybrid instrument. _____ s are senior to common stock, but subordinate to bonds in terms of claim and may have priority over common stock in the payment of dividends and upon liquidation. Terms of the _____ are described in the issuing company`s articles of association or articles of incorporation.

Exam Probability: **Medium**

44. *Answer choices:*

(see index for correct answer)

- a. Preferred stock
- b. Growth investing
- c. OpenIPO
- d. Qualified institutional placement

Guidance: level 1

:: Management accounting ::

In business, a _____ is a division that gains revenue from product sales or service provided. The manager in _____ is accountable for revenue only.

Exam Probability: **Low**

45. *Answer choices:*

(see index for correct answer)

- a. Job costing
- b. Revenue center
- c. Backflush accounting
- d. Variable Costing

Guidance: level 1

:: ::

_____ is capital that is contributed to a corporation by investors by purchase of stock from the corporation, the primary market, not by purchase of stock in the open market from other stockholders . It includes share capital as well as additional _____ .

Exam Probability: **Low**

46. *Answer choices:*

(see index for correct answer)

- a. co-culture
- b. deep-level diversity
- c. Paid-in capital
- d. process perspective

:: Management accounting ::

An _____ is a classification used for business units within an enterprise. The essential element of an _____ is that it is treated as a unit which is measured against its use of capital, as opposed to a cost or profit center, which are measured against raw costs or profits.

Exam Probability: **High**

47. *Answer choices:*

(see index for correct answer)

- a. Throughput accounting
- b. Inventory valuation
- c. Investment center
- d. Construction accounting

:: Accounting ::

_____ is the recording of financial transactions, and is part of the process of accounting in business. Transactions include purchases, sales, receipts, and payments by an individual person or an organization/corporation. There are several standard methods of _____ , including the single-entry and double-entry _____ systems. While these may be viewed as "real" _____ , any process for recording financial transactions is a _____ process.

Exam Probability: **High**

48. *Answer choices:*

(see index for correct answer)

- a. Accounting period
- b. FreeAgent
- c. Pipeline planning
- d. Bookkeeping

Guidance: level 1

:: Corporate governance ::

The _____ is the officer of a company that has primary responsibility for managing the company's finances, including financial planning, management of financial risks, record-keeping, and financial reporting. In some sectors, the CFO is also responsible for analysis of data. Some CFOs have the title CFOO for chief financial and operating officer. In the United Kingdom, the typical term for a CFO is finance director . The CFO typically reports to the chief executive officer and the board of directors and may additionally have a seat on the board.The CFO supervises the finance unit and is the chief financial spokesperson for the organization. The CFO directly assists the chief operating officer on all strategic and tactical matters relating to budget management, cost–benefit analysis, forecasting needs, and securing of new funding.

Exam Probability: **High**

49. *Answer choices:*

(see index for correct answer)

- a. Taylor Report
- b. King Committee
- c. King II
- d. Corporate headquarters

Guidance: level 1

:: International taxation ::

_____ is the levying of tax by two or more jurisdictions on the same declared income , asset , or financial transaction . Double liability is mitigated in a number of ways, for example.

Exam Probability: **Low**

50. *Answer choices:*

(see index for correct answer)

- a. Euromod
- b. Common Reporting Standard
- c. European Union withholding tax
- d. Double taxation

Guidance: level 1

:: Negotiable instrument law ::

_____ of a financial instrument, such as a cheque, is only a signature, not indicating the payee. The effect of this is that it is payable only to the bearer – legally, it transforms an order instrument into a bearer instrument . It is one of the types of endorsement of a negotiable instrument.

Exam Probability: **Medium**

51. *Answer choices:*

(see index for correct answer)

- a. Regulation CC
- b. Negotiable Instruments Act, 1881
- c. Clearfield Trust Co. v. United States
- d. Real defense

Guidance: level 1

:: Free accounting software ::

A _____ is the principal book or computer file for recording and totaling economic transactions measured in terms of a monetary unit of account by account type, with debits and credits in separate columns and a beginning monetary balance and ending monetary balance for each account.

Exam Probability: **Low**

52. *Answer choices:*

(see index for correct answer)

- a. Grisbi
- b. Ofuz
- c. Ledger
- d. JGnash

Guidance: level 1

Generally speaking, a _____ begins on the New Year's Day of the given calendar system and ends on the day before the following New Year's Day, and thus consists of a whole number of days. A year can also be measured by starting on any other named day of the calendar, and ending on the day before this named day in the following year. This may be termed a "year's time", but not a " _____ ". To reconcile the _____ with the astronomical cycle certain years contain extra days .

Exam Probability: **Medium**

53. *Answer choices:*

(see index for correct answer)

- a. Calendar year
- b. surface-level diversity
- c. empathy
- d. interpersonal communication

Guidance: level 1

:: Stock market ::

A _____ , securities exchange or bourse, is a facility where stock brokers and traders can buy and sell securities, such as shares of stock and bonds and other financial instruments. _____ s may also provide for facilities the issue and redemption of such securities and instruments and capital events including the payment of income and dividends. Securities traded on a _____ include stock issued by listed companies, unit trusts, derivatives, pooled investment products and bonds. _____ s often function as "continuous auction" markets with buyers and sellers consummating transactions via open outcry at a central location such as the floor of the exchange or by using an electronic trading platform.

Exam Probability: **Medium**

54. *Answer choices:*

(see index for correct answer)

- a. Stock Exchange
- b. H share
- c. Super-majority amendment
- d. Widow-and-orphan stock

Guidance: level 1

:: Debt ::

A _____ is a monetary amount owed to a creditor that is unlikely to be paid and, or which the creditor is not willing to take action to collect for various reasons, often due to the debtor not having the money to pay, for example due to a company going into liquidation or insolvency. There are various technical definitions of what constitutes a _____ , depending on accounting conventions, regulatory treatment and the institution provisioning. In the USA, bank loans with more than ninety days' arrears become "problem loans". Accounting sources advise that the full amount of a _____ be written off to the profit and loss account or a provision for _____ s as soon as it is foreseen.

Exam Probability: **Low**

55. *Answer choices:*

(see index for correct answer)

- a. Bad debt
- b. Arrears
- c. Museum of Foreign Debt
- d. Interest

Guidance: level 1

:: Asset ::

In financial accounting, an _____ is any resource owned by the business. Anything tangible or intangible that can be owned or controlled to produce value and that is held by a company to produce positive economic value is an _____ . Simply stated, _____ s represent value of ownership that can be converted into cash . The balance sheet of a firm records the monetary value of the _____ s owned by that firm. It covers money and other valuables belonging to an individual or to a business.

Exam Probability: **High**

56. *Answer choices:*

(see index for correct answer)

- a. Current asset
- b. Asset

Guidance: level 1

:: Expense ::

An _____ is the right to reimbursement of money spent by employees for work-related purposes. Some common _____ s are: administrative expense, amortization expense, bad debt expense, cost of goods sold, depreciation expense, freight-out, income tax expense, insurance expense, interest expense, loss on disposal of plant assets, maintenance and repairs expense, rent expense, salaries and wages expense, selling expense, supplies expense and utilities expense.

Exam Probability: **Medium**

57. *Answer choices:*

(see index for correct answer)

- a. Expense account
- b. Operating expense
- c. Corporate travel
- d. Business overhead expense disability insurance

Guidance: level 1

:: ::

A tax is a compulsory financial charge or some other type of levy imposed upon a taxpayer by a governmental organization in order to fund various public expenditures. A failure to pay, along with evasion of or resistance to _____ , is punishable by law. Taxes consist of direct or indirect taxes and may be paid in money or as its labour equivalent.

Exam Probability: **Medium**

58. *Answer choices:*

(see index for correct answer)

- a. Taxation
- b. empathy
- c. open system
- d. Sarbanes-Oxley act of 2002

:: International Financial Reporting Standards ::

_____ , usually called IFRS, are standards issued by the IFRS Foundation and the International Accounting Standards Board to provide a common global language for business affairs so that company accounts are understandable and comparable across international boundaries. They are a consequence of growing international shareholding and trade and are particularly important for companies that have dealings in several countries. They are progressively replacing the many different national accounting standards. They are the rules to be followed by accountants to maintain books of accounts which are comparable, understandable, reliable and relevant as per the users internal or external. IFRS, with the exception of IAS 29 Financial Reporting in Hyperinflationary Economies and IFRIC 7 Applying the Restatement Approach under IAS 29, are authorized in terms of the historical cost paradigm. IAS 29 and IFRIC 7 are authorized in terms of the units of constant purchasing power paradigm.IAS 2 is related to inventories in this standard we talk about the stock its production process etcIFRS began as an attempt to harmonize accounting across the European Union but the value of harmonization quickly made the concept attractive around the world. However, it has been debated whether or not de facto harmonization has occurred. Standards that were issued by IASC are still within use today and go by the name International Accounting Standards , while standards issued by IASB are called IFRS. IAS were issued between 1973 and 2001 by the Board of the International Accounting Standards Committee . On 1 April 2001, the new International Accounting Standards Board took over from the IASC the responsibility for setting International Accounting Standards. During its first meeting the new Board adopted existing IAS and Standing Interpretations Committee standards . The IASB has continued to develop standards calling the new standards " _____ ".

Exam Probability: **Low**

59. *Answer choices:*

(see index for correct answer)

- a. IAS 2
- b. IAS 39
- c. IFRS 2
- d. IAS 37

Guidance: level 1

INDEX: Correct Answers

Foundations of Business

1. a: Partnership

2. c: Capitalism

3. : Working capital

4. : Cash flow

5. b: Marketing research

6. b: Bankruptcy

7. d: Sony

8. a: Evaluation

9. : Revenue

10. a: Empowerment

11. : Expense

12. b: Regulation

13. c: Direct investment

14. a: Demand

15. a: Entrepreneur

16. : Six Sigma

17. c: Office

18. d: Import

19. a: Quality control

20. d: Globalization

21. a: System

22. d: Competitor

23. b: Balance sheet

24. d: Procurement

25. a: Marketing mix

26. c: Property rights

27. c: Small business

28. d: Performance

29. a: Debt

30. a: Currency

31. : Board of directors

32. d: Creativity

33. a: Market value

34. c: Trade

35. d: Document

36. c: Sexual harassment

37. : Industrial Revolution

38. d: Quality management

39. d: Variable cost

40. d: Duty

41. a: Financial services

42. : Limited liability

43. a: Career

44. a: Energies

45. c: Marketing strategy

46. : Sustainability

47. : Common stock

48. a: Business model

49. c: Need

50. a: Number

51. d: Innovation

52. : ASEAN

53. a: INDEX

54. : Copyright

55. a: Stock market

56. b: Asset

57. c: Free trade

58. a: Economic growth

59. a: Insurance

Management

1. d: Profit sharing

2. a: Questionnaire

3. : Supply chain management

4. d: Trade

5. a: Overtime

6. c: Frequency

7. b: Quality circle

8. b: Proactive

9. d: Performance appraisal

10. b: Planning

11. d: Mass customization

12. : Offshoring

13. b: Corporate governance

14. c: Organizational culture

15. : Schedule

16. b: Risk management

17. c: Distance

18. d: Employee stock

19. c: Brand

20. d: Justice

21. d: Project manager

22. b: Mission statement

23. b: Virtual team

24. c: Training and development

25. a: Vertical integration

26. b: Bounded rationality

27. b: Six Sigma

28. c: Grievance

29. b: Quality control

30. b: Procurement

31. b: Information

32. : Strategy

33. b: Property

34. b: Scientific management

35. c: Research and development

36. : Case study

37. d: European Union

38. c: Social capital

39. b: Collaboration

40. : Dilemma

41. : Size

42. d: Total quality management

43. b: Subsidiary

44. c: Cross-functional team

45. a: Organizational structure

46. a: Strategic planning

47. c: Assessment center

48. b: Myers-Briggs type

49. : Office

50. d: Social loafing

51. d: Bias

52. d: Decision-making

53. c: Benchmarking

54. d: Inventory control

55. : Intellectual property

56. b: Corporation

57. b: Patent

58. a: Forecasting

59. a: Transformational leadership

Business law

1. b: Standing

2. c: Forgery

3. d: Board of directors

4. d: Presentment

5. b: Common carrier

6. : Operating agreement

7. b: Trade

8. c: Verdict

9. d: Probate

10. b: Trespass

11. : Prohibition

12. : Committee

13. c: Management

14. a: Inventory

15. b: Utilitarianism

16. b: Advertisement

17. : Stock

18. c: Sexual harassment

19. : Revocation

20. c: Advertising

21. d: Credit

22. : Appeal

23. a: Disclaimer

24. d: Petition

25. d: Void contract

26. d: Cooperative

27. b: Affirmative action

28. : Subsidiary

29. d: Shares

30. a: Res ipsa

31. a: Operation of law

32. b: Interest

33. a: Contract law

34. b: Injunction

35. a: Punitive

36. : Sole proprietorship

37. : Rescind

38. b: Statutory Law

39. : Specific performance

40. b: Supreme Court

41. c: Uniform Electronic Transactions Act

42. b: Identity theft

43. c: Administrative law

44. b: Reasonable person

45. b: Brand

46. c: Eminent domain

47. b: Consumer Good

48. a: Security agreement

49. a: Real property

50. : Warehouse receipt

51. a: Duty

52. a: Condition precedent

53. b: Due diligence

54. a: Garnishment

55. b: Marketing

56. d: Policy

57. b: Insolvency

58. c: Damages

59. c: Misrepresentation

Finance

1. c: Taxation

2. a: Capital lease

3. : Investment

4. d: Derivative

5. c: Tax expense

6. d: Cost of goods sold

7. a: Retained earnings

8. a: Patent

9. : Accounting method

10. c: Accounts payable

11. : Gross profit

12. b: Equity method

13. b: Initial public offering

14. c: Technology

15. : Financial accounting

16. c: Corporate governance

17. : Source document

18. a: Expense

19. d: Compounding

20. : Chart of accounts

21. a: Sales

22. : Accountant

23. b: Partnership

24. c: Preferred stock

25. d: Accounting period

26. : Financial analysis

27. : Convertible bond

28. : Wall Street

29. a: Accounts receivable

30. d: Total cost

31. d: Absorption costing

32. d: Hedge

33. a: Loan

34. b: Debt

35. c: Income

36. : Bank of America

37. c: Payment

38. b: Fixed asset

39. b: Cost object

40. d: Cash management

41. b: Stock

42. d: Inventory

43. b: Amortization

44. : Vacation

45. : Going concern

46. d: Stock exchange

47. c: Return on assets

48. d: Debit card

49. d: Risk

50. b: Capital market

51. : Merchandising

52. c: Gross margin

53. c: Working capital

54. a: Coupon

55. d: Property

56. c: Purchasing

57. : Utility

58. : Exercise

59. d: Cost allocation

Human resource management

1. c: National Institute for Occupational Safety and Health

2. a: Realistic job preview

3. a: Aggression

4. b: Public administration

5. d: Business process outsourcing

6. d: Interdependence

7. : Survey research

8. a: Problem solving

9. : Worker Adjustment and Retraining Notification Act

10. a: Age Discrimination in Employment Act

11. a: Self-assessment

12. b: Empowerment

13. b: Workforce planning

14. c: Knowledge worker

15. a: Family violence

16. d: Affirmative action

17. d: National Association of Colleges and Employers

18. a: Hazard

19. c: Flexible spending account

20. c: Occupational Information Network

21. a: Resignation

22. d: Card check

23. d: Mining

24. c: Works council

25. c: Trade union

26. c: Leadership development

27. d: Independent contractor

28. : Compa-ratio

29. b: Job fair

30. a: Unemployment insurance

31. a: Bottom line

32. : Social network

33. c: Unemployment benefits

34. d: Employee surveys

35. d: Individualism

36. : Employee assistance program

37. d: Nearshoring

38. b: Interactional justice

39. b: Coaching

40. : Cost of living

41. : Career development

42. b: Intellectual capital

43. c: Union shop

44. c: Organizational socialization

45. : Unfair labor practice

46. b: Task force

47. : Needs analysis

48. d: Organizational commitment

49. c: Service Employees International Union

50. b: Behavior modification

51. c: Construct validity

52. c: Physician

53. : Pregnancy discrimination

54. c: Evidence-based

55. : Performance improvement

56. b: Performance

57. c: Organizational structure

58. a: Intuition

59. : Price Waterhouse v. Hopkins

Information systems

1. : Infrastructure

2. b: Query language

3. b: Manifesto

4. b: Random access

5. b: Zynga

6. : Open source

7. a: Database management system

8. d: Automation

9. : Telnet

10. d: Cookie

11. c: Payment system

12. : Fraud

13. a: Digital rights management

14. : Operational system

15. d: Semantic Web

16. : Search engine

17. c: System

18. d: Personalization

19. a: Database design

20. a: Edge computing

21. a: Entity-relationship

22. d: Health Insurance Portability and Accountability Act

23. b: Data dictionary

24. c: Economies of scale

25. c: Dashboard

26. c: Payment card

27. c: Database model

28. : Big data

29. c: First mover advantage

30. b: Joint application design

31. b: Social shopping

32. a: E-commerce

33. b: Botnet

34. : Text mining

35. a: Throughput

36. : Kinect

37. : Domain name

38. : Gmail

39. c: World Wide Web

40. : Netscape

41. c: Domain Name System

42. d: Data warehouse

43. : Consumerization

44. a: Vertical integration

45. d: Diagram

46. a: YouTube

47. b: Crowdsourcing

48. d: Data mart

49. c: Blog

50. a: Google Maps

51. : Groupware

52. c: Social network

53. d: Disaster recovery plan

54. b: Government-to-business

55. : Blogger

56. a: Intrusion detection system

57. a: Code

58. : Data cleansing

59. b: Change control

Marketing

1. d: Brand management

2. d: Innovation

3. d: Regulation

4. c: Questionnaire

5. b: Copyright

6. b: Empowerment

7. : Commercialization

8. b: Loyalty program

9. c: Return on investment

10. d: Social network

11. a: Supply chain

12. a: Audit

13. : Advertisement

14. d: Demand

15. : Marketing mix

16. a: Trademark

17. d: Inventory

18. b: Monopoly

19. c: Business model

20. a: Partnership

21. c: Wall Street Journal

22. c: Research and development

23. d: Creativity

24. a: Ford

25. a: Trade association

26. d: Consumer behavior

27. d: Security

28. d: Franchising

29. a: New product development

30. a: Hearing

31. a: Committee

32. c: INDEX

33. d: Merchandising

34. c: Globalization

35. c: Feedback

36. b: Consultant

37. b: Retailing

38. a: Market share

39. c: Social media

40. d: Supermarket

41. a: Advertising agency

42. c: Direct selling

43. b: Goal

44. a: Purchasing

45. c: Problem Solving

46. : Intranet

47. d: Blog

48. a: Sales

49. c: Sales promotion

50. a: Early adopter

51. b: Logo

52. b: Marketing plan

53. : Federal Trade Commission

54. d: Microsoft

55. b: Situation analysis

56. : Unique selling proposition

57. b: Exchange rate

58. c: Choice

59. d: Firm

Manufacturing

1. a: Consensus

2. c: Distillation

3. d: Bill of materials

4. c: E-commerce

5. b: Asset

6. c: Value engineering

7. d: Reflux

8. : Vendor

9. a: Service quality

10. : EFQM

11. d: Certification

12. b: Process engineering

13. a: Acceptance sampling

14. b: American Society for Quality

15. c: Service level

16. a: Process control

17. d: Check sheet

18. d: Sputnik

19. a: Economies of scope

20. b: Concurrent engineering

21. : Poka-yoke

22. : Quality management

23. c: Materials management

24. d: Minitab

25. a: Total productive maintenance

26. d: Interaction

27. a: Goal

28. c: Purchasing manager

29. c: Thomas Register

30. a: Blanket

31. a: Project

32. a: Consortium

33. c: Change control

34. c: Throughput

35. b: Root cause

36. c: Process capital

37. a: Product differentiation

38. c: Ball

39. c: Supply chain network

40. b: Retail

41. a: Sales

42. d: Reboiler

43. c: Process management

44. a: Metal

45. : Forecasting

46. b: Business process

47. a: PDCA

48. c: Inspection

49. a: Durability

50. b: Transaction cost

51. b: Capacity planning

52. a: Bullwhip effect

53. b: Resource allocation

54. c: Malcolm Baldrige National Quality Award

55. : Toshiba

56. d: Ishikawa diagram

57. : Material requirements planning

58. : Kaizen

59. b: Quality control

Commerce

1. d: Economies of scale

2. : Wholesale

3. c: Corporation

4. b: Basket

5. c: Wall Street Journal

6. b: Americans with Disabilities Act

7. c: Jury

8. b: Empowerment

9. b: Risk management

10. : American Express

11. b: Outsourcing

12. c: Economic regulation

13. b: Human resources

14. : Long run

15. b: Vickrey auction

16. a: Subsidy

17. d: Purchasing manager

18. a: Audit

19. : Electronic funds transfer

20. c: Collaborative filtering

21. a: Interest

22. c: Confirmed

23. d: Investment

24. d: Entrepreneur

25. : Chief executive officer

26. a: Committee

27. a: Case study

28. a: Marketing strategy

29. : Mining

30. d: Real estate

31. : Total cost

32. : Inventory control

33. a: Pizza Hut

34. d: Joint venture

35. a: E-commerce

36. a: Mobile commerce

37. b: Control system

38. d: Quality management

39. c: Affiliate marketing

40. d: Cooperative

41. a: Technology

42. b: Minimum wage

43. a: Trade show

44. : Consumer-to-consumer

45. d: Contract

46. c: Anticipation

47. c: Pop-up ad

48. d: Planning

49. c: Uniform Commercial Code

50. : Statutory law

51. : Webvan

52. d: Social shopping

53. : Shopping cart

54. b: Inflation

55. b: Netflix

56. b: Supranational

57. a: Exchange rate

58. d: Customs

59. a: Marketing mix

Business ethics

1. c: Accounting

2. d: Great Depression

3. d: Working poor

4. : Medicaid

5. d: Clean Water Act

6. c: Socialism

7. b: Lanham Act

8. d: Organic food

9. c: Individualistic culture

10. a: Risk assessment

11. b: Patriot Act

12. : Greenpeace

13. b: Clayton Act

14. c: Dual relationship

15. d: Statutory law

16. a: Patent

17. d: Utopian socialism

18. a: Cause-related marketing

19. c: Martin Luther

20. b: WorldCom

21. c: Electronic waste

22. a: ExxonMobil

23. : Whistleblower

24. a: Global Fund

25. c: Partnership

26. a: Stanford International Bank

27. : Financial Stability Oversight Council

28. : Petroleum

29. a: Collusion

30. a: Subprime lending

31. d: Exxon Valdez

32. d: Nepotism

33. b: Fraud

34. a: Authoritarian

35. : Oil spill

36. c: Greenwashing

37. d: Empowerment

38. c: Better Business Bureau

39. : Urban sprawl

40. d: Consumerism

41. : Locus of control

42. : Building

43. d: Environmental audit

44. b: Disclaimer

45. c: Affirmative action

46. a: Risk management

47. b: Corporation

48. a: Referent power

49. c: Corporate social responsibility

50. : Micromanagement

51. c: Qui tam

52. b: Skill

53. d: Undue hardship

54. d: Habitat

55. a: Communist Manifesto

56. d: Marketing

57. a: Sherman Antitrust Act

58. b: Lawsuit

59. a: Living wage

Accounting

1. d: Internal control

2. c: Embezzlement

3. d: Petty cash

4. c: Accounting

5. d: Securities Exchange Act

6. d: Income approach

7. d: Chief executive officer

8. : Securities and Exchange Commission

9. : Accounting period

10. c: Generally Accepted Accounting Principles

11. d: Controlling account

12. a: Dividend

13. : Certified Public Accountant

14. d: Single Audit

15. b: Responsibility center

16. a: Financial Accounting Foundation

17. c: Pension

18. : Callable

19. a: Taxpayer

20. b: Disability insurance

21. a: Limited liability partnership

22. d: Matching principle

23. c: Maturity date

24. : Tax rate

25. b: Sole proprietorship

26. a: Customer profitability

27. d: Control environment

28. b: Land

29. b: Financial analysis

30. a: Flowchart

31. b: Activity-based management

32. a: Trend analysis

33. b: Controversy

34. d: Public company

35. d: Capital account

36. c: Bank

37. a: Common stock

38. d: Bank account

39. d: MACRS

40. c: Variable Costing

41. d: Standard cost

42. b: American Express

43. c: Tax reform

44. a: Preferred stock

45. b: Revenue center

46. c: Paid-in capital

47. c: Investment center

48. d: Bookkeeping

49. : Chief financial officer

50. d: Double taxation

51. : Blank endorsement

52. c: Ledger

53. a: Calendar year

54. a: Stock Exchange

55. a: Bad debt

56. b: Asset

57. a: Expense account

58. a: Taxation

59. : International Financial Reporting Standards

CPSIA information can be obtained
at www.ICGtesting.com
Printed in the USA
LVHW041023301019
635717LV00002B/85/P